Connemara, Ireland

CONTENTS

PREFACE

Home Baked is a book filled with recipes for the average home baker like your-self. No need to be a skilled *pâtissier*. I will guide you through the hard parts, just like that.

For some techniques I'll use step-by-step illustrations; for others I'll give you a clear and simple description. This book only contains goods I like to bake my-self. These can be classics, but also concoctions of my own making. Recipes that I came up with, for instance, after having decided to live a little healthier from time to time.

This is why I sometimes try to bake wheat-free, sometimes gluten-free, and sometimes sugar-free, but just as often I don't. I follow my instincts, like I do in life itself, really.

When, like me, you suffer from baking urges, you'll notice that there is some-thing to bake pretty much every day. I like to bake because it is relaxing. It's a nice routine during the day. Nicer, even, when you have something delicious to eat or treat.

Baking will not only make you very happy; it will make you beloved.

Home Baked contains homey recipes: from spelt bread and homemade oat crackers to chic French *cannelés*, savory Irish pies, and formidable birthday cakes brimming with sugar and whipped cream. Nothing is impossible. You can do it too. Easily.

Of course, once you begin to master the basic recipes, you can start your own baking experiments; my recipes could very well offer you ideas to expand on. This is why I will also present you recipes for all sorts of universal pie crusts and tart shells, basic pound cakes, and beginner's bread, along with anything you can use to top, fill, and garnish them. In short: everything you need to get your bake on.

I wish you lots of success, and fun,

x YVETTE

Amsterdam

Paris

CROISSANTS
BAGUETTES
& BRIOCHE

Paris

in front of the oven in the middle of the night

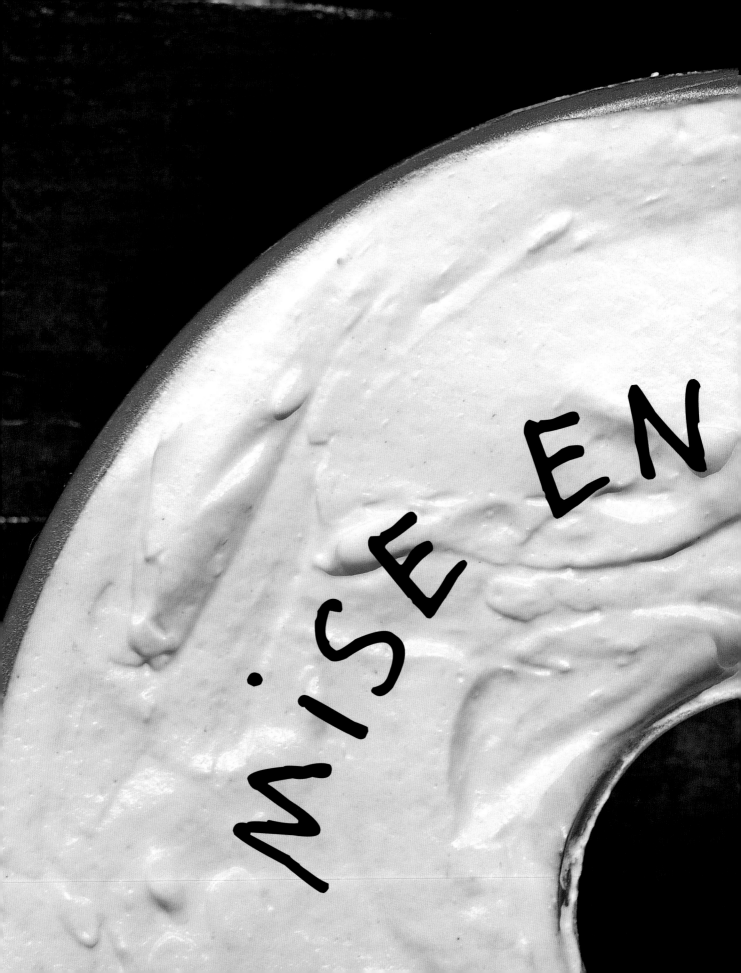

BAKING GEAR

Fairly essential tools to have at hand

DOUGH SCRAPERS
MADE OUT OF PLASTIC OR METAL
≫→ INDISPENSABLE ←≪

A HAND MIXER WITH DOUGH HOOKS!

HOWEVER, OFTEN A QUALITY WHISK & CLEAN HANDS WILL DO JUST FINE.

AN OVEN THERMOMETER IS A MUST HAVE! IT COSTS ALMOST NOTHING & IT WILL RESCUE YOU. NO MATTER HOW FANCY YOUR OVEN IS, YOU WILL STILL NEED THIS DEVICE!

ROLLING! PIN!

→ PIZZA STONE

ALTHOUGH I DON'T HAVE A PIZZA STONE, I USE DOUBLE-KILNED FLOOR TILES, WHICH I PLACE ON TOP OF A BAKING SHEET.
THAT WAY MY OVEN WILL TRULY GET SCORCHINGLY HOT. →
→ PERFECT FOR SOURDOUGH BREAD OR PIZZA, FOR INSTANCE

A SMALL SIEVE, FOR CONFECTIONERS' SUGAR OR CINNAMON

A BRUSH

A PASTRY BAG → OPTIONAL!

A DIGITAL SCALE, WHILE NOT A MUST, DOES COME IN HANDY

A BAKERS' SPATULA OR PALETTE KNIFE (I GOT MINE FROM A HARD-WARE STORE)

RUBBER (OR SILICONE) SPATULAS!

WHISKS

→ MEA-SURING SPOONS

BAKING PANS!

A BAKING (LOAF) PAN OF 6 CUPS (1,5 L)

A LOW-RIMMED 9- OR 10-INCH (24 CM) PIE PAN, WITH REMOVABLE BOTTOM

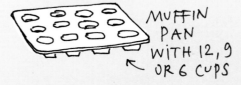

A 9- OR 10-INCH (24 CM) SPRINGFORM PAN

MUFFIN PAN WITH 12, 9 OR 6 CUPS

BAKING SHEETS ARE ESSENTIAL, SMALL, LARGE, MEDIUM: IN ALL SIZES PLEASE!

A FOOD PROCESSOR MAY COME IN HANDY. ALTHOUGH I OFTEN TRY TO WORK WITHOUT ONE.

COOKIE CUTTERS ARE NICE, BUT A GLASS WILL ALSO DO THE TRICK

BOWLS IN SEVERAL SIZES

ALSO IN GLASS OR METAL FOR AU BAIN-MARIE (IN A DOUBLE BOILER)!

FINE GRATER

A RACK. A TRIVET WILL OFTEN WORK TOO!

MEASURING CUPS!

BLIND-BAKING BEANS!

DRY, UNSOAKED BEANS THAT YOU CAN USE & REUSE, SO KEEP THEM. ONCE THEY'RE BAKED YOU CAN'T EAT THESE, BY THE WAY. COOKING STORES SELL CERAMIC BEANS OR PIE WEIGHTS, BUT REGULAR BEANS WORK JUST AS WELL.

BAKING ADVICE FOR EVERY DOMESTIC ADVENTURER

ROOM TEMPERATURE

Make sure that all your ingredients are at room temperature, unless the recipe states otherwise. It will decrease the risk of your dough curdling.

This means you should also make sure your eggs aren't too cold. To be safe, remove them from the fridge an hour in advance.

CLEANLINESS

Always work on a clean surface, with clean tools. Especially when you're whisking egg whites, everything should be spotless and free of any grease, otherwise your meringue won't fly.

PRECISION

Be precise. Weigh your ingredients carefully. Baking demands a higher level of accuracy than, say, making a soup. Always follow the recipes to the letter. If a recipe says you should "whisk for a long time," that means you should really do that; if it says "fold carefully with a spatula," don't plunge in the hand mixer.

These descriptions are included for a reason: Only when following them will you achieve the result you were aiming for. Once you've gained enough experience with a certain recipe, you will know which ingredients to shift around, use less of, or more, and what to leave out in order to tweak the final result. Don't start tinkering right away. Always try out a recipe first.

GREASING & PARCHMENT PAPER

Always thoroughly grease a baking pan. Most of the time I also cut a sheet of parchment paper to size and line my pan. Then I grease the paper, too. There's really nothing worse than a perfect cake that won't come out of the pan in one piece. Then all the work has been for naught. When, instead of neatly cutting the paper into the right size, you only casually press it in place into the pan (something I see often), your pie or cake will get rumpled edges, which I consider somewhat of a waste of work too.

With a little more effort, you will achieve a result just a tad better looking and definitely more professional.

SIFTING

Yes, sifting is mandatory. By sifting you'll thoroughly combine all ingredients, making sure everything is evenly spread throughout the mixture. Sifting will also bring air into your baked goods, which is great for everything. Cakes will become lighter, pie dough more crisp.

No strainer? No problem: Put all the dry ingredients in a bowl and stir with a whisk. Works just as well.

MIXER OR SPATULA?

When making a cakelike batter, always thoroughly combine the wet ingredients, using a hand mixer, for instance, to get air into your mixture.

Always use a spatula as soon as you add flour. Flour shouldn't be whisked or mixed for too long. You want an airy, crumbly cake, not a tough, dry one.

The rule of thumb therefore is: Adding flour? Grab a spatula, and carefully fold it in.

PREHEATING

Always begin preheating the oven about 20 minutes before you start baking. You know your own oven better than I do. Preheating times vary for each oven. To be certain, always check the temperature on your oven thermometer before putting your cake in.

OVEN THERMOMETER

Always use an oven thermometer. They can be bought for as little as five dollars at the average housewares store. Not a big investment, I'd say. No matter how outrageously expensive or dead cheap your oven may be, the temperature indicated on the display will always differ from the actual temperature inside.

Therefore: Buy an oven thermometer. It will save you a whole lot of baking sorrow. My oven tends to get way hotter than the temperature I set it at. Curious, but now at least you know what you can do to prevent unpleasant surprises.

CONVECTION VS. REGULAR OVEN

I do my baking in a convection oven. These tend to get hotter than regular ovens but they also tend to dry out your baked goods faster. When using a regular oven, always add 10 minutes to the cooking times mentioned in the recipes.

PLACEMENT

Unless stated otherwise, pies, cakes, cookies, and pound cakes are usually baked on a rack set in the middle of the oven.

UNEVEN BROWNING

Always make sure your batter reaches the same level throughout the pan. If you notice your pound cake or bread is baking unevenly (meaning one side gets darker or rises higher), simply rotate the pan after two-thirds of the baking time, to ensure all sides get the same amount of heat. Some ovens just happen to be more powerful on one side than the other.

POUND CAKE DONE? OR NOT YET?

A baked pound cake should bounce back after you gently press it. The edges must have shrunk a little in comparison to the baking pan. A bamboo skewer inserted into the middle should come out clean. If these things aren't the case, the cake has to go back into the oven for a while.

TURNING OUT

Always let everything you bake rest in the baking pan on a wire rack for at least 10 minutes. First, assess whether the pound cake or bread will easily release from the pan. When in doubt, you can run a thin knife between the cake and the pan to make sure you'll be able to smoothly release it.

Then, place a small rack (or plate) on top of the pan and flip (using oven mitts) the whole thing over. Feel how the cake is coming loose from the pan and let it slide out onto the rack. Allow it to cool further. You won't be able to neatly slice warm bread. Once it's lukewarm, you can slice it more easily. Let a pound cake cool for at least 1 hour before you finish decorating it.

TYPES OF FLOUR THAT ARE USED IN THIS BOOK

WHAT'S THE DIFFERENCE BETWEEN MEAL AND FLOUR?

I'll start off discussing a topic that I have noticed many people find confusing. Meal is made by grinding grains (or nuts, beans, or roots). When the kernels are used whole, the meal will contain bran and germ. This often results in much tastier bread recipes.

Flour is made from grain that has been re-fined, meaning that the chaff has been removed and the flour has been sifted so that it doesn't contain any more fibers and bran. Flour is better for pound cakes, cookies, et cetera.

Sometimes a package might note that it's "bolted"—this is just a way of sifting, nothing complicated.

So, from coarse to fine: whole-wheat meal > wheat meal > wheat flour > cake flour.

WHEAT FLOUR

This is the most common type of flour—it's sold in supermarkets. Made from ground wheat, which is then refined, it is perfect for baking cookies and pound cakes.

You should probably know that wheat flour does contain gluten.

All-purpose flour is even finer than regular wheat flour and contains even more gluten proteins, which makes it even more suitable for baking cookies and cakes. It also makes for fine bread. Because a lot of flour is made from genetically modified wheat or because of sensitivity to gluten, some people no longer like

to consume it. In that case, light spelt flour (see below) is a good alternative. Using spelt, I've been able to bake some wonderful breads and pound cakes. Of course there's also whole-wheat flour. Made by grinding whole kernels, this flour contains more fiber, something that makes health food experts wildly enthusiastic because it puts your body to work.

SPELT FLOUR

Spelt is a primitive wheat species. At some point in history, the type of wheat we consume today gained popularity over spelt because it commands higher prices and is easier to peel than spelt. Nowadays, spelt is *en vogue* again, for the reasons mentioned in the previous paragraph.

This strong wheat species needs little fertilizer or pesticides. Even with a moderate gluten content, spelt is very suitable for baking. You could say I'm a bulk user. Take note: Organic spelt may be easier to digest than industrial wheat flour, but, unfortunately, people with a severe wheat intolerance should avoid it.

When buying spelt flour, always make sure it's made from 100% spelt instead of a combination of wheat and spelt. This does happen sometimes, and if so, you're being duped. People with a wheat sensitivity should be especially aware of this possibility.

Most of my recipes call for light spelt flour. If you can't find light spelt flour, use regular spelt flour, but expect a darker color and heartier flavor.

RYE FLOUR

Rye flour is rye meal that has been sifted. It has a white color and no longer contains any bran or germ. Rye meal, which has a gray color, is used for baking rye bread and crackers, among other things. Rye has a much lower gluten content than wheat. Therefore, it doesn't leaven as well. It is, however, very tasty, especially in a mixture with other types of flour. It is a little more bitter. I'm a rye flour fan. You will notice me using it quite a lot in this book.

RICE FLOUR

Rice flour is made from fine-ground white or brown rice. It is gluten-free, which is good news for people who are gluten-intolerant. Baking with rice flour does take a little getting used to. The lack of gluten makes the dough impossible to knead. This may feel weird at first. This flour bakes really well, though, and unlike what you may think, it doesn't taste radically different. It's really a good alternative to wheat flour if, for instance, you want to bake a pie crust.

Rice flour is available in most organic stores, but you can also make it yourself by finely grinding dry rice in a clean coffee grinder.

CORNMEAL / POLENTA

Cornmeal is a fine-ground version of polenta. And polenta is available in various versions: some finer, some more coarse.

Cornmeal—naturally—has a yellow color and has no gluten content, though it may have been processed or grown close enough to gluten-containing grains that it is not entirely gluten-free. Some supermarkets sell 100% gluten-free (organic) cornmeal, so that's good news for some.

Be aware that corn is almost always genetically modified, so if you subscribe to a strict orthomolecular diet, corn is a no-go for you.

ALMOND FLOUR / HAZELNUT MEAL

Almond flour is made from ground blanched almonds. It's that simple. (Almond meal, meanwhile, is made from ground unblanched, or "natural," almonds.) This means you can easily make it yourself if you own a food processor. You can also buy it in the gluten-free or organic baking sections. In some supermarkets and natural foods stores, you can also buy hazelnut meal, which can serve as a delicious substitute. Hazelnut is a little more savory than almond and I like to use it on occasions where I'd otherwise use whole wheat. Try it yourself.

Nut meal is always gluten-free, and as you can see, it's easy to make.

OATMEAL / ROLLED OATS

Oatmeal is made by washing, husking, and heating oat grains. Also known as "rolled oats," oatmeal consists of flattened whole oat groats, while oat flour is the finer, ground version.

Pay attention when buying oatmeal, because there are different varieties available: There is a huge difference between *fast-cooking* oatmeal (quick oats) and *instant* oatmeal. Quick oats are made from broken and steamed oats. The pre-cooked *instant* varieties have all sorts of flavorings and other stuff added, something I don't like all that much. It's better to buy organic oatmeal; it is pure and natural.

Oats don't contain any gluten, but they are usually processed in plants where other types of grain are also processed. If you really want to be strict, you should buy oatmeal that has "gluten-free" on the package.

People who want to lose weight or watch their health would do well eating a lot of oatmeal. It contains few calories, a lot of fiber, and a lot of antioxidants, and it satisfies hunger.

Anyway, I especially love oatmeal because it provides structure to everything I bake. It makes everything crispy, giving it a crunchy bite. Delicious for bread, tasty in cookies, and excellent for crumble pies.

Oatmeal also absorbs a lot of water. When baking from a recipe, you can't just replace flour with oatmeal. You'd have to add more liquid as well.

WHEAT GERM

The germ forms the core of a wheat kernel. You could say it is the storage place of all the kernel's nutrients. Wheat germ is rich in vitamins, minerals, proteins, omega-3/-6, lecithin, and many different fibers, making it a welcome addition to any bread, muesli, or crumble recipe.

Like oatmeal, wheat germ provides a great coarse texture to all your baked goods, making them nicely crispy. Organic wheat germ is available at supermarkets specializing in natural foods.

FURTHERMORE . . .

There are many other types of flour, flakes, and so on in natural food stores or the organic baking or gluten-free sections of many supermarkets that I like to use once in a while (or all the time). Please do experiment! Other grain and nut meals, baked quinoa flakes (gluten-free and awesome), amaranth (South American seeds—gluten-free!), buckwheat flour (perfect for pancakes or bread—a little bitter, though), teff (cereal from Egyptian grass, also gluten-free!), barley meal—way too many to mention, really. Just try out many different things, because hey, it's fun!

HANDY

*For each recipe in this book,
I'll indicate whether it's*

*wheat-free, gluten-free, lactose-free,
sugar-free, or refined sugars–free.*

People with a wheat allergy don't necessarily have a gluten allergy. Although spelt is a type of wheat, our body digests it better and more naturally. Hence, many people with a wheat intolerance can *in fact eat spelt even though it contains gluten. This means that when I indicate a recipe is "gluten-free," I won't also mention that it's "wheat-free," because to me that's a given.*

*More about recipes being free of
refined sugars on page 26.*

Connemara, Ireland

LEAVENING AGENTS

BAKING SODA

Also commonly called sodium bicarbonate, sodium hydrogen carbonate, bread soda, cooking soda, bicarbonate, or bicarb. In this book, I'll use the term "baking soda."

Baking soda reacts with acidic components in your batter. This is why you add acidic dairy such as buttermilk, sour cream, or yogurt, or other acidic ingredients like lemon or dried cranberries, to recipes that involve baking soda. This will release carbon dioxide and result in a nicely leavened dough.

Baking soda has a direct effect so it is important to place your dough or batter in the oven immediately after adding it, or to only stir it in at the very last moment. Baking soda can lose its effectiveness over the course of time.

If you'd like to test whether the baking soda that has been sitting in your cupboard for so long still works, add a dash of the baking soda to a small bowl of vinegar. If it starts to effervesce right away, it's still good. Without the addition of an acidic component to your recipe, your baked product could taste a little soapy, so do pay attention. Baking soda is sold at most supermarkets and pharmacies.

Baking soda is somewhat of a magic household potion, by the way. It works ridiculously well when used to get rid of smells in your fridge or to clean ovens, for example. To find out more about these uses, I advise you to do some research online.

CREAM OF TARTAR

Also known as potassium bitartrate or potassium hydrogen tartrate.

Not to be confused with tartaric acid: It is the potassium acid salt *of* tartaric acid, but that may be too technical for now.

Cream of tartar is the acidic component of baking powder, for baking powder consists of baking soda (basic) and hydrogen tartrate (acidic). Just add a little extra cream of tartar to the dough for scones and they will leaven beautifully. In the Netherlands, cream of tartar and baking powder are not commonly used. In the Anglo-Saxon cooking tradition, they're very common, and I recommend you try to play with the quantities of cream of tartar and baking soda to get a nicely leavened bread.

You can buy cream of tartar in most stores in the baking section.

Tip: A pinch of cream of tartar added to whisked egg whites will result in a perfectly stable, frothy meringue.

BAKING POWDER

As mentioned, baking powder is a mixture of baking soda and cream of tartar. Easy as that.

Store-bought baking powder often contains cornstarch to prevent lumps and to slow down the reaction between the two main components. Therefore, baking powder doesn't have a long shelf life. Be careful if you are sensitive to certain chemicals or if you only use it once in a while. It's best to make it yourself whenever you need it (see the recipe on the opposite page).

Also: When a recipe already contains many acidic ingredients, baking soda alone should suffice. By adding cream of tartar, your baked goods could end up tasting a bit too sour. To test whether your baking powder is still good, stir ¼ teaspoon into a cup of hot water. If it starts to foam, it still works; if not, you should make a new batch.

HOW TO MAKE BAKING POWDER

Making baking powder is easier than you think. Baking powder sold in stores often contains cornstarch. You can leave this out when making yours at home. This way, you can also use your own baking powder for a gluten-free recipe.

When making a large portion of baking powder at once, remember that it only keeps for about 2 months. Better not to make too much.

Use 2 parts cream of tartar to 1 part baking soda (plus, if you want to, 1 part cornstarch. It's not necessary, especially when you use your powder straightaway.)

HOW TO MAKE SELF-RISING FLOUR

I stopped buying self-rising flour after I found out how easy it is to make it yourself—especially useful if you live in a place where it's hard to find.

For self-rising flour, you need 1 cup (125 g) all-purpose flour, 1 teaspoon (5 g) baking powder, and ½ teaspoon salt.

Because the effects of baking powder significantly decrease after 2 months, I would recommend not to buy self-rising flour but to make it instead. That way you can play around with the measurements to achieve a different result *and*—not unimportant—you know what you're putting in your mouth.

YEAST

Yeast is a living microorganism that feeds on the proteins and sugars in flour. When liquid and some kind of sweetener (sugar, honey) are added to the flour, the yeast becomes active. Salt slows down the process, so it's better to add it after you've already added the sugar and the liquid. Yeast also works slower when heavy ingredients like cream, eggs, and butter are added. When adding any of these, you should allow more time for your dough to leaven.

There are various yeast types: fresh, active dry, and instant.

FRESH YEAST

You can buy fresh yeast at a bakery. It looks like compact, soft, beige clay and it's sold in cubes. It should smell fresh—old yeast smells worse than dirty socks. Be aware: Keep fresh yeast loosely wrapped in plastic wrap in your fridge, but not for too long! Or you will be unpleasantly surprised.

You can, on the other hand, freeze fresh yeast in small portions.

Fresh yeast yields wonderful baking results. To use, crumble it over a small bowl of luke-warm liquid—never more than 86°F (30°C), or you'll kill the yeast and it won't work any longer.

ACTIVE DRY YEAST

This granular beige yeast is sold in little packages. Carefully weigh the amount you need and immediately close the package, making sure to press out all the air. Active dry yeast should be soaked in lukewarm water for a while (10 to 15 minutes) in order to dissolve, preferably with some sugar to feed it. Water temperatures exceeding 106°F (41°C) will kill the dry yeast, so be careful.

Because active dry (and instant) yeast are several times more concentrated than fresh yeast, you need to use way less of it. On the next page, I've provided a little conversion table. Once opened, active dry and instant yeast keep for 2 months.

INSTANT YEAST

Since these particles are more porous than those in active dry yeast, they work faster. Often the package states that the yeast doesn't need to be dissolved and can be directly mixed in with the flour, but I don't have positive experiences with that. After taking baked bread out of the oven, I would often find tiny pellets of bitter instant yeast throughout.

It dissolves much more quickly than active dry yeast, though, often in no longer than 6 minutes. It is therefore a small effort to briefly let it soak in a small bowl while you are gathering the other ingredients for your recipe. Here the same rule applies: When dissolving the yeast, never use liquid warmer than 106°F (41°C).

YEAST CONVERSION TABLE

Because different sources don't seem to agree on the numbers, these are rounded quantities. I always use the following:

From fresh to dry yeast: 2.5 : 1

Which comes down to: 1 tbsp + 2½ tsp (25 g) fresh yeast = 2¼ tsp (10 g) active dry yeast.

From fresh to instant yeast: 3 : 1

Which comes down to: 2 tbsp + ¾ tsp (30 g) fresh yeast = 2¼ tsp (10 g) instant yeast.

SOURDOUGH STARTER

A sourdough starter is the oldest method of leavening a dough. Long before the beginning of our modern calendar, it was used for baking bread. A sourdough starter is a mixture of water and flour inoculated by bacteria that cause fermentation. We call this wild yeast.

To create a starter, you need to put aside a mixture of lukewarm water and flour for a couple of days. The bacteria culture that then develops causes that typical sour aroma. I will explain how to make a sourdough starter and how to use it when baking on page 108. As opposed to the aforementioned factory-made yeast, a sourdough starter is an organic product. These days in Holland you can buy a dried version at the organic food store. I've achieved wonderful results using it.

BLIND BAKING?

Blind baking means prebaking a pie crust with a replacement filling before putting in the real one. This way you can be sure the crust will cook properly.

Simply line your baking pan with dough and perforate it with a fork. Cover with a sheet of parchment paper, gently pressing it into the edges of the pan. Fill with dry beans (or baking beans from a kitchenwares store).

Blind bake the pie crust for about 15 minutes in a preheated oven. Then remove the parchment paper and the beans and bake the crust for another 6 minutes or so (depending on the size), until it's golden brown, or put in the actual filling and proceed as directed in the recipe.

"FAST" AND "SLOW" SUGARS

For all recipes in this book, I've indicated whether they are completely sugar-free or just free of refined sugars. I've done this because many people no longer want to, or cannot, eat sugar or refined sugar. Of course, sometimes sugar is just delicious. Therefore I use all sorts of sugar throughout this book. Now I will briefly tell you what I mean by "fast" (refined) and "slow" sugars. I will also list a few slow sugars for you. It's a bit of a technical story, really. But I promise, I'll be as brief as possible.

REFINED SUGARS

Eating refined sugar will cause a spike in your blood sugar level. This will give you a short burst of energy; your body will then produce insulin, a hormone that regulates the transport of sugars to your liver and your muscles, thus restabilizing your blood sugar level.

Shortly afterward, you will experience a dip: Now your body asks for even more sugar. To meet this demand, you will increasingly eat more (sugar), and so on and so forth. Each time I read the labels of grocery products in the store, I'm shocked by the amounts of sugar they contain! We are being made addicted. Nearly everything contains sugar.

Therefore, it's best to prepare as much of your own food as possible and to buy fewer processed food products, since they always contain flavor enhancers like sugar (and salt).

I have started to use less and less sugars, and I've been increasingly replacing them with alternative sweeteners.

I also often completely omit sugar. It's a myth that sugarless pastry is boring. Just look at many of my recipes! In the end it's up to you, however. Of course you can often also use table sugar wherever I use a sugar substitute. I

just like to point out that sometimes you can actually do without as well.

You'll also notice that brown sugar is called for in some of my recipes. When working with brown sugar, it's important to pay attention to the different types and what the recipe calls for. If you don't have light brown sugar, please use white sugar and not dark brown. If you don't have dark brown sugar, you can replace it with light brown sugar.

GLYCEMIC INDEX

The glycemic index (GI), ranging from 0 to 100, represents the speed at which specific types of food are broken down by the human body. The highest number, a GI of 100, is based on the metabolization of white table sugar.

Sugars with a low GI (slow sugars) are better because they are broken down more slowly. Thus their cached energy is released over a longer period of time and doesn't need to be stored in the form of body fat.

At natural foods stores, you can buy all sorts of sweeteners that, provided they're the 100% pure product, have a low GI. Their use leads to a more stable blood sugar level. This will decrease your body craving for that next "shot." Often these sugar substitutes also contain more minerals and antioxidants than traditional sweeteners.

AGAVE SYRUP

Agave syrup is the boiled-down sap of the agave plant (native to Mexico). Be careful which one you buy: Many brands use the cheaper, lower-quality parts of the agave plants, rendering the syrup less healthy. Buy the high-quality, 100% organic syrup.

HONEY

Not only does honey contain quite a lot of sugars, it's also rich in minerals and nutrients—which is why honey is still preferable over refined sugar. Using raw honey would be ideal. Because this product hasn't been pasteurized, it also contains antibacterial and antiviral components.

STEVIA

Stevia is a plant. As a sweetener, it's about four times as strong as regular sugar, so be careful when you use it. Stevia's GI is ZERO, so it doesn't provide any calories. Make sure you buy 100% stevia, though, and not some kind of mixture—some products only contain a teeny tiny bit of stevia; the rest is filler, just powder, and therefore fake. I don't particularly like the taste of stevia—it's a tad bitter—so I don't use it too often. There are people, however, who adore it.

MAPLE SYRUP

Maple syrup is a runny liquid produced by reducing the sap of (Canadian and U.S.) maple trees. It can be a little pricey, but it's absolutely one of the most delicious syrups I know. Always check that you have real 100% maple syrup and not some sort of watered-down product. This syrup has a caramel-like flavor, contains a lot of minerals, and has a low GI. The darker the syrup, the richer it will taste.

PALM SUGAR AND COCONUT SUGAR

These unrefined sugars, produced from the sap of palm trees (in Southeast Asia), are wonderful. Both are rich in vitamins and minerals and both have a low GI, making them ideal sugar substitutes. Palm sugar, made from the sap of the sugar palm, is just as sweet as regular table sugar and can be used as a substitute at a 1:1 ratio. Its taste somewhat resembles cane sugar. Coconut sugar, made from the sap of coconut palm flower buds, is slightly less sweet but has a lovely nutty caramel taste.

DATE SYRUP

Date syrup is produced by boiling down dates in water. Because dates, like raisins, contain a lot of sugar, you shouldn't drink whole bottles of this syrup (at least not when you are on a health kick). It is still one of my favorite sugar substitutes, though. Rich in taste and full of vitamins and minerals.

FRUIT CONCENTRATE

I use fruit concentrate when I really feel like drinking a glass of lemonade. I'll also stir it into my yogurt. Concentrate is produced by boiling down fruit juice, so it does have a high level of fructose. Use sparingly. It's also great in smoothies or over pancakes, or other pastries like the Dutch Baby (page 80), for instance. These days there are many different varieties available. Go and try them to see which ones you like!

County Mayo, Ireland

SPELT & OAT
BREAD
€3.50

Connemara, Ireland

HOMEMADES
products you can make yourself

Sesame Nougatine

FOR about ⅔ cup (110 g)
PREP 30 min.

gluten-free
lactose-free

6 tbsp (75 g) sugar
¼ cup (35 g) sesame seeds, toasted

In a heavy saucepan, heat the sugar and a drop or two of water over medium heat. Softly shake the pan and use a wet brush to swipe down any sugar granules from the pan's edge. As soon as the sugar acquires a golden color, add the sesame seeds. Thoroughly stir, then pour the warm caramel directly onto a sheet of parchment paper. Cover with another sheet of parchment paper and use a rolling pin to roll out the caramel into a thick slab. Let cool until the caramel has solidified.

Without removing the parchment paper (this will prevent the crumbs from flying throughout the room), crush the caramel using a hammer or a rolling pin. You can also grind the caramel coarse (or fine, depending on what you like to use it for) in a food processor, if you have one.

TIP: Do the same with toasted & coarsely chopped nuts.

Lemon Curd

FOR about 1½ cups (350 ml)
PREP 15 min. plus at least 2 to 3 hours for cooling down

gluten-free

5 egg yolks
scant 1 cup (200 g) brown sugar
grated zest of 1 lemon
juice of 2 lemons (about 7 tbsp / 100 ml)
7 tbsp (100 g) butter, cubed

Combine the egg yolks, brown sugar, lemon zest, and lemon juice in a saucepan. Bring to a boil while slowly stirring and continue boiling and stirring for about 5 minutes, until the sauce has the consistency of yogurt. Take the pan off the heat and stir in the butter cubes. Pour into a sterilized jar and close with a lid. Allow to further cool and solidify in the fridge. Lemon curd only really reaches its proper consistency when completely cold.

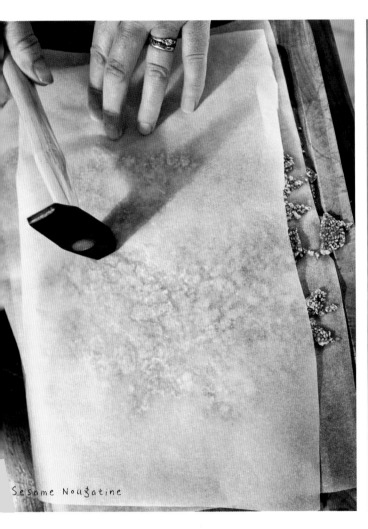

Sesame Nougatine

Lemon Curd

Vanilla Extract

You can easily make vanilla extract by allowing vanilla beans to steep in alcohol. You can use any kind of liquor: whiskey, vodka, cognac, or rum. Whatever you prefer. Vodka is my preference since it has the most neutral flavor. I also like cognac, though. It's up to you.

FOR 1 cup (250 ml)
PREP 5 min.
INACTIVE at least 1 month

gluten-free
lactose-free

4 vanilla beans
1 cup (250 ml) alcohol

Slice open the vanilla beans and drop them in a jar or bottle. If necessary, you can cut them into shorter pieces to make them fit. Pour in enough alcohol to completely submerge the vanilla. Set aside for at least 1 month before using, preferably longer.

If you keep refilling the bottle with alcohol, you will never run out of vanilla extract. You can also add scraped vanilla beans each time you have some leftover from baking a cake. After a while, your extract will turn deep dark brown, almost black. So aromatic, you can keep smelling it forever!

Vanilla Sugar

FOR 1¼ cups (250 g)
PREP 5 min.
INACTIVE at least 2 weeks

gluten-free
lactose-free

1¼ cups (250 g) sugar (preferably superfine)
1 vanilla bean, whole or scraped

Put the sugar in a jar with a good lid. Using a sharp knife, slice open the vanilla bean and scrape out the seeds (you can use the seeds in a recipe). Chop the bean pod into four or more pieces and add to the sugar. Close the lid and thoroughly shake the jar to mix everything. Set aside for at least 2 weeks before using.

Each time you have a scraped pod leftover from baking, add it to the jar. Meanwhile, keep refilling the sugar—this way you'll have a bottomless homemade vanilla sugar reservoir.

TIP: Do the same with lavender blossom or dried rose petals. Delicious for sprinkling over a pie or over yogurt.

Vanilla Extract

Flavored Buttercream

FOR 1 cake
PREP 45 min.

gluten-free

1 cup (200 g) sugar
1 flavor element such as: 1 vanilla bean,
    1 bunch fresh basil or mint, et cetera
2 eggs

1⅓ cups (2⅔ sticks / 300 g) butter,
    at room temperature
grated zest and juice of ½ lemon

Heat the sugar and 3 tbsp water with the flavor element in a heavy saucepan over medium heat. Let the sugar syrup gently boil for 12 minutes, until the sugar has been fully dissolved and is softly boiling. I use a wet, heat-resistant brush to swipe down any sugar crystals from the side of the pan. If you have a candy thermometer, you should check for when the sugar reaches a temperature of 240°F (116°C), or soft ball stage. Then, immediately take the pan off the heat. Remove the flavor element, using tongs because the syrup is very hot.

In a bowl, beat the eggs to a nice foam. While whisking, pour in the hot syrup in a thin stream. Keep whisking while the mixture slowly cools down, until it reaches room temperature. This will take 4 to 5 minutes. When the mixture has cooled, gradually add the soft butter. Thoroughly whisk after each addition. Finally add the lemon zest and juice. If the cream becomes too soft, chill it in the fridge and whip it up again later. Afterward, use the buttercream on a cake.

TIP: Here is a piece of advice from my wonderful editor Martine: If your buttercream starts to curdle, just heat it up *au bain-marie* (in a double boiler) while whisking, and it will become fluffy and smooth again. Good to know, I figured.

Meringue Icing

Officially, this is called Italian meringue. Ridiculously sweet, but insanely good! Use it to top a cake or in combination with a fresh, tangy counterpart such as grapefruit or red berries (see recipe on page 304) or artfully pipe it over lemon tarts and briefly caramelize the meringue with a torch.

FOR 1 cake
PREP 30 min.

lactose-free
gluten-free

1¼ cups (250 g) sugar
5 egg whites

pinch of salt
3 drops fresh lemon juice

Making
Flavored Buttercream

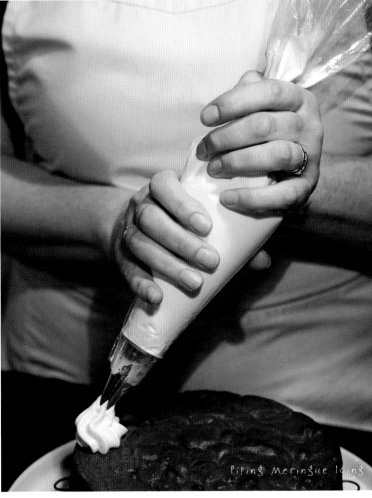

Piping Meringue Icing

Combine the sugar and 7 tbsp (100 ml) water in a saucepan and bring to a boil, then heat to 250°F (121°C)—measure this with a candy thermometer. If you don't have one, just allow it to boil for about 15 minutes. The syrup has to still be translucent and colorless. You can also check whether it's done by sticking a teaspoon into the syrup and then dipping it into a glass of water. If you are able to tear the syrup into a thin thread, it is done.

Whisk the egg whites with the salt in a clean, grease-free bowl until foamy. Add the lemon juice. While continuing to beat the egg whites with a hand mixer—or better still, a stand mixer—pour in the boiling syrup in a thin stream. Keep beating until the foam has cooled. This will *truly* take a while.

Spoon the foam into a pastry bag. Place in the fridge for later use. If needed, you can prepare meringue 1 day in advance.

Orange Pastry Cream

Instead of cardamom and oranges, you could also just use vanilla, or 1 tbsp lavender blossom, or a tiny splash of orange blossom water. What I mean to say is: The amount of possible flavors is limited only by the size of your own imagination. This is wonderful in the croquembouche *on page 356.*

FOR about 2 cups (500 ml)
PREP 25 min.

1¼ cups (300 ml) milk
8 crushed cardamom pods
finely grated zest of 1 orange
3 egg yolks
⅓ cup (70 g) sugar

2 tbsp cornstarch
2 tbsp all-purpose flour
2 tbsp butter
3 tbsp Cointreau or Grand Marnier
 (optional)

In a saucepan, heat the milk, cardamom, and orange zest to a near boil and simmer for 15 minutes over low heat.

In a bowl, beat the egg yolks until foamy. Add the sugar, cornstarch, and flour and stir everything until smooth.

Strain the warm milk and, while stirring, pour it into the yolk mixture. Pour the mixture back into the saucepan and continue stirring until you get a nice thick consistency. Spoon in the butter and, if you like, add a splash of liqueur.

Allow the cream to cool in a bowl. Cover, placing plastic wrap on the cream's surface to prevent any skin from forming. You can also put it in a pastry bag and allow it to further set in the fridge.

CLOTTED CREAM

Naturally, when serving scones, you also offer clotted cream. However, I do know that outside of England and Ireland it can be difficult to find the right heavy cream. Fortunately it's not that hard to make it yourself. With a little patience, you'll have your own clotted cream. Whatever cream you may have leftover after skimming the thick stuff from the top can be used in a soup or something. No need to throw away anything.

FOR ⅔ cup (150 ml)
PREP 16 hours (overnight plus 1 day)

gluten-free
sugar-free

2 cups (500 ml) heavy cream

Preheat the oven to 175°F (80°C) shortly before going to bed. Be sure to place an oven thermometer in the oven to check the temperature (see page 15). Pour the cream into a wide bowl or dish: The wider the bowl, the more clotted cream you will make. Not too large, though, because the bowl will have to fit in your fridge.

Cover the dish with aluminum foil and place it in the oven for at least 8 hours, or for one whole night. The more cream you use, the longer it will have to sit in the oven. Don't worry, you don't have to stay up to watch it. You'll get your 8 hours of sleep.

The clotted cream is ready if a thick yellow layer has formed on top of the cream in the bowl. This layer is your clotted cream. Leave the dish on the kitchen counter to cool until it reaches room temperature. Subsequently cover it and place it in the fridge for another 8 hours.

Scrape the thick layer from the liquid cream sitting at the bottom of the dish and thoroughly stir it loose. Store the clotted cream in a clean jar. It should keep for another 4 to 5 days, provided you use clean spoons whenever you scoop some out.

The leftover thin cream in the dish can be used in your coffee or in a soup; it may be a little thinner but is perfectly edible. You can no longer whip it, though. Just so you know.

Almond Milk

FOR a scant 2 cups (450 ml)
PREP 15 min.
INACTIVE 1 to 2 days

lactose-free
gluten-free
sugar-free

1 cup (150 g) blanched almonds

Soak the almonds in a bowl of water for at least 1 day, but preferably 2 days (for a smoother result).

Drain in a strainer and throw out the water.

Put the almonds in a blender, add 1¼ cups (300 ml) fresh water, and blend until completely smooth. As smooth as possible. Take your time; the result will only be better.

Now you have the most delicious almond milk you've ever tasted. Use less water to get an even richer taste. Never make more than you intend to use. It will only keep a day or two in the fridge.

Ganache

Ganache is that finger-licking chocolate glaze, that firm truffle filling, or that irresistibly creamy chocolate hiding between the cake layers. Although ganache basically isn't more than a mix of melted chocolate and heavy cream, the ratio varies depending on the way you use it.

YIELD varies
PREP 15 min.
INACTIVE 2 hours to a whole night

gluten-free

When glazing a cake you need a thinner ganache than when making a filling. Therefore, I'll start off by giving you some ratios. If you want equal proportions, make sure to use 3½ oz (100 g) chopped chocolate and 3½ oz (100 g) cream (weigh, don't measure volume). The ratio will be 1 : 1.

A thin glaze: 1 : 2.

I always add 1 tbsp oil or butter for some extra shine. When you plan to use the glaze immediately, you can also use 1½ : 2.

Cake filling and firm glaze 1 : 1.

Chocolate truffles 2 : 1. 🐟

Chop the chocolate as finely as possible. Heat the cream. Don't let it boil, but bring it to just below the boiling point. Turn off the heat. Pour in the chocolate and let rest for 5 minutes without stirring. If you want to use a little butter, add that as well. The same goes for a touch of flavoring, like a splash of liqueur or some espresso grounds. After 5 minutes have passed you can stir the ganache with a soft spatula. Don't beat it, just a gentle stir.

Always allow the ganache to cool before processing it further. This way it will set considerably.

Glaze: Allow the ganache to cool in a bowl in the fridge. Check on it once in a while—it will continue to set. Once it has reached the preferred consistency—which should be after an hour or two—you can pour the ganache over the cake.

Cake Filling: Allow the ganache to cool completely before placing it in the fridge to further set. This will take at least 4 hours, although waiting 1 night is even better as it allows the cream to further "ripen" (this is a bit of *haute* pastry-chef wisdom, but it really does result in a nicer ganache, believe me).

Once your ganache has fully set, you can whisk it into a light and fluffy mousse with a hand mixer. You can spoon the mousse into a pastry bag for piping between your cake layers.

Truffle Filling: When making truffles, you need a firm ganache. Therefore, you should always allow it to fully cool in the fridge, at least 4 to 6 hours, but preferably over-night. Then scoop out little balls and roll them into delicious truffles.

EXTRA ADVICE: To give your ganache a different taste, steep a flavoring in the cream, something like Lapsang Souchong tea, tonka beans, or lavender.

Marzipan

FOR almost 4 cups (900 g)
PREP 20 min.

gluten-free
lactose-free

Making marzipan is very easy. Just make a bunch at once because you can store it in the freezer, where it will keep for 3 months. Instead of brandy you can use a liqueur, or some other type of flavoring, as well. You can also add some coloring if you like. It's important to use real almond oil, if you can find it. It has a subtle, slightly bitter almond flavor that really enhances the marzipan. Artificial flavoring is far too sweet and not subtle at all—never use it!

¾ cup plus 2 tbsp (175 g) packed light brown sugar
1¾ cups (175 g) confectioners' sugar, plus a little extra for dusting
4 cups (450 g) almond flour

seeds of 1 vanilla bean
2 eggs, beaten
1 tsp brandy, orange blossom water, or fresh orange juice
1 or 2 drops of real almond oil (optional)

Combine both sugars, the almond flour, and the vanilla seeds in a large bowl. Make an indentation in the middle and pour in the eggs and brandy. Add a drop or two of almond oil, if using (be careful: one drop too many and the taste will be ruined). Swiftly combine everything into a cohesive dough.

Dust your work surface with confectioners' sugar and continue kneading the marzipan for a short while until you have a smooth dough. Don't knead for too long or it will render your marzipan a bit greasy. If needed, add a little extra confectioners' sugar. Form the dough into a ball and wrap it in plastic wrap. Store in the fridge for up to 2 days (or in the freezer for up to 3 months).

Pistachio Cream

ENOUGH FOR 1 cake
PREP 20 min.
INACTIVE 2 hours

gluten-free
lactose-free

This cream is so heavenly, I could eat it straight from the bowl. But if you manage a little more restraint than me, this could be the perfect filling for between two cake layers or inside a puff pastry crust, like on page 286 of this book.

1⅓ cups (200 g) pistachios
⅓ cup (60 g) sugar

7 tbsp (50 g) almond flour
1 drop of real almond oil (optional)

Put everything in a blender with ¾ cup plus 1 tbsp (200 ml) water and grind for a long time until you get a soft cream. Spoon it into a pastry bag or into a sealable container and let it rest in the fridge for at least 2 hours. The cream will continue to set.

Marzipan

Pistachio cream

HOW TO MAKE YOUR OWN NUTELLA

(FOR 1 JAR)
PREP: 12 MIN.

LACTOSE-FREE   WHEAT-FREE

GRIND 1 CUP (125g)
HAZELNUTS INTO
VERY FINE POWDER
IN A BLENDER

THIS WILL TAKE AT LEAST 5 MIN. PEOPLE!

ADD 5 TBSP (25g)
COCOA

AND ¾ CUP (75g)
CONFECTIONERS'
SUGAR

AND SALT!
AND VANLLA EXTRACT   1 TSP

GRIND FOR ANOTHER 3 MIN. INTO AN EVENLY
COLORED DARK-BROWN PASTE.

WHILE GRINDING, POUR IN
ABOUT 6 TBSP (90ML) OIL.
BE CAREFULL: NOT TOO MUCH
OR IT WILL BECOME
TOO THIN!

REGULARLY STOP THE BLENDER TO SCRAPE THE
PASTE FROM THE BOTTOM & CONTINUE GRINDING

STORE YOUR HOME MADE NUTELLA IN THE FRIDGE
IT WILL KEEP FOR AT LEAST 15 MONTHS.

Saintes-Maries-de-la-Mer, France

NATURAL COLORING

It's very easy to color icing or frosting—or whatever you want, really—with natural colorants. No doubt you'll have some of the necessary ingredients sitting in your pantry already. As a matter of fact, I'm almost certain of it.

For some products, like spinach juice or parsley juice, you will need a juicer or a very strong blender. If you don't have one, don't worry; there are other ways to achieve the desired colors.

GREEN

Japanese matcha tea powder, spirulina powder, wheatgrass powder, fresh parsley juice, fresh spinach juice. That last one is the best in my opinion. Spinach juice has no taste but it gives off an even, truly beautiful green color.

YELLOW

Ground turmeric or saffron dissolved in some lukewarm lemon juice or water; use carefully, as both colorants are highly effective.

ORANGE

Strained fresh carrot juice, paprika.

RED

Pure pomegranate juice.

PINK

Strained fresh beet juice; pure cranberry juice; strained juice of red fruits such as strawberries, red currants, or raspberries.

PURPLE

Boil chopped red cabbage leaves in water until the water is dark purple. Use a few drops of this cooking water.

BLUE

Make the purple colorant as described above and in the end stir in a pinch of baking soda. Yes, I know it sounds a bit scary and brings back memories of that first chemistry class, but trust me on this one.

BROWN

Instant coffee powder, espresso coffee grounds, well-steeped black tea, cacao, cinnamon.

BLACK

Charcoal, ground in a mortar or grated with a fine grater; squid ink.

SOS!
emergency rescue...

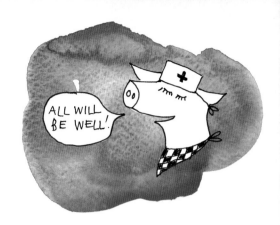

ALL WILL BE WELL!

Of course there are all sorts of things that can go wrong in the kitchen, even though I try my best to keep instructions as clear as possible. Sometimes things simply go awry, no matter how strictly you followed the recipe. Baking, after all, is a complicated process, a kind of magic that takes time to master, during which some people may encounter more hurdles than others. In general my recipes aren't too complicated. And if they are, I hope my explanations will guide you through the tricky parts, with pictures and illustrations if necessary.

Be sure to read my general baking tips on page 14 before you get started. This will probably prevent the worst disasters . . .

Now, the last thing I want to do is scare you, because baking isn't that difficult. Nevertheless, if you do encounter some sort of baking emergency, I hope the following section will offer you some hands-on solutions.

EGG WHITES WON'T STIFFEN

Two reasons:

- There is some yolk residue in your egg white. You didn't separate your eggs meticulously enough. Throw everything out and start over in a spotless bowl.

- Your whisk or mixing bowl weren't completely free of grease. Before you start beating eggs, it is best to first wash all your tools with soap and really hot water. Then dry off everything with a clean dish towel. Purists even polish the bowl with a little lemon juice, but if you just make sure you're working with clean tools, nothing should go wrong. Otherwise: Throw everything out and start over in a spic-and-span bowl.

CAKE IS STUCK IN THE BAKING PAN

Start by buying a quality baking pan.

Always carefully grease the baking pan. I cut parchment paper to the exact size and use it to line my pan. Then, to be on the safe side, I also grease the paper.

But regardless: It won't come out.

- Slide a thin knife between the cake and the wall of the baking pan to ensure it comes loose. Then tap the outside of the pan in several spots along the edges.

- Allow the cake to cool for a bit; often, it won't come loose as easily when it's still hot.

- If—oh, horror—it has already broken into several pieces, you can try to reassemble it by sealing the edges with a thick layer of frosting. Some examples of frosting can be found a couple of pages back in this chapter.

- Use the pieces of the "failed" cake and turn them into a trifle or a tiramisù. Never throw them out.

THE CAKE SANK IN THE MIDDLE

• You used too much or too-old (meaning, no longer working) baking powder. In the first case, your cake will rise enormously and then suddenly collapse.

• You opened the oven door too many times during baking, thus allowing too much cold air to come in. This can cause the cake to collapse. In any case, try not to open the oven door during the first 15 minutes.

• You stirred the batter for too long after adding the flour.

THE CAKE'S CENTER ISN'T DONE YET BUT THE CRUST IS ALREADY BEGINNING TO BURN

• The oven temperature is too high. For next time, buy an oven thermometer; they're only a few bucks and you can find them at most housewares stores. You'll be surprised how much hotter your oven gets than the temperature you set it to.

• Lower the temperature and cover the cake with aluminum foil. Then bake it at the lower temperature for 10 to 15 minutes more and check on it regularly.

• Later you can carefully cut off the burned edges and, if you want, cover the edges with frosting or whipped cream or something.

THE CAKE WON'T RISE

• You forgot to use a leavening agent, or the leavening agent was too old and wasn't as effective anymore. See page 22 about leavening agents and their shelf life.

• The batter was too thick or too dry, either because the flour absorbed too much liquid, the weather was too dry, or the eggs were too small. It helps to add the liquid *gradually*, not all at once, and see if the batter needs a bit more or less.

• You stirred the batter for too long after adding the flour, which beats the air out of, instead of into, the batter.

• If the oven didn't get warm enough, your pastry won't properly rise. Always check the temperature with an oven thermometer. See my remarks about oven thermometers on page 15.

AFTER BAKING, THE FILLING (RAISINS, FOR INSTANCE) HAS SUNK TO THE BOTTOM

Most likely the batter was too thin or didn't have the right firmness. Next time it would be a good idea to toss the filling with some flour before folding it in with the batter.

CAKE BURSTS IN THE MIDDLE AND THE EDGES ARE BURNING

The oven temperature is too high. Measure with an oven thermometer. See my remarks on page 15.

PASTRY ISN'T DONE

Immediately put your pastry back in the oven and extend the baking time. Check the temperature with an oven thermometer—perhaps it was too low.

It also helps when you wrap a cake in aluminum foil. This will help retain the heat and prevent the crust from burning. After about 7 minutes, check again.

CAKE IS TOO DRY

- Your batter was too dry. Most likely you used too much flour. The size of the eggs can also be a factor; make sure they weren't too small.

- You beat the batter for too long.

- It can also be that your baking temperature was too low.

- In a situation like this, generously dousing your cake with homemade syrup is a good solution. Make a syrup by dissolving 1 cup (200 g) sugar in ¾ cup plus 1 tbsp (200 ml) water. Add a flavoring like lemon zest, cardamom, or lavender and let the syrup slowly steep over low heat for 20 minutes. Strain over a jug and throw out the flavoring. Pour one-third of the syrup over the cake, immediately after you have turned the cake out of the pan. Then, each time you walk by, add a little more syrup. Continue until you're out of syrup and the cake has absorbed all of it. Store the cake covered with plastic wrap. You can also make a trifle or something like that. Never throw out anything. That would be a waste.

CAKE IS BAKING UNEVENLY

- It can be that you didn't sufficiently mix the flour into the batter, causing the leavening agent to not be evenly spread throughout as well.

- Did you rotate the cake when you checked the oven halfway through baking? Some ovens don't heat up evenly. In that case, you have to rotate your pastry yourself to make sure each side gets the same amount of heat.

- For now, cut the slanted top off with a bread knife and turn the cake over. This way it will look sharp again and you can go ahead and finish it.

THE PIE DOUGH IS TOO STICKY

You have kneaded the dough for too long.

AFTER BAKING, THE PIE DOUGH FALLS APART

You didn't use enough liquid or butter.

CAKE is BURNED BLACK

OVEN WAS TOO HOT
OR YOU FORGOT
THE TIME.

CAKE IS SLANTED

BUY A TORPEDO LEVEL
AND LEVEL YOUR OVEN.

CAKE iS LIQUID

DID YOU EVEN
BAKE IT?

BATTER IS SALTY AS BRINE

GO AND VISIT YOUR OPTICIAN.

PIE CRUST ISN'T SUFFICIENTLY DONE

- You didn't blind bake it and the filling you put in is too wet.

- The oven temperature was too low, or there was too little heat coming from below. Next time, try to bake the pie at a lower position in the oven and/or raise the oven temperature. What you can do now is turn it over on a parchment paper–lined baking sheet (only do this if the filling is properly cooked!) and put the pie back in the oven, bottom up. I sometimes do this with quiches.

THE PIE DOUGH SEVERELY SHRINKS AFTER BAKING

You kneaded the dough for too long.

COOKIES ARE TOO HARD

You used too little liquid or too much flour for the dough. The sugar and the butter (or some other type of fat) have begun to caramelize, making the cookies too crunchy. Next time, make thinner cookies with this dough. That way, the crunchiness actually becomes delightful.

COOKIES ARE TOO SOFT

- You used too much liquid or too little flour for the batter. You used relatively too much sugar and butter for this recipe.

- The cookies haven't been baked long enough or they are too thick or too large relative to the baking time.

COOKIES SPREAD OUT TOO FAR DURING BAKING

It really helps to cool your dough in the fridge before baking. Also, make sure your oven has been properly preheated.

THE BREAD TEXTURE IS TOO DENSE

- You used too much salt; salt breaks down the effectiveness of yeast.

- You didn't use enough liquid in the dough.

- You didn't use enough yeast.

- The bread hasn't risen long enough.

OH NOoo!

Cinnamon & Caramel Pull-Apart Loaf

SERVES 12
PREP 30 min.
RISE 1 hour and 45 min.
BAKE 40 min.

FOR THE DOUGH
3 cups (375 g) all-purpose
    flour, or more as needed
¼ cup (50 g) sugar
scant 2 tsp (7 g) instant
    yeast
½ tsp salt
½ cup (120 ml) milk
¼ cup (½ stick / 60 g) butter,
    plus more for the pan
seeds of 1 vanilla bean
2 eggs, at room temperature

FOR THE FILLING
¼ cup (½ stick / 60 g)
    butter, at room
    temperature
¾ cup (150 g) packed light
    brown sugar or cane
    sugar
2 tsp cinnamon

FOR THE CARAMEL
9 tbsp (125 g) butter
½ cup plus 1 tbsp (125 g)
    packed dark brown sugar
3 tbsp milk or heavy cream

First, make the dough: In the bowl of a stand mixer fitted with the dough hook, thoroughly combine 2 cups (250 g) of the all-purpose flour with the sugar, yeast, and salt.

Heat the milk, butter, and vanilla in a small saucepan over medium heat until the butter has just melted. Allow it to cool somewhat. Add the lukewarm milk-butter mixture to the dry ingredients and knead everything into a firm dough. Then, one by one, add the eggs and continue mixing until everything is blended and the dough has become very smooth.

Now add the rest of the flour and, with flour-dusted hands, knead the dough on the kitchen counter until it's soft and supple. Go on kneading for at least 8 minutes. If needed, you can add some more liquid (milk or water) if the dough seems dry, or flour if the dough is sticky. Form the dough into a ball and place it in a greased bowl. Cover with plastic wrap and set aside in a warm spot for at least 1 hour to rise.

Meanwhile, make the filling: In a small bowl, combine the butter, brown sugar, and cinnamon into a spreadable paste.

Once the dough has doubled in volume, remove it from the bowl and, on a flour-dusted countertop, roll it out into a large flat rectangle of 16 by 9½ inches (40 by 24 cm). Using a spatula, spread the cinnamon butter over the entire dough rectangle. Then, using the back of a knife, slice the dough lengthwise into 4 or 6 long strips. Stack them and cut them into squares. Stack the dough squares vertically inside a well-greased 1½-qt (1.5-L) loaf pan. This should be done somewhat loosely, leaving the dough some room to rise. Cover it with some plastic wrap and allow it to rise for another 45 minutes.

About 20 minutes before bake time, preheat the oven to 340°F (170°C). Bake the bread for 35 to 40 minutes. If the top is browning too fast, you can cover it loosely with some aluminum foil. Allow the bread to cool on a rack, then carefully turn it out onto a large plate.

Meanwhile, make the caramel: Melt the butter and brown sugar together in a heavy saucepan over low heat. Gently stir in the cream (careful, the syrup's hot!) and pour the hot caramel over the bread in a thin stream, making sure it reaches all spots. You can keep some of the caramel for later when you're serving. Eat the bread while still warm and the caramel is deliciously soft and melted. Or serve it cold, so you get crispy caramel.

Strawberry Roll-up Scones

SERVES 6
PREP 20 min.
BAKE 30 min.

3¼ cups (500 g) strawberries, washed and
sliced
¼ cup plus 2 tbsp (75 g)
sugar
finely grated zest of 2 limes
juice of 1 lime
2¾ cups (350 g) all-purpose
flour, plus some extra for
dusting
1½ tsp baking powder
pinch of salt
7 tbsp (100 g) cold butter,
cubed, plus some extra
for greasing
about ½ cup plus 1 tbsp
(140 ml) buttermilk (you
can also use regular milk,
but I prefer buttermilk;
the acidity works better
to activate the baking
powder)

FOR SERVING
confectioners' sugar
whipped cream, lightly
sweetened

Put the strawberries in a bowl, sprinkle with ¼ cup (50 g) of the sugar, the zest of 1 lime, and the lime juice, then set aside.

Preheat the oven to 400°F (200°C). Grease an 8-inch (20-cm) round baking pan with some butter.

Sift together the flour, baking powder, salt, and the remaining sugar over a bowl. Swiftly combine this mixture with the remaining lime zest and the butter cubes. Knead until you get a coarse crumb while pouring in the buttermilk in splashes. You may not need all the buttermilk. Swiftly knead the mixture into a soft dough. Make sure you don't knead for too long—scones should be light, and too much kneading will result in a tough dough.

On a flour-dusted work surface, pat the dough into a square sheet ¼ inch (0.5 cm) thick. Sprinkle with half of the marinated strawberries. Spread them so you have a single layer of sliced strawberries, leaving a 1-inch- (2.5-cm-) wide strip bare at one edge. Now, starting at the opposite edge, roll up the dough.

Cut the roll into six even pieces and place them upright in the baking pan; they will rise some more, then they will merge together. Bake the rolled-up scones for 30 minutes, until golden brown and done. Let them cool for 5 minutes before serving them, garnished with the rest of the strawberries. Sprinkle with confectioners' sugar and serve some lightly sweetened whipped cream on the side.

Good times.

Raspberry Jam Cookies

FOR 8 to 12 cookies   **PREP** 20 min.   **BAKE** 20 min.

¾ cup (150 g) sugar, plus about 1 tbsp extra
2 tsp baking powder
1 tsp salt
2¼ cups (300 g) all-purpose flour, plus some extra for dusting
½ cup (1 stick / 120 g) cold butter, cut into small cubes
finely grated zest of 1½ lemons
½ cup (120 ml) buttermilk
1 egg, beaten
1 jar lovely (homemade) raspberry jam

WHAT YOU ALSO NEED
a cookie cutter about 2½ inches (6 cm) in diameter or a glass of the same size
sour cream or whipped cream, for serving

Preheat the oven to 350°F (180°C). In a large bowl, combine the sugar, baking powder, salt, and flour. Using your (cold) fingers, mix in the butter and lemon zest and rub until your dough has the appearance of coarse crumbs. Add the buttermilk and mix with a fork until the mixture holds together, then stop. Don't mix any further—place the dough on a lightly floured work surface and carefully knead everything into an even dough ball. This way your cookies will come out of the oven all crumbly, light, and crisp.

Roll out the dough to a slab of about ⅜ inch (1 cm) thick. Cut out as many cookies as you can and place them on a parchment paper–lined baking sheet. Scrape together the scraps, form them into a ball, roll out, and repeat until all the dough has been used. Using your thumb, press a dimple at the center of each cookie. Brush them with the egg and fill each dimple with 1 tablespoon raspberry jam. Sprinkle with a little sugar and bake to a golden brown, about 20 minutes. Serve the cookies with cream and the remaining raspberry jam in a little dish on the side.

De Kempen, Belgium

Scones

I repeat the following recipe from my book Home Made—*in case you don't have that book—because I thought it fits in this collection. These scones are terribly easy to make and since you most likely already have the necessary ingredients, you'll always be able to prepare the perfect breakfast in no time.*

The next recipe will be a richer version, for when you add crème fraîche and eggs, scones will suddenly transform into luxury pastry. Ideal for Easter, or for a birthday brunch.

FOR 8 to 10 easy-peasy scones
PREP 15 min.
BAKE 15 min.

3½ cups (450 g) all-purpose
  flour, plus extra for
  dusting
1 tbsp baking powder
½ cup (50 g) confectioners'
  sugar
pinch of salt
9 tbsp (125 g) cold butter,
  cubed, plus more for
  greasing
approx. ⅔ cup (150 ml) milk
  or buttermilk, plus more
  for brushing

Preheat the oven to 425°F (220°C). That means hot.

Combine all the ingredients except for the milk in a stand mixer or a large bowl. Knead briefly but thoroughly, until the butter and flour have turned into coarse crumbs. In Ireland, people use two knives in order to not warm up the butter with their hands, but I find that inconvenient. If you knead fast, it will be all right. Pour in the milk and knead everything into a cohesive ball. You may not need to use all the milk, or you may need to use more.

Dust a work surface with flour. Press the ball into a disc about ¾ inch (2 cm) thick. Cut out the scones using a 2½-inch (6-cm) cookie cutter or a glass. Keep kneading and rolling out the dough scraps until you have used everything. Place the scones on a greased or parchment paper–lined baking sheet, brush them with milk, and slide them into the oven. Bake for about 15 minutes, depending on the size of the scones, until golden brown.

Serve with jam, lightly salted butter, or whipped, unsweetened crème fraîche.

Luxury Scones

This is the Sunday version of my regular scones. Because I make them with spelt flour and because they contain egg, crème fraîche, and raisins, they are richer than regular scones. A happy medium between bread and pound cake, you could say. Really something for a chic brunch, or for an Easter morning. Serve with some homemade jam and crème fraîche. Delicious.

FOR 8 scones
PREP 10 min.
BAKE about 45 min.

wheat-free

4 cups (400 g) light spelt
   flour
2 tsp baking powder
¼ tsp salt
½ cup (100 g) plus 2 tbsp
   sugar, plus extra for
   sprinkling
⅔ cup (1⅓ sticks / 150 g)
   cold butter, cut into small
   cubes
heaping ½ cup (100 g)
   raisins, steeped for
   30 min. in warm water or
   tea, drained
1 egg
½ cup (125 ml) crème
   fraîche
½ cup (125 ml) buttermilk
1 egg yolk, beaten with
   3 drops of water
lightly salted butter or sour
   cream, for serving

Place a rack in the middle of the oven and preheat the oven to 350°F (180°C). In a bowl, combine all the dry ingredients until they are properly mixed. With cool hands, swiftly knead in the butter and rub until the flour looks like coarse crumbs. Mix in the raisins. Whisk the whole egg, crème fraîche, and buttermilk in a pitcher and pour the mixture into the flour mixture. Quickly knead everything into a cohesive dough ball.

You can add some flour if the dough is too wet, or some buttermilk if it's too dry. Be careful not to add too much, though—just a few drops may be enough.

Form the dough into a ball and flatten it into a disc about ¾ inch (2 cm) thick. Place it on a parchment paper–lined baking sheet. Use a knife to divide the dough into 8 even triangles, barely cutting down to the bottom.

Brush the top with the beaten egg yolk and sprinkle with some sugar.

Bake the scones for 45 to 50 minutes, until they're nicely golden brown. They should sound hollow when you tap the bottom. Allow to cool a bit and serve with some lightly salted butter or sour cream.

Oatmeal Loaf

In my opinion this bread—or, well . . . cake—is the most healthy thing on earth. I received the recipe from Cil, who's an orthomolecular health coach, but I have since given it my own personal twist. That's how it goes with recipes; they receive a new life with each owner.

I often bake one of these over the weekend. After it's cooled, I slice it and I wrap each of the slices separately. This way I'll have treats for an entire week. I also eat this loaf for breakfast often. Very delicious.

Forget porridge—we use oatmeal to bake bread. Far tastier.

By the way, you can leave out the sweetener—such as date syrup—if you like. I find the cake too savory without it, but your taste may be different.

FOR 10 slices
PREP 10 min.
RESTING 30 min.
BAKE 45 min.

wheat-free
refined sugar–free

6 eggs, beaten
6 tbsp (90 ml) date syrup, maple syrup, or honey
¼ cup (60 ml) olive oil, plus some extra for greasing
1 tbsp cinnamon
3¾ cups (350 g) rolled oats (not instant) from the natural foods store (see page 18)
½ cup (75 g) dried figs, halved
⅔ cup (100 g) dried apricots (no sulfites), halved
1 handful of hazelnuts
1 handful of pumpkin seeds
¾ cup (100 g) sesame seeds (black, if possible—looks better!)

In a wide bowl, whip the eggs with the date syrup, oil, cinnamon, and 1 cup (250 ml) water until foamy. Add the oatmeal. Then spoon in the figs, apricots, hazelnuts, pumpkin seeds, and sesame seeds. Pour the batter into a greased, 1½-qt (1.5-L) loaf pan. Leave for 30 minutes.

Meanwhile, preheat the oven to 350°F (180°C).

Bake the cake for 40 to 45 minutes in the middle of the oven, until brown and firm. Let cool on the countertop for a bit, then remove from the pan and let it cool further. Cut into slices and serve.

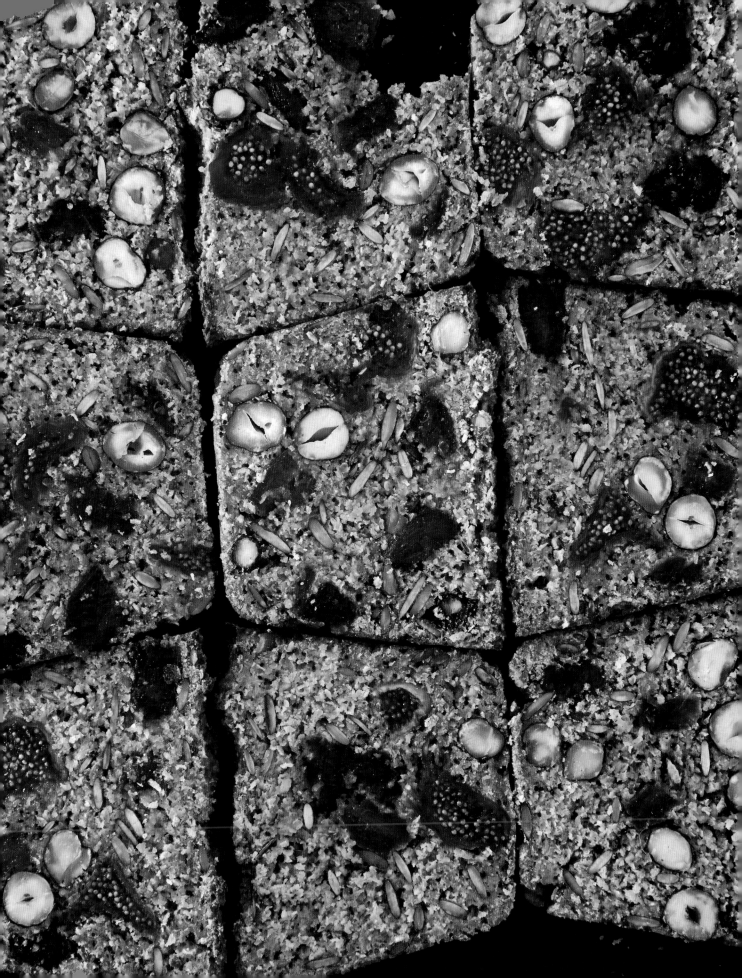

Chocolate Cinnamon Brioche

In order to test whether this recipe can be made without a stand mixer, I also tried making it completely by hand. That went really well, although it takes some persistence because, well . . . brioche dough isn't for wusses. Some experience with baking bread doesn't hurt, either, when you're trying to make this improbably wonderful bread.

You could say this bread is for the advanced home baker.

And . . . if you happen to have some leftovers the next day, this bread—sliced and sprinkled with some extra cinnamon sugar—makes perfect French toast. Oh!

FOR 1 loaf
PREP 30 min.
RISE almost 3 hours
BAKE 35 min.

FOR THE DOUGH

3½ tbsp (50 ml) lukewarm
    milk
scant 2 tsp (7 g) instant
    yeast
5 tbsp (65 g) sugar
2 cups (250 g) all-purpose
    flour, plus a little extra
½ tsp salt
3 eggs
¾ cup (1½ sticks / 175 g)
    butter, cubed, at room
    temperature

FOR THE FILLING

about 3 tbsp butter, at room
    temperature
5 tbsp (65 g) sugar
1 tsp cinnamon
pinch of sea salt
5¼ oz (150 g) dark chocolate,
    chopped
1 egg, beaten, for brushing

Make the dough: Pour the milk into a bowl. Add the yeast and 1 tablespoon of the sugar and allow the yeast to dissolve and foam for 7 minutes.

Combine the flour with the rest of the sugar and the salt in a bowl. Pour in the dissolved yeast mixture and break the eggs over the bowl.

Take a sturdy spatula or use a stand mixer fitted with the dough hook and stir until you get a cohesive dough. This can take a while, especially if you do this by hand. But not to worry, eventually it will come together.

Then, while kneading, keep adding small cubes of butter. Only throw in a new cube once the previous one has been fully incorporated.

Keep going until all the butter has been added and you have a firm dough that no longer feels sticky and has a soft sheen.

By now you're kneading with your hands. A spatula won't do the job anymore. If using a stand mixer: Lower its speed.

Now transfer the dough to a clean bowl. Cover with plastic wrap and set aside in a draft-free, warm spot to rise for at least 2 hours. This will take a while because the butter and the eggs slow down the leavening process considerably. ✒

Paris, France

Meanwhile, make the filling: Combine the butter, sugar, cinnamon, and salt in a small bowl.

Lift the leavened dough from the bowl and place it on top of a large flour-dusted sheet of parchment paper on the counter. The dough will be very soft. Using a flour-dusted rolling pin, roll out the dough to a thick rectangle of about 10 by 14 inches (25 by 35 cm)—doesn't have to be precise.

Spread the top with the cinnamon-butter mixture and sprinkle with the chopped chocolate. On one side you should leave bare a strip about ¾ inch (2 cm) wide. With that side facing away from you, start rolling up the dough. Carefully roll up the dough, using the parchment paper like a sushi rolling mat. Brush the empty strip with some egg and press down. Let the dough rest on the parchment paper with the seam facing down. Close off the two ends of the roll by folding them down.

Allow the dough to rise again, this time for 45 minutes to 1 hour. It will again nicely leaven into a beautiful soft and plump loaf.

About 20 minutes before baking time, preheat the oven to 350°F (180°C).

Place the bread on its parchment paper on a baking sheet. Brush the bread with the beaten egg and bake for 35 minutes, until nicely brown.

Allow your brioche to cool a little before slicing it. The filling will be piping hot!

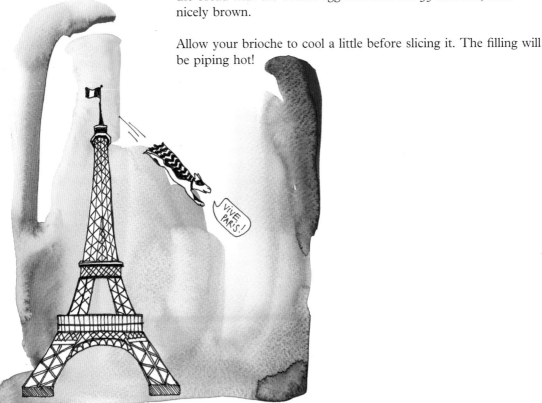

Whole-Wheat Oatmeal & Honey Cakes

FOR 12 cakes
PREP 7 min.
BAKE 20 min.

refined sugar–free

2 cups (175 g) quick oats
1½ cups (175 g) whole-wheat
    flour
2 tsp baking powder
½ tsp cinnamon
½ tsp ground ginger
¾ tsp sea salt
scant 1 cup (225 ml)
    buttermilk
½ cup (125 g) honey
6 tbsp (90 ml) coconut oil,
    melted (or another type
    like canola or sunflower
    oil), plus extra for
    greasing
2 eggs

Preheat the oven to 350°F (175°C). Grease 12 small ramekins (or a 12-cup muffin pan).

In a bowl, combine the oats with the flour, baking powder, cinnamon, ginger, and salt.

Beat the buttermilk with the honey and oil using an electric beater or a whisk. Then, while beating, add the eggs.

Pour the egg mixture into the dry ingredients and beat into a smooth, even batter.

Divide the batter among the 12 ramekins and bake for about 20 minutes, until a bamboo skewer inserted into the middle comes out clean. Let cool, then turn out of the ramekins.

Île Saint-Louis, Paris

Breakfast Muffins with Yogurt & Fruit

FOR 12 muffins
PREP 20 min.
BAKE 25 min.

wheat-free option

FOR THE CRUMB TOPPING
scant ¼ cup (40 g) unrefined cane sugar
3 tbsp wheat or light spelt flour
1 tbsp butter, at room temperature
pinch of salt
½ tsp cinnamon

FOR THE MUFFINS
2⅔ cups (300 g) wheat or light spelt flour
2 tsp baking powder
pinch of sea salt
2 eggs
¾ cup (150 g) unrefined cane sugar
1 tbsp butter (or coconut oil), melted, plus extra for greasing
1½ cups plus 1 tbsp (375 ml) yogurt
finely grated zest of ½ lemon
2¼ cups (350 g) pitted cherries, blueberries, and blackberries (frozen ones are fine as well)
sour cream, for serving

Make the crumb topping: In a bowl, combine all the ingredients and mix into a coarse crumble. Set aside in the fridge until ready to use.

Preheat the oven to 350°F (175°C).

Make the muffins: Grease a muffin pan or 12 individual ramekins with some butter (or coconut oil) or nonstick cooking spray.

In a bowl, combine the flour with the baking powder and salt.

In a large bowl, beat the eggs until foamy. Use a hand mixer, if you can: It's much faster. Add the sugar and butter and beat until the mixture has become light and airy.

Now, first stir in the yogurt and lemon zest, then the flour mixture. Stir carefully, making sure that the batter retains as much air as possible.

Fold in the fruit. Then spoon the batter into the prepared muffin cups, filling them three-quarters full. Sprinkle the crumb topping over the top.

Bake the muffins for about 25 minutes, or until a skewer inserted into the middle comes out clean. Let them cool on a rack for 5 minutes, then remove them from the cups. Serve for breakfast, nicely warm and with some sour cream on the side.

Whole-Wheat Oatmeal & Honey Cakes

Breakfast Muffins with Yogurt & Fruit

Bram Brack Scones

These scones hold a middle ground between a cake and a roll, which makes them perfect for your breakfast table. Sliced and toasted, they are still delicious the next day.

FOR 6 large or 12 small rolls
INACTIVE 30 min.
PREP 15 min.
BAKE 35 min.

wheat-free option
refined sugar–free

⅔ cup (100 g) raisins
⅔ cup (100 g) currants
½ cup plus 2 tbsp (150 ml)
    hot black tea (Lapsang
    Souchong or Earl Grey,
    for instance)
3 cups (300 g) wheat or light
    spelt flour
2 tsp baking powder
½ tsp cinnamon
¾ tsp nutmeg
1 tsp caraway seed (optional)
½ tsp salt
5 tbsp (75 g) cold butter,
    cubed
1 egg
1 tbsp honey
scant 1 cup (225 ml)
    buttermilk
3 tbsp chopped preserved
    orange peel (optional)

Soak the raisins and currants in the tea for at least 30 minutes to 1 hour (or better still: Soak them overnight).

Preheat the oven to 350°F (180°C).

Combine the flour, baking powder, spices, and salt in a bowl. With cold hands, rub the butter into the flour until the mixture forms coarse crumbs. Add the egg, honey, and buttermilk. Stir into a smooth, consistent batter. Now mix in the raisins and currants. Any liquid left in the bowl can be added as well. You can also add the orange peel at this point, if you'd like.

Spoon the batter into 6 large or 12 smaller greased baking forms. Bake for 35 minutes—the small ones should be done after 25 minutes, so keep an eye on the oven.

Eat them while they are still warm with some salted butter and marmalade or some aged cheese.

Dutch Baby

Before leaving for New York to promote our cookbook Home Made Winter, *Oof and I hosted a brunch at home for our friends. I had the idea to prepare them something very American. Something that could be made savory as well as sweet. Therefore, I made Dutch babies. Although a popular brunch dish in the United States, Dutch babies are all but unknown in the Netherlands. Surprisingly so, since they are named after us. At least, so it seems. Not exactly, as it turns out: This is originally a German recipe derived from* Pfannkuchen. *So actually they should be called* Deutsche *babies.*

Be that as it may, it is a ridiculously nice brunch dish. Americans like to eat this pancake with confectioners' sugar and lemon, although a savory version is just as tasty. For our brunch, I first braised some leeks until they were tender and also baked some pear wedges. I laid these in the batter and then crumbled some blue cheese (Stilton) on top before sliding the cakes into the oven. I served the sweet version with a bowl of red fruits. It turned into a very lengthy and entertaining brunch. Could be that the large quantities of champagne we drank with our Dutch babies played a role in this, though . . .

FOR 1 large pancake
PREP 10 min.
BAKE 12 min.

¼ cup (50 g) granulated
    sugar
finely grated zest of ½ lemon
3 eggs, at room temperature
½ cup plus 2 tbsp (150 ml)
    whole milk
scant ⅔ cup (75 g) all-
    purpose flour
½ tsp vanilla extract
pinch of cinnamon
pinch of nutmeg
pinch of salt
about 2 tbsp butter

FOR SERVING
lemon wedges

EXTRA
a 10- to 12-inch (25- to 30-cm)
    ovenproof cast-iron skillet
    or tarte tatin pan

Place the cast-iron skillet in the center of the oven and preheat the oven to 500°F (255°C)

In a small bowl, mix the granulated sugar and lemon zest and set aside.

Using a hand mixer, beat the eggs on high speed until frothy. Then, using a whisk, stir in the milk, flour, vanilla, cinnamon, nutmeg, and salt. Whisk until the batter becomes smooth.

Open the oven door and slide the pat of butter into the hot pan. It will melt immediately, so gently sway the pan back and forth (wearing oven mitts) to spread the butter all around. Directly pour all of the batter into the scorching pan and close the oven. Bake until it's nicely puffed up and done; this should take 12 to 14 minutes.

Remove from the oven and slide onto a large plate.

Serve with lemon wedges and the lemon sugar. The Dutch baby will deflate somewhat, but that's normal.

Pretty tasty, no?

Brabant-Style Sausage Buns

In the southern Dutch province of Brabant, they eat worstenbroodjes *(sausage buns), while in the rest of the Netherlands they eat* saucijzenbroodjes *(sort of sausage turnovers) instead. Though both are similar to American "pigs in a blanket," there is a difference between the two: their dough wrap. For* worstenbroodjes, *the bun is made of bread dough and for* saucijzenbroodjes, *it's puff pastry dough. My mother's sausage buns became sort of world famous after I featured them in my book* Home Made Winter. *She made her first batch in Ireland because she missed these buns, which she loved to eat so much when she was growing up in the Dutch south. Because she didn't know how to make the bread dough, she used puff pastry dough that first time. I also adore these wonderful buns, and this is how I make them: with real bread dough.*

SERVES 12 to 16
PREP 40 min.
RISE 2 hours
BAKING 25 min.

sugar-free

FOR THE DOUGH
4 tsp (15 g) instant yeast
¾ cup plus 1 tbsp (200 ml) lukewarm milk, plus extra as needed
3½ cups (450 g) all-purpose flour, plus extra as needed
2 tsp salt
3½ tbsp (50 g) soft butter, plus extra for greasing
1 egg

FOR THE FILLING
9 oz (250 g) ground beef
9 oz (250 g) ground pork
homemade bread crumbs from 1 or 2 slices stale white bread (see page 142)
1 egg
salt and freshly ground black pepper
pinch of nutmeg
pinch of ground cloves

1 egg, beaten, for brushing

Make the dough: Soak the yeast in the milk for 10 minutes until it has dissolved. Sift the flour and salt over a bowl. Pour the yeast mixture into the flour mixture while kneading. Add the butter and egg as well. Knead into a soft and elastic dough. You may need to add some extra flour or some more milk. Continue kneading for 10 minutes more on a flour-dusted countertop. Then shape the dough into a ball and set it aside in a covered bowl. Allow it to rise for 1 hour and 30 minutes, or until the dough has doubled in volume.

In the meantime, make the filling: In a bowl, combine all the ingredients and knead into a properly seasoned meat mixture that no longer feels sticky. Divide the meat mixture into 2 parts and roll into 2 sausages.

Grease a baking sheet with butter. Roll out the dough into a rectangle about ¼ inch (½ cm) thick and cut the dough into 2 smaller rectangles (or 4, if you have a smaller oven; just check what will fit and divide the meat mixture into 4 sausages instead of 2). Using a soft brush, glaze the dough sheets with a little beaten egg and place a roll of ground meat on top of each of them. First fold the short edges around the meat, then the long ones. Seal the edges with some egg. Make sure the dough fits together neatly. Place the sausage buns, the seams facing down, slightly apart from each other on the prepared baking sheet. Cover them with a flour-dusted dish towel and let them rise for 30 minutes. Meanwhile, preheat the oven to 400°F (200°C).

Brush the sausage buns with some egg and bake them for about 25 minutes, until they're golden brown. Cut into even pieces and arrange them on a platter. Serve immediately.

Poppy Seed Popovers

Poppy Seed Popovers

Popovers are American puff rolls that are generally eaten for breakfast. The English have a similar pastry called Yorkshire pudding, although that dish is usually served as a main course. I think popovers are cool. In the oven they rise enormously, causing the insides to become hollow, which makes them perfect vessels for rich layers of butter and jam. You can make the batter some time in advance (the night before, for instance). This will actually benefit your batter because rest always improves the texture. Keep in the fridge until you need it. Before use, simply beat the batter into shape with a hand mixer.

FOR about 8 rolls
PREP 10 min.
BAKE 25 min.

sugar-free

1 cup (250 ml) milk
2 eggs
1¼ cups (150 g) all-purpose
    flour
pinch of salt
2 tbsp poppy seeds

Preheat the oven to 425°F (225°C).

Thoroughly grease 8 conical cups or a 9- or 12-cup muffin pan with butter. If using separate cups, place them on a baking sheet (it will be more convenient later). Once the oven has reached its temperature, put the greased cups in so they can heat up.

Combine the milk and eggs in a bowl with a hand mixer. Combine the flour with the salt and poppy seeds in a separate bowl and stir the flour mixture into the milk mixture until you get a frothy batter.

Open the oven. Quickly fill all the cups three-quarters full, then put them back in the oven and close the door again. Be fast so you keep the heat inside the oven. Turn down the heat to 400°F (200°C).

Bake the popovers until they are nicely browned, 20 to 25 minutes. They will rise considerably—which is perfectly fine. After you've removed them from the oven, they will deflate a little. Which is fine too.

Let the popovers cool a little on a rack and pinch the hollow rolls so that the hot steam can escape.

Serve them while they're warm, with butter and jam or some kind of cream cheese.

TIP: Popover pans should *always* be greased with butter.

Connemara, Ireland

Sweet Potato Cinnamon Rolls

FOR 4 fat ones
PREP 35 min.
BAKE 25 min.

FOR THE DOUGH
1 cup (150 g) cubed sweet
    potatoes
⅓ cup (75 ml) maple syrup
1 tsp *speculaas* spices (see
    page 245) or pumpkin
    pie spice
1 tsp cinnamon
pinch of salt
1 tsp vanilla extract
1 cup (125 g) all-purpose
    flour, plus extra for
    dusting
1 cup plus 1 tbsp (125 g)
    whole-wheat flour
1½ tsp baking powder
5 tbsp (75 g) butter, at room
    temperature, plus extra
    for greasing

FOR THE FILLING
2 tbsp butter, at room
    temperature
2 tbsp cane sugar
1 tsp cinnamon
½ cup (45 g) pecans, briefly
    toasted in a dry skillet

FOR THE TOPPING
¼ cup (50 g) cream cheese,
    at room temperature
2 tbsp milk
1 cup (100 g) confectioners'
    sugar, or to taste

Make the dough: Cook the potatoes for 20 minutes, drain thoroughly, and let them cool down.

Preheat the oven to 400°F (200°C) and grease an 8- to 9-inch (22-cm) baking pan. Put the sweet potatoes, maple syrup, spices, salt, and vanilla extract in a food processor and beat to a smooth puree.

Combine the two flours with the baking powder in a bowl. Fold the flour mixture into the puree to make a smooth and cohesive dough. If it's too dry, add a few drops of milk or water.

On a flour-dusted work surface, roll out the dough to a slab ⅜ inch (1 cm) thick.

Spread the softened butter over the dough.

Make the filling: In a food processor, pulse all the ingredients into coarse crumbs. Sprinkle most of the filling over the dough slab. Do reserve some crumbs for topping later, however.

Roll up the dough and cut the log into 4 even portions. Of course, you can cut more portions if you want.

Place the rolls cut side up in the prepared baking pan, making sure there's some space left in between them because they will rise further. Bake the cinnamon rolls for 25 minutes max, until nicely crisp. The baking time depends on the size of the rolls.

Meanwhile, make the topping: Beat the cream cheese and milk together in a bowl and stir in the confectioners' sugar, until the mixture has the consistency of yogurt. Spoon the sauce over the rolls and sprinkle with the reserved pecan-cinnamon filling.

Eat warm. So good I could cry!

BREAD

Pecan Rye Bread

Baking bread with instant yeast is not difficult. You have to knead well to allow the gluten in the dough to develop, and let the dough rise for about an hour. Shape it into a nice loaf and allow it to rise for a bit longer. Then you can slide it into the oven.

That's pretty much it. It's up to you to let your creativity roam free. This works best with a gluten-rich flour—see page 17 for suggestions.

For a basic bread recipe: 4 cups (500 g) all-purpose flour, 1¼ cups (300 ml) water (or milk), scant 2 tsp (7 g) yeast, and 1 teaspoon salt.

I make this bread with either wheat flour and rye flour or just all-purpose flour (as I did for the loaf in the picture)—it's up to you. I'm also adding nuts and a flavoring (fennel seeds).

You can do this too—this way, you can bake great bread to perfectly match any dish you serve. Delicious.

For this and all bread recipes, make sure to carefully weigh all the ingredients.

FOR 1 loaf
PREP 10 min.
RISE 1 hour and 30 min.
BAKE 35 min.

lactose-free

scant 2 tsp (7 g) instant
    yeast
1¼ cups (300 ml) lukewarm
    water
2⅓ cups (300 g) wheat flour
    or all-purpose flour, plus
    some extra
1½ cups (200 g) rye flour
1 tbsp fennel seeds
pinch of salt
½ cup plus 1 tbsp (65 g)
    pecans, coarsely chopped
some oat flakes and/or bran,
    for garnish

Pour the yeast into a small bowl and add ¼ cup (50 ml) of the lukewarm water. Let stand for 7 minutes to dissolve.

Combine the wheat flour, rye flour, fennel seeds, salt, and pecans in a bowl and mix thoroughly.

Add the yeast mixture to the flour mixture. Pour in almost all of the remaining water and start kneading. Knead until you have a nice cohesive mixture. You may need to add some more water, perhaps some extra flour. ✒

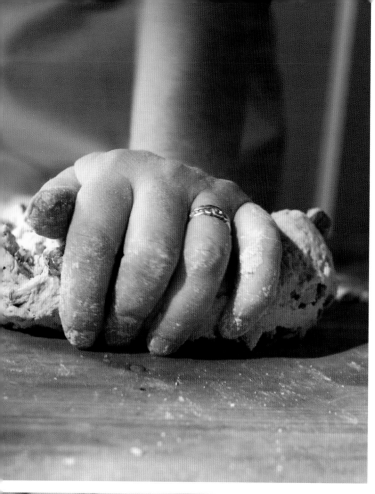

Once everything has come together into a smooth dough, continue kneading for at least another 10 minutes on your kitchen counter. Dust the counter with some extra flour if necessary, but use it sparsely. The dough loses its elasticity if you use too much flour.

Place the dough ball in a lightly greased bowl, cover with a towel or plastic wrap, and let rise in a warm place for 1 hour, or until it's doubled in size. Sometimes it needs more time.

When the dough has doubled in size, knead it again. Push the air out of the dough. Knead briefly, about 5 minutes.

Form the dough into an oval ball and place it on a sheet of parchment paper or a greased baking sheet. With a sharp knife, make a shallow cut lengthwise in the loaf and brush the surface of the loaf with water. Sprinkle with some oat flakes or bran and let the dough rise for 30 minutes more.

Meanwhile, preheat the oven to 350°C (180°C).

Bake the bread for about 35 minutes, until golden brown.

Pain d'Épi Bread

Pain d'Épi is a French name for bread that looks like the top of a wheat stalk, because of the way the dough is clipped before it goes into the oven. It's pretty bread for when you have a dinner party: You can place the loaf in the middle of the table and everyone can tear a piece off.

FOR 2 loaves
PREP 35 min.
INACTIVE 2 hours and 5 min.
BAKE 30 min.

sugar-free
lactose-free

2¼ tsp (10 g) instant yeast
scant ½ cup (350 ml) lukewarm water
4¼ cups (425 g) light spelt flour, plus some extra
⅔ cup (75 g) rye flour, plus some extra
1½ tsp sea salt
a generous handful of ice cubes

Put the yeast in a small bowl and add a splash of the lukewarm water. Let stand for 6 minutes to dissolve. Combine the spelt flour and rye flour in a large bowl and make a well in the middle. Pour in the dissolved yeast and the rest of the water (gradually, never all at once!) and stir with a spatula until you have a smooth dough. Let rest for 20 minutes. Only then add the salt (salt delays the rising process) and knead the dough on the counter for a long time: at least 10 minutes. Place the dough in a bowl lightly greased with oil, cover with some plastic wrap, and set aside to rise in a warm place for about 45 minutes, or until it's doubled in size.

Place the risen dough on a lightly floured countertop. Stretch the dough until it resembles a long, flat sausage. Roll it up lengthwise and divide it in two crosswise. If you don't divide it and only make one large braid, it will become too big and won't have those pretty tips after baking. Believe me, I've often tried. Working with one piece of dough at a time, turn over the dough so the seam faces downward. Roll and stretch the dough into a long sausage. Form it into a ring and push the ends together—you may need a drop of water for that. Lift the ring onto a large sheet of parchment paper and dust with flour. Repeat to make a second ring. Cover both dough rings loosely with clean dish towels and let rise for another hour.

Preheat the oven to 425°F (225°C). Position a pizza stone in the middle of the oven and place a baking dish on the bottom of the oven.

Holding a pair of scissors at a 45-degree angle to the top of the dough, make cuts on a dough ring every 1½ inches (4 cm)—cut through almost to the parchment! As you go, alternate moving these "leaves" to the left and right. If you can't fit both breads in the oven at the same time, don't clip both dough rings yet. Only clip the dough just before you slide it into the hot oven. Lift the clipped dough using the parchment paper and slide it onto the pizza stone. Throw a handful of ice cubes in the baking dish at the bottom to create steam and close the door as quickly as possible. Bake the bread for 30 minutes, until nicely dark brown.

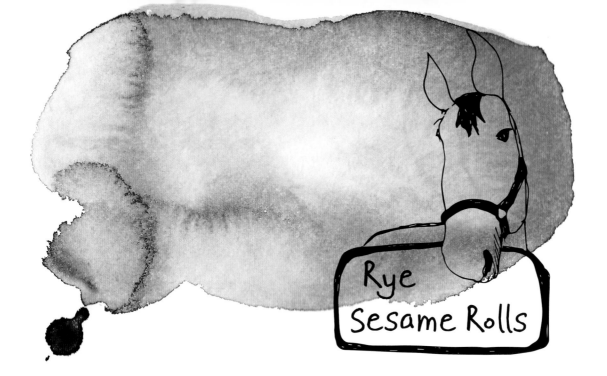

Rye Sesame Rolls

FOR 8 rolls
PREP 15 min.
RISE 2 hours
BAKE 30 min.

refined sugar–free option

scant 2 tsp (7 g) instant
    yeast
1 tbsp honey or sugar
¾ cup (175 ml) lukewarm
    water
1¾ cups (225 g) all-purpose
    flour
⅔ cup (75 g) rye flour, plus
    some extra
olive oil, for greasing
2 tbsp sesame seeds, plus
    some extra
1 tsp salt

Put the yeast in a small bowl and add the honey or sugar and some of the lukewarm water. Stir until the honey or sugar is dissolved. Let stand until it begins to foam: about 7 minutes.

Combine the flour, rye flour, sesame seeds, and salt in a large bowl and make a well in the middle. Add the dissolved yeast and the rest of the water. With clean hands, knead into a smooth dough. Once the dough has come together in a ball, continue kneading on the counter. Knead for a long time: at least 10 minutes.

Place the dough in a bowl lightly greased with olive oil and cover with plastic wrap. Set aside to rise in a warm place for 1 hour and 30 minutes. (Rye flour of course doesn't contain much gluten, so the leavening process is slower.)

Once the dough has doubled in size, knead again but for a shorter time (5 minutes max).

Form a thick roll and divide that roll into 8 equal parts. Roll each portion into a small ball and place them slightly apart in a greased pan with a removable bottom.

Cut a shallow X into the tops of the balls, then brush with water and sprinkle with some extra rye flour and/or sesame seeds.

Let the balls rise once more, for about 30 minutes this time.

Meanwhile, preheat the oven to 350°F (180°C).

Bake the rolls until golden brown, about 30 minutes.

Potato Rolls

These rolls are really amazing. Soft and spongy and terrific for mopping up sauce—so bake them for dinner or to serve with a warm lunch. You could make juicy pulled pork to go with them, and white beans in tomato sauce as a side dish. (You can find these recipes in my book Home Made Winter, *if you have that lying around.)*

FOR 20 rolls
PREP 15 min.
RISE 1 hour and 30 min.
BAKE 15 min.

scant 2 tsp (7 g) instant yeast
about 1 cup (250 ml) lukewarm milk
1¼ cups (250 g) mashed potato, at room temperature
⅔ cup (1⅓ sticks / 150 g) butter, at room temperature
2 eggs
¼ cup (50 g) sugar
1 tsp salt
5 cups (625 g) all-purpose flour, plus extra for dusting

Dissolve the yeast in ¼ cup (50 ml) of the lukewarm milk.

In a large bowl, combine the mashed potatoes, butter, eggs, sugar, and salt and mix with a hand mixer for about 2 minutes on medium speed. (It's also fine to use a stand mixer, of course.)

Add the yeast mixture and the rest of the lukewarm milk. Mix well.

Replace the beaters with dough hooks and, bit by bit, add the flour until everything is absorbed. Knead for at least another 5 minutes. Form a nice smooth ball and place the covered dough in a warm place to rise for at least 1 hour.

Knead the dough by hand on a flour-dusted countertop and shape it into a long sausage. Divide the dough into 20 equal parts of about 3 oz (85 g) each. Roll each portion into a nice ball. Line a baking sheet with parchment paper and place the balls on top, spacing them about ¾ inch (1.5 cm) apart. Sprinkle the balls with some flour and let rise again for 30 minutes. Meanwhile, preheat the oven to 400°F (200°C).

Bake the rolls until golden brown, about 15 minutes.

Irish Whole-Wheat Bread

The Irish can bake; I learned this at my mother's knee. Most of my childhood memories are about bread and pastry. The taste of freshly baked dark bread with salted butter and a dollop of my mother's homemade marmalade instantly takes me back to our Irish kitchen in Dublin.

The Irish often bake soda breads, but they do bake with yeast as well, trust me.

This foolproof bread is an example of that. You'll see that you don't always have to knead bread with yeast. It will be a wet dough that simply can't be kneaded.

It turns into a whole other type of bread. And a very delicious one at that.

FOR 1 loaf
PREP 7 min.
RISE 30 min.
BAKE 45 min.

lactose-free

4 tsp (15 g) instant yeast
1 tsp date syrup, molasses, honey, or treacle
1¾ cups plus 2 tbsp (450 ml) lukewarm water
scant 2 cups (250 g) (five-grain) whole-wheat flour (see Note)
1½ cups (150 g) light spelt flour
¼ cup (50 g) millet or scant ½ cup (50 g) wheat germ
1 tsp salt
a handful of mixed seeds like sesame seeds, pumpkin seeds, flaxseeds, or sunflower seeds

Note: Instead of the whole-wheat flour, light spelt flour, and millet or wheat germ, you could just use 3½ cups (450 g) total whole-wheat flour.

Put the yeast in a small bowl and add the syrup and some of the lukewarm water. Let stand for 5 minutes, until the yeast dissolves and starts to foam.

Combine the flours with the salt and three-quarters of the seeds in a large bowl and make a well in the center.

Add the dissolved yeast and the rest of the water and stir with a wooden spoon into a wet mixture.

Grease a loaf pan (of at least 1½ qts / 1.5 L) with coconut oil or baking spray and pour in the batter. The batter will rise a lot, and the bread will rise some more in the oven, so choose a large pan. Sprinkle with the rest of the seeds. Loosely cover the pan with plastic wrap and set aside for 30 minutes in a warm place.

Meanwhile, preheat the oven to 425°C (225°C).

Bake the risen bread for about 30 minutes. Remove the loaf from the pan and return it to the oven rack to bake for another 15 minutes, so the bread gets a nice crispy crust.

You can easily freeze this bread, but if well wrapped it will stay fresh at room temperature for a week.

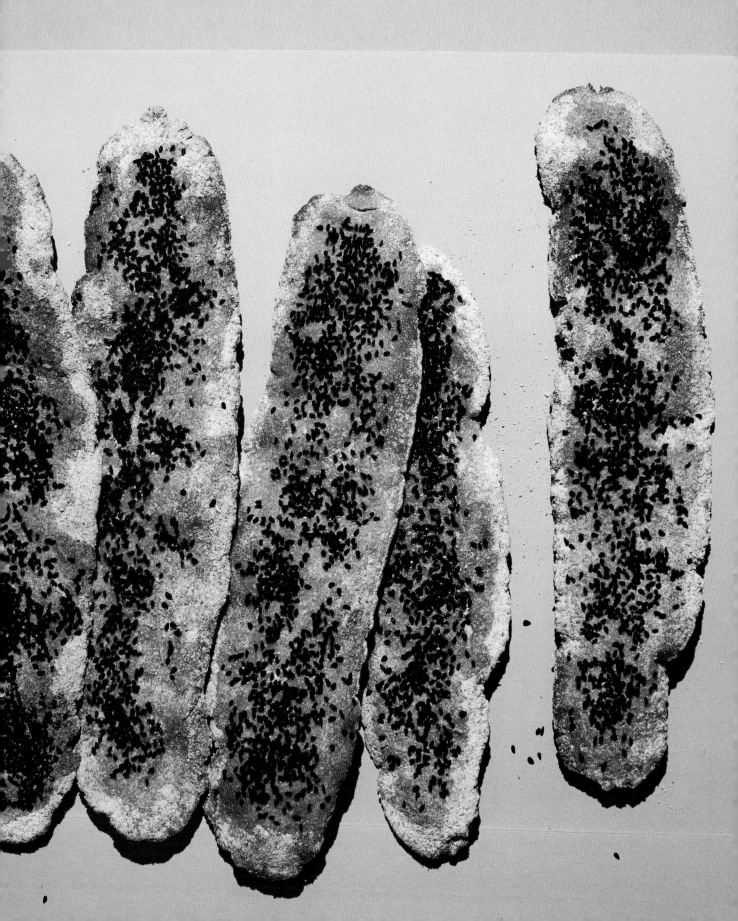

Rye Crackers

Oh! So delicious! Eat them for breakfast, or serve them later in the day with some cheese, cured sausage, and some spreads like hummus. I sprinkled these with nigella seeds (sometimes called onion seeds). They can be hard to find—I bought mine abroad, but you can find them in specialty stores, like Indian or Middle Eastern stores, or online of course. They taste heavenly: very aromatic—a bit like dark, bitter toast, and slightly peppery. The seeds and herbs aren't mandatory, however; the crackers are very tasty au naturel as well.

FOR 12 crackers
PREP 30 min.
RISE 1 hour
BAKE 9 min.

wheat-free
refined sugar–free
lactose-free

1 tsp instant yeast
1 tbsp honey
¾ cup plus 1 tbsp (200 ml)
    lukewarm water
1 tsp salt
2 cups (250 g) rye flour, plus
    extra
seeds or herbs for
    garnishing: nigella seeds,
    fennel seeds (briefly
    bruised in a mortar),
    caraway seeds, sesame
    seeds, or dried rosemary,
    for example (optional)
flaky sea salt, such as
    Maldon (optional)

Put the yeast in a wide bowl and add the honey and some of the lukewarm water. Let stand for 10 minutes, until the yeast dissolves and starts to foam.

In a bowl, mix the salt with the rye flour and about 1 teaspoon seeds or herbs of choice, if using.

Add the dissolved yeast and stir everything together with a spatula. It should look a little like sticky mortar.

Cover with plastic wrap and let stand for 1 hour.

Meanwhile, preheat the oven to 400°F (200°C).

The dough will be less sticky after 1 hour, although still somewhat sticky. Take a piece of dough the size of a Ping-Pong ball and roll this into a ball with flour-dusted hands. On a heavily flour-dusted countertop, roll out the dough into a thin round slab or a rectangle (that way, more will fit onto the baking sheet); continue dusting with flour if necessary.

With a metal spatula, carefully lift the cracker onto a baking sheet lined with parchment paper or a silicone baking mat. If you wish, brush lightly with water and sprinkle with seeds, herbs, or sea salt. Repeat with more balls of dough.

Bake the crackers in batches for about 9 minutes (depending on the size of the crackers), or until crispy.

Let cool and keep them in an airtight container; they will stay fresh for about a week.

Spicy Italian Anchovy-Garlic Bread

This little bread roll really tastes like Italy. Do use durum wheat, which you can buy in natural foods stores or online. Durum is a very hard wheat that gives this bread a completely different texture.

Cut two slices as thinly as possible and serve with your best olive oil for dipping. Drink some red wine with it and be happy.

FOR 1 loaf
PREP 20 min.
RISE 2 hours and 30 min.
BAKE 35 min.

lactose-free
sugar-free

FOR THE DOUGH
2¼ tsp (11 g) instant yeast
½ cup plus 2 tbsp (150 ml)
    lukewarm water
1¼ cups (150 g) all-purpose
    flour, plus some extra
1 cup plus 3 tablespoons
    (150 g) durum wheat
    flour
1 tsp salt
2 tbsp extra-virgin olive oil,
    plus some extra

FOR THE FILLING
7 tbsp (100 ml) extra-virgin
    olive oil
1 tbsp dried oregano
1 tbsp very finely chopped
    fresh rosemary
2 cloves garlic, minced
6 canned anchovies, drained
    and finely chopped
a pinch of sea salt & freshly
    ground black pepper

Make the dough: Put the yeast in a small bowl and add some of the lukewarm water. Let stand for 7 minutes, until the yeast is dissolved and foaming.

Combine the flour with the durum wheat and the salt in a large bowl. Pour in the dissolved yeast, the rest of the water, and olive oil. Stir until a dough forms, then knead with clean hands into a cohesive dough ball.

Place the dough in a bowl lightly greased with olive oil and cover with plastic wrap. Set aside to rise in a warm place for 1 hour and 30 minutes.

Make the filling: Stir together the filling ingredients in a bowl.

Grease a 1-qt (1-L) loaf pan.

Roll out the dough on a flour-dusted countertop into a rectangle about ⅛ inch (4 mm) thick. The short side should be as long as the loaf pan.

Brush the whole piece of dough with the filling and roll it tight. Place the dough seam side down in the pan. Cover with plastic wrap and allow the dough to rise for 1 hour in a warm place.

Meanwhile, preheat the oven to 350°F (180°C).

Once the loaf has doubled in size, you can bake it. Bake for about 35 minutes. It should remain quite light in color.

Let cool slightly, remove from the pan, and cut the bread into very thin slices. Serve with your best olive oil as an apéritif with some olives and a drink.

Making a Starter

A fermentation starter (or "mother") is, unlike store-bought instant yeast packets, a homemade wild yeast. The wild yeast is made through fermentation of bacteria that have a bit of a sour taste. You make this sourdough starter pretty much with flour and water alone.

It's that easy.

As is true for everything: The better the product, the better the result. So make a quick detour to a good natural foods store for quality flour. Preferably use flour milled on a millstone. It contains more cultures that later on will push the development of wild yeast. And fresh-bought flour contains more live cultures than a pack that has been in your pantry for over a year.

I use rye flour for my starters, because rye flour is more sour than regular flour and it is faster. You don't have to. You can also just use wheat flour. (Or all-purpose flour—but wheat flour contains more bacteria, kickstarting the fermentation process.) After that you can feed your starter with anything you wish—for example, light spelt flour or all-purpose flour. Or half and half.

DAY 1:

Combine ¾ cup plus 1 tablespoon (100 g) whole-wheat flour (or in my case: half whole-wheat flour and half rye flour) and 7 tbsp (100 ml) water in a plastic or glass jar (no metal!). Stir everything together to form a smooth batter, cover loosely, and place in a warm place (so not on the windowsill). Maybe that simply means on your counter.

DAYS 2 AND 3 AND MAYBE EVEN 4:

Stir the starter 2 or 3 times every day until small bubbles appear, then add ¾ cup plus 1 tablespoon (100 g) flour (rye flour, whole-wheat flour, or light spelt flour, whatever you wish) and stir in 7 tbsp (100 ml) water. If the bubbles only appear on day 4, wait another day as the yeast isn't ready yet. By stirring you're adding oxygen and that boosts the number of microcultures.

DAY 5:

By now you should have a glop with bubbles. It should have a slightly sour smell. Discard half of it and fill up the rest with equal parts flour and water. For example, 100 g (¾ cup plus 1 tablespoon) whole-wheat flour (or half light spelt flour and half whole-wheat flour) and 100 ml (7 tbsp) water. Repeat this process for a few days.

There are people who start baking with their starter after 5 days, but in my experience the bread's flavor deepens if you refresh your starter a few times. View it as an exciting project—every day is a party. Try to do the "feedings" at the same time every day. Every 24 hours. This is when you discover the starter has a ritual: In the hours after its feeding, it rises enormously and then it sags. My starter acquired its own personality. I followed her every day and was curious to see what mood she was in every morning. Really fun. I named her Fiona.

When the starter is very bubbly and doubles in volume within an hour or two after refreshing, it's ready to use. This will take anywhere from 7 to 10 days. 🐦

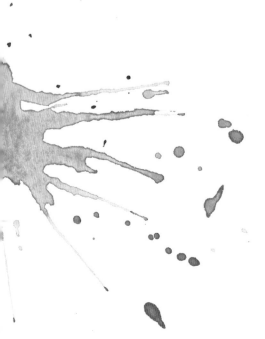

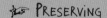 ## PRESERVING

If you want to preserve your starter, put it in the fridge, as this will temper its growth. Make sure to discard half and replace with equal parts flour and water once a week. Think of it as taking care of a plant. Provided you feed and stir it every week, your starter will be with you for life.

It's okay if a small layer of liquid forms on top of the starter—you can just stir it in. But if it turns pink, you need to throw it out and start all over again.

If you need more starter because you're baking two breads, give your starter some more flour and water the day before.

You'll need to get a handle on it, but over time you will get to know your starter really well, like with a new pet, and then this whole description will suddenly no longer be needed.

Paris, France

Baking Sourdough Bread

Baking bread with instant yeast is fast—you'll usually be finished within 2 hours. This is not the case for sourdough bread. The good news is you barely need to knead sourdough. In the hours it needs to rise, the flavor for which it is so famous develops as well. So if you are impatient, think about how you're going to benefit from all that waiting.

In these waiting hours, the wild yeast will do its work as well, so give it some time. It's important to draw up a schedule before you start making sourdough. Oh well, I'll talk you through it.

Make sure to feed the starter 8 to 12 hours before use. For example, feed it before you go to bed.

When you're ready to make the bread dough, test if the yeast has developed well enough. You can do this by dropping a teaspoon of the starter into a small bowl of water. If it floats, it contains sufficient gas for the baking process; if not, you'll have to wait a little longer (sometimes up to an hour).

FOR 1 loaf
PREP 1½ hours
RISE 7 hours
BAKE 45 min.

sugar-free
lactose-free

FOR THE STARTER
7 oz (200 g) starter (see
    page 108)
¾ cup plus 1 tablespoon
    (100 g) flour

FOR THE BREAD
1⅔ cups (200 g) wheat flour
scant ½ cup (50 g) whole-
    wheat flour, for example
    rye flour or light spelt flour
1½ tsp salt
rice flour, rye flour, wheat
    germ, or all-purpose flour,
    for dusting

Feed the starter: Place the starter dough in a bowl and add 7 tbsp (100 ml) water and the flour, so you've refreshed the starter immediately.

Make the bread: Add ½ cup plus 2 tbsp (150 ml) water to the starter dough in the bowl and stir to combine. Add the flour. I often use 1⅔ cups (200 g) wheat flour and a scant ½ cup (50 g) rye or whole-wheat flour. It's a good combination and gives the bread more depth. You can experiment with a slightly different combination. I always feed my starter the night before with the same combination, so with 7 tbsp (100 ml) water and a scant ½ cup (50 g) wheat flour and a scant ½ cup (50 g) rye or whole-wheat flour.

Stir with a spoon until you have a smooth, thick batter.

Cover the bowl and let stand for 30 minutes, so the cultures can do their work. This phase is officially called *autolysis*.

Add the salt and thoroughly stir the dough. (Salt slows down the development of the cultures, so only add it after autolysis.) The dough will be damp and sticky.

Now the fun part begins.

Scoop the dough with a dough scraper onto the counter. You may dust the counter minimally with flour, but you don't have to. Wet your hands (to prevent sticking), then lift the dough and throw it forcefully onto the countertop. Lift once more with the dough scraper and throw the dough onto the counter again. ✍

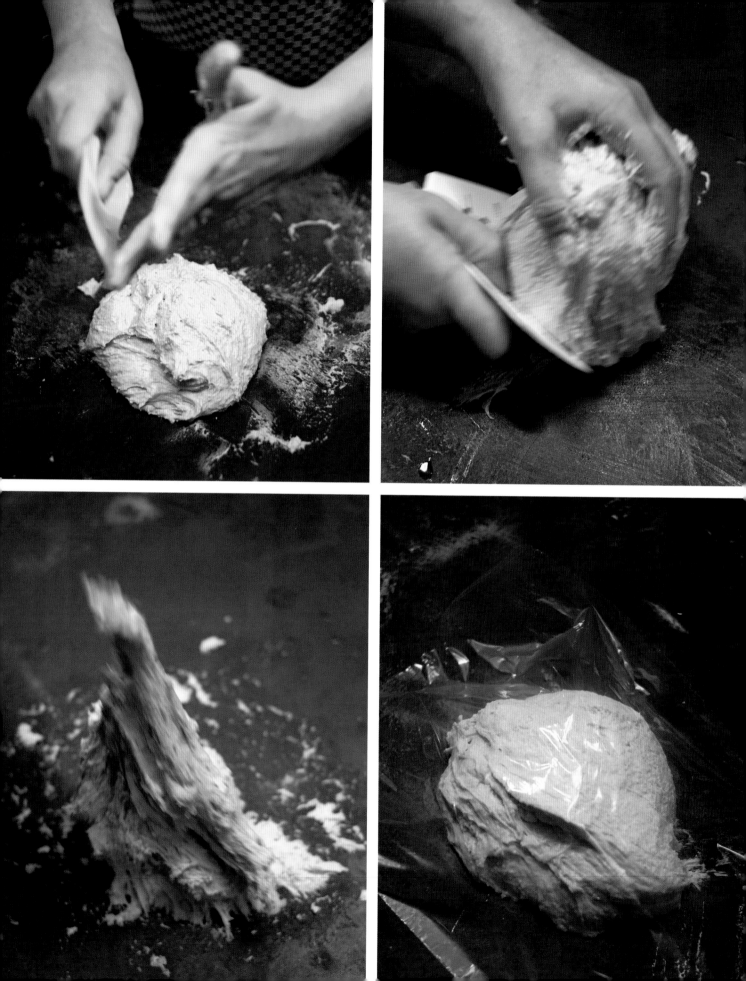

Repeat this about 8 times. Leave the dough ball on the counter after the last slam. Grease a sheet of plastic wrap or parchment paper with some oil or baking spray and cover the dough with it. Set your timer for 10 minutes.

Repeat the process twice.

You will notice that the dough becomes firmer after every 10 minutes and doesn't stick as much to the counter. After the third time, lift the dough into a clean bowl, cover with plastic wrap greased with oil or baking spray and a dish towel, and let rise for 4 hours.

After 4 hours, very carefully lift the dough with a dough scraper onto a flour-dusted countertop. Make sure it doesn't tear. Place the smooth, risen top on the counter so that the bottom faces upward. Stretch the dough lightly. With floured hands, fold the bottom one-third of the dough over the rest, then fold down the bottom third, as you'd fold a letter. (See the pictures on page 116.) Gently press the dough. Pull and stretch the other sides carefully over the dough and shape it into a ball. Turn the dough over so the seam is down. With open palms, gently turn the ball clockwise so it becomes more tight. If you look at the pictures, it will likely become more clear what I mean.

This way, you pull the skin of the unbaked bread beautifully tight and you will get a pretty ball.

Shaping the Bread

Place a dish towel in a bread basket and dust it with rice flour, rye flour, wheat germ, or all-purpose flour. The first three have more texture, which will result in a very thin barrier between the dough and the cloth so that it will loosen more easily later on.

Place the dough in the basket with its seam facing up and cover it with the overhanging dish towel. Let rise for 2 to 3 hours.

Place a big cast-iron pan with a lid in the oven and preheat the oven to 475°F (250°C—or even 500°F / 260°C!). Let everything become piping hot—check your oven thermometer carefully.

Lay out a razor or surgical knife and oven mitts.

Open the oven. With oven mitts, lift the lid of the pan and flip the bread from the basket lickety-split into the scorching hot pan. Score the top of the bread with the razor or surgical knife and quickly return the lid to the pan. This is necessary for the bread to rise.

Close the oven and lower the oven temperature to 450°F (230°C).

Bake the bread for 20 minutes, then remove the lid using oven mitts and bake for 20 to 25 minutes more, so the top browns nicely.

The crust may become very dark brown. That's what it should be.

Take the bread out of the pan with a pair of tongs and place it on a rack to cool.

When you've gotten a handle on making your own dough, you can start making variations: I now make double quantities for a nice big loaf, but that requires some more practice in kneading. That's why I first give you a recipe for a smaller loaf.

If you'd like to add ingredients like cumin seeds or olives or something, do that when you add the salt.

Adjust the baking time for a bigger loaf. All in all, it needs 10 to 15 minutes longer.

Sourdough Roll with Ramp-Feta Filling

You can forage for ramps in spring. If you live in a city and don't know where to find them, you can also opt for a pesto of arugula, watercress, parsley, or nettle from the park, as that's of course also delicious. If you pick that last ingredient, you're a bit of a forager too, and thus very hip.

FOR 1 loaf
PREP 35 min.
RISE 4 hours and 30 min.
BAKE 30 min.

sugar-free

FOR THE DOUGH

7 oz (200 g) starter (see page 108)
½ cup (120 ml) lukewarm water
2½ cups (320 g) all-purpose flour, plus some extra
1 egg, beaten
½ tsp salt
olive oil, for greasing

FOR THE FILLING

½ cup (50 g) chopped ramps (or arugula or watercress or parsley or nettle tops)
2 cloves garlic
⅓ cup (40 g) pine nuts, toasted in a dry skillet
1½ oz (40 g) grated Parmesan cheese
about 7 tbsp (100 ml) olive oil
coarse sea salt & freshly ground black pepper
2½ oz (75 g) feta

Make the dough: Mix the starter with the water in a bowl. Add half the flour and stir until all the lumps of flour have dissolved. Cover the bowl with plastic wrap and let the batter rest in a warm spot for 30 minutes.

Add the egg and salt to the batter, stir well with a spoon, and then add the rest of the flour. Knead for a long time, then lift the dough ball onto the counter and knead for at least 10 minutes. Add more flour as you knead. The dough is probably a little wet. After kneading, the dough should feel like a soft baby belly. Place the dough in a bowl greased with olive oil, cover with plastic wrap, and let rise for at least 3 hours. The dough should double in volume.

Make the filling: Grind the ramps, garlic, pine nuts, and cheese in a food processor. Add as much olive oil as you need to get a smooth pesto that's firm enough that if you stick a small spoon in, it remains standing up. Taste for salt and pepper. It may be quite salty; this saltiness will diminish once the bread is baked. I like to add the feta later on.

Press the air out of the dough with your fist and knead again, this time for just a few minutes. Roll out the dough on a flour-dusted counter into a rectangle of 16 by 10 inches (40 by 25 cm).

Crumble the feta over the pesto and stir. Generously spread the pesto over the dough and roll up the dough very tightly, starting from one long side.

Place the roll seam side down on a baking sheet lined with parchment paper. With a sharp knife, cut very deep slashes in the dough every 1 inch (2.5 cm), almost to the parchment paper (the bottom of the dough should stay connected). Alternating left and right, push the pieces 45 degrees sideways. Cover loosely with greased plastic wrap and let the bread rest for another hour. Meanwhile, preheat the oven to 400°F (200°)C.

Bake the bread for 10 minutes, then lower the oven temperature to 350°F (180°C) and bake for 20 minutes more. Serve warm, naturally, as an apéritif or with soup.

Sourdough Pizza with
Spicy Smoked Tomato Sauce & Mozzarella

FOR 4 small or 2 large pizzas   **DOUGH PREP** 12 hours   **PIZZA PREP** 1 hour   **BAKE** 10 min.   *sugar-free*

FOR THE DOUGH
Dough for 1 small sourdough
    bread (page 112)

Note: I like to make the dough
with 2 cups (250 g) all-purpose
flour and a scant ½ cup (50 g)
whole-wheat flour, for some
extra bite. (I feed my starter 12
hours in advance with 7 tbsp /
100 ml water and ½ cup / 50 g
wheat flour and a scant ½ cup /
50 g whole-wheat flour).

FOR THE SAUCE
2 tbsp wood chips or tea
    (optional)
2 (14-oz / 400-g) cans whole
    peeled tomatoes (not diced)
3 cloves garlic, peeled and
    crushed
1 tsp red pepper flakes, or to
    taste
7 tbsp (100 ml) extra-virgin
    olive oil, plus more for
    drizzling
salt & freshly ground black
    pepper

FOR THE TOPPING
2 balls mozzarella (not buffalo
    mozzarella, as that contains
    too much moisture), sliced
a few kalamata olives, pitted
a handful of fresh basil leaves

ADDITIONAL
a smoker (or create one
    yourself in a wok or roasting
    pan with a rack and some
    aluminum foil. You can find
    instructions in my first book,
    Home Made.)

Make the dough: Prepare the dough as described, but when you
get to the "shaping the bread" section, form 2 or 4 equal-size
balls and let them rise for 2 to 3 hours on a flour-dusted tray or
baking sheet, covered with plastic wrap or in a plastic bag.

Make the sauce: Scatter the wood chips or tea, if using, over the
bottom of the smoker, position the plate or lay aluminum foil on
top, and place a rack on top of that. Pour one can of tomatoes
into a saucepan. Pour the other can into a strainer set over the
saucepan. Very gently squeeze the whole tomatoes in the strainer
until most of the seeds have come out. Place these seeded tomatoes on the rack in the smoker and close the lid.

Smoke the tomatoes for about 30 minutes.

Fill the empty tomato cans with water and pour it into the saucepan with the tomatoes. Add the garlic, red pepper flakes, and
olive oil and bring it all to a boil. Simmer over low heat for 30
minutes. If the sauce becomes too dry, add some water.

Add the smoked tomatoes and puree the sauce directly in the pan
with an immersion blender until completely smooth (or transfer
the sauce to a blender in batches and puree—be careful, it's hot!).

Season with salt and pepper. If the sauce is too thin, simmer it a bit more to reduce it a little. Turn off the heat once the sauce has the consistency you like. Let it cool until you're ready to use it.

Preheat the oven to its highest temperature. Mine can go to 475°F (250°C), but can become even hotter with a pizza stone, almost to 575°F (300°C).

Make the pizzas one by one. Gently lift one dough ball with your dough scraper onto a floured baking sheet. Press it gently. With your fingers, make a rim by pushing into the dough ¾ inch (1.5 cm) from the edge. Then stretch the inside of the dough. You'll feel how far you can stretch it. Be careful—you put so much effort into the dough, it would be a shame if it tears. Push it apart until you have the desired size.

Pour a few tablespoons of the sauce onto the middle of the dough and spread it evenly, leaving a border. Place a few slices of the mozzarella on top, leaving the rim uncovered, and some olives. Drizzle some good olive oil around the edge (which you've kept clear).

Slide the baking sheet onto the pizza stone in the scorching-hot oven.

Bake for 10 minutes. Sprinkle with basil leaves about 2 minutes before you take it out. (While this one's in the oven, get the next one ready, and so on.) Serve immediately.

Connemara, Ireland

with baking powder

with baking soda

Soda Bread with Nuts, Grains, and Seeds

Recently, I met Dan Lepard in London. He is a great baker and that's why I wanted to talk to him. He experiments with his ingredients: "What happens if I roast the grains before I add them?" is one of the things he asks himself, and that is inspiring.

Leafing through his book Short & Sweet, *I saw a recipe for soda bread that looked fantastic. And it was. It was the best soda bread I'd ever eaten. The secret? The rolled oats were first soaked in water before they were baked into the bread. This gave the bread the bouncy structure that I was looking for.*

Inspired, I decided to get going myself. And I dare say: not without results.

I tried using baking powder first, then baking soda. With the latter, the bread becomes many times darker inside, the structure is more supple, and it simply results in a tastier bread, with a more intense taste. I now eat this bread almost every day.

FOR 1 loaf
PREP 7 min.
RESTING 2 hours
BAKE 1 hour and 15 min.

wheat-free
lactose-free
refined sugar–free

2 tbsp coconut oil,
    plus extra for the pan
2 cups (500 ml) hot water
2 tbsp agave syrup
1 cup (150 g) sunflower
    seeds
5 tbsp (50 g) flaxseeds
¼ cup (50 g) chia seeds
¾ cup (100 g) almonds (or
    other nuts), raw
1⅔ cups (150 g) oat flakes or
    rolled oats (not instant),
    from the natural foods
    store (see page 18)
1 tsp salt
2 tsp baking soda

Put the coconut oil in a jar or bowl. Pour the hot water and syrup on top and let everything melt.

Thoroughly mix the sunflower, flax, and chia seeds along with the almonds, oats, salt, and baking soda in a bowl. Pour in the coconut oil mixture and stir well.

Let stand on your countertop for 2 hours, stirring occasionally when you walk by.

After 2 hours your batter should be so thick that it comes loose from the edge of your bowl—if not, then let it stand for a while longer.

Preheat the oven to 350°F (175°C) (use convection heat). Set a rack in the middle of the oven.

Grease a 1-qt (1-L) loaf pan. Line the bottom with parchment paper and grease this as well.

Scoop in the sticky batter, then slam the pan on the counter a few times to let the air bubbles escape and smooth out the batter.

Bake for about 1 hour, then turn the bread out of the pan and return it to the oven rack to bake for another 15 minutes.

Let the bread cool on a rack. I usually wrap the bread immediately in plastic wrap and keep it in the fridge. You can easily keep it there for up to a week.

Soda Bread with Rye, Flaxseed & Yogurt

FOR 1 loaf
PREP 7 min.
INACTIVE 1 hour
BAKE 1 hour and 30 min.

wheat-free
sugar-free

1⅔ cup (150 g) rolled oats (not instant), from the natural foods store (see page 18)
1¼ cups (300 ml) boiling water
2 cups (250 g) rye flour
1½ tsp sea salt
2 tsp baking soda
7 tbsp (75 g) flaxseeds
2 eggs
¾ cup plus 1 tbsp (200 g) plain yogurt
2 tbsp coconut oil or butter, melted, plus extra for greasing

Pour the oats into a large bowl, pour in the boiling water, and let stand for 1 hour.

Preheat the oven to 350°F (175°C). Mix the rye flour, salt, baking soda, and flaxseeds in a small bowl and then add it to the oats in the bowl. Beat the eggs in a medium bowl, then add the yogurt, coconut oil, and 7 tbsp (100 ml) water and stir to combine. Pour this mixture in with the dry ingredients and stir into a smooth, homogenous mass.

Grease a 1½-qt (1.5-L) loaf pan with coconut oil or butter. Cut a sheet of parchment paper to fit the bottom of the pan and grease this as well.

Pour the batter into the pan and smooth out the top.

Bake the bread for 1 hour and 15 minutes, until nicely brown. Turn the bread out of the pan and return it to the oven rack to bake for another 15 minutes.

Let cool a little before you slice it.

Oat Crackers

When I discovered this recipe, I was sold. These super-easy, delicious crackers have an almost nutlike flavor. It's up to you to decide when to take them out of the oven: A longer baking time results in a darker cracker with a more intense nutlike taste than a cracker that only baked for 20 minutes. You can also lower the oven temperature and bake them even longer. They will become more brittle.

Eat them like you would eat any cracker: as breakfast or lunch with cottage cheese and tomatoes, or with butter and marmalade, or serve them as an apéritif with some cheese.

Notice how you can vary this recipe endlessly: Add herbs or other grains to make a completely different cracker. Replace part of the rolled oats with finely ground nuts. Anything is possible—it's your cracker. Sometimes I replace ¾ cup (75 g) rolled oats in this recipe with rye flour, that's delicious too.

FOR 16 crackers
PREP 15 min.
INACTIVE 1 hour
BAKE 20 to 30 min.

wheat-free
sugar-free
lactose-free

2¾ cups (250 g) rolled oats (not instant) from the natural foods store (see page 18), plus some extra as needed

¼ tsp flaky sea salt, such as Maldon

¾ tsp baking powder

1 tbsp coconut oil or extra-virgin olive oil or soft butter

about 7 tbsp (100 ml) boiling water

some oat flakes to garnish and perhaps some flaky salt (optional)

Preheat the oven to 350°F (170°C). Combine the oats, salt, and baking powder in the bowl of your stand mixer or in a regular large bowl.

Add the coconut oil and as much of the boiling water as needed to form a smooth dough. It entirely depends on the grind of the oats and the humidity in the air, so add little splashes, not all at once. If your dough becomes too moist, add some more oats. Mix briefly in a stand mixer or with a hand mixer into a firm dough. Let cool in the bowl to room temperature, about 1 hour.

The dough will be drier when it has cooled, so add a few drops of cold water and mix a few times until the dough comes back together. Dust a silicone mat or a parchment paper–lined baking sheet with rolled oats and some oat flakes and salt flakes, if you like. Pat the dough into a flat ball and roll it out over the oats as thinly as possible. Slice the dough into 16 equal-size rectangles the size of a cracker. Use a pizza cutter for easy slicing. Prick with a fork. Sprinkle with some oat flakes and salt flakes. Press them into the dough with your rolling pin, if you wish, but it isn't mandatory.

Bake for 20 to 30 minutes, until crispy and just light brown. Rotate the baking mat or sheet halfway through for even browning.

Quick Whole-Wheat
Sunflower Seed Bread with Beer

If you don't have much time, but you still wish to serve a fresh whole-wheat bread, this is the solution. Provided you have a can of beer. There's no need to knead the bread as the baking powder and the yeast in the beer will leaven it. The beer also gives the bread an intense and full flavor, and it transforms it into a very hearty bread, almost like sourdough. I make this often with all types of beer, so go ahead and try with your favorite.

This bread is nice with cheese fondue, or with soup. We are crazy for it.

I don't have a faster and easier recipe than this one.

FOR 1 loaf
PREP 5 min.
BAKE 45 min.

lactose-free option
refined sugar–free

2 tbsp coconut oil or butter, melted
2¾ cups (350 g) whole-wheat flour (or whatever you prefer: you can also use light spelt flour or all-purpose flour)
1 tbsp baking powder
1½ tsp salt
¼ cup (50 g) coconut sugar, honey, or agave syrup
⅓ cup (50 g) sunflower seeds (or other seeds: flaxseeds, pumpkin seeds, and so on)
1 can beer (about 10 oz / 300 ml)

Preheat the oven to 350°F (180°C). Grease a 1- to 1½-qt (1- to 1.5-L) loaf pan with 1 tablespoon of the coconut oil.

Combine the flour, baking powder, salt, and coconut sugar in a bowl. Mix in almost all the sunflower seeds, though keep a few for garnishing. Pour in the beer and mix until it just about comes together, no kneading necessary. Pour the batter into the prepared pan.

Pour the rest of the coconut oil over the batter.

Bake for about 45 minutes, maybe a tad longer, or until a bamboo skewer inserted into the center comes out dry, just like with regular cake.

P.S.: In the picture you see two different breads: The one on the right was made with whole-wheat flour and high-fermenting specialty beer—certain types of ale or stout might work, but ask your local beer specialist. The one on the left was made with all-purpose flour and an organic pilsner.

Whole-wheat bread doesn't rise as well as white bread, but the taste of whole-wheat bread with dark beer is cool. Try to bake your favorite combination.

My Favorite Chili with a Thousand Beans, Chorizo, Chocolate, and Corn Bread

Yes, you're reading this correctly: This recipe contains chocolate, and it's delicious. Try it before you start muttering. It's very common in Latin America, they do it all the time. Because of the chorizo there's no need to add salt—be careful. This is ultra-comfort food. I'm already picturing an open fire pit in the garden with a bench in front of it.

SERVES at least 6
PREP 45 min.
BAKE about 25 min.

sugar-free

FOR THE CHILI
2 tbsp olive oil
2 onions, chopped
1 green bell pepper, diced
1 red bell pepper, diced
4 cloves garlic, minced
1 (9-oz / 250-g) dried chorizo
    sausage, cubed
½ tsp dried chile, or to taste
1 tbsp ground cumin
1 tbsp dried oregano
1 tsp cinnamon
2 (14-oz / 400-g) cans diced
    peeled tomatoes
zest and juice of 1 lime
1 tbsp coarsely chopped jala-
    peño peppers, or to taste
2 (14-oz / 400-g) cans
    black & kidney beans,
    drained and rinsed
corn kernels from 1 cob, or 1
    small can organic corn
1¾ oz (50 g) extra-dark
    chocolate (at least 75%
    cacao), coarsely chopped
sea salt & freshly ground
    black pepper
leaves from 1 small bunch
    fresh cilantro

FOR THE CORN BREAD
1 cup (150 g) fine-ground
    polenta or cornmeal (see
    page 18)
½ cup (60 g) all-purpose flour
5 tsp baking powder
generous pinch of salt
2 large eggs, beaten
1¼ cups (300 ml) buttermilk
7 tbsp (100 g) butter, melted,
    plus some extra

Make the chili: Heat up the oil in a heavy saucepan. Add the onion and sauté until soft. Add the green and red peppers, garlic, and chorizo and fry for 5 minutes. Add the dried chile, cumin, oregano, cinnamon, and tomatoes. Bring to a boil. Lower the heat, cover, and let simmer for 30 minutes, stirring occasionally. Add a splash of water if it becomes too dry. At the last moment, add the lime zest and juice, jalapeño, beans, and corn and heat up. Remove from the heat and stir in the chocolate. Cover and let stand for 5 minutes, then taste for salt and pepper. Chances are you don't need to add anything. Chop the cilantro and sprinkle it on top.

Make the corn bread: Preheat the oven to 350°F (180°C). In a large bowl, thoroughly mix the polenta, flour, baking powder, and salt. In a separate bowl, beat the eggs, buttermilk, and melted butter into a smooth mixture. Pour this into the polenta mixture while stirring with a wooden spoon and stir until you have a smooth batter.

Set 6 oven-safe mason jars or individual baking dishes in a baking pan. Fill them just over halfway with the chili. Spoon the corn bread batter on top. Slide the pan into the oven and bake for about 25 minutes, or until the bread is well baked and the chili bubbles nicely. Serve immediately.

Turkish Pide

The first time I tasted Turkish bread, I was sold. It was a long time ago, I think possibly somewhere in the 1980s. The bread has never bored me since. Not even after it has been served a thousand times at parties with some dreadfully dull dips.

Baked fresh, this might be the most delectable bread in the book.

And the nigella seeds are a must, you hear? A must.

FOR 2 breads
PREP 30 min.
RISE 2 hours
BAKE 8 min.

lactose-free
refined sugar–free

4 tsp (15 g) instant yeast
1 tsp honey
1⅔ cups (400 ml) lukewarm water
4 cups (500 g) durum wheat flour, type 65 or higher
1 tsp salt
3½ tbsp (50 ml) extra-virgin olive oil, plus more for greasing
1 egg, beaten with a few drops of water
1 tbsp nigella seeds (see page 105)
1 tbsp sesame seeds

Put the yeast in a medium bowl and add the honey and ½ cup plus 2 tbsp (150 ml) of the lukewarm water. Set aside for 10 minutes, until the yeast has dissolved and started to foam.

Stir in ¾ cup (100 g) of the flour. Cover the bowl with a dish towel and set aside in a warm place to rise for 30 minutes.

In a bowl, combine the salt with the rest of the flour and make an indentation in the middle. Pour the yeast mixture in and add the rest of the water and the oil. Stir well—I use a spatula to mix, as the dough is soft and gooey.

Once the dough is smooth, knead with a hand mixer for at least 10 minutes, until you have a soft and supple dough.

Turn the dough out into a bowl lightly greased with olive oil and let rise for 1 hour.

Place a pizza stone on the middle rack in the oven. Preheat the oven to the highest temperature.

Divide the dough in two and roll each piece into a ball. Brush the balls with the egg and flatten them with the palm of your hand. Make dents with your fingers. Let the flattened dough balls rest under a dish towel for 30 minutes.

Dust your pizza stone with some flour. Place one ball of dough on top and stretch it a little bit. You'll get the hang of it after a while.

Sprinkle the stretched dough ball with nigella and sesame seeds and close the oven immediately so as not to lose too much heat. Bake the bread until nicely brown, about 8 minutes. Bake the second dough ball the same way.

Filled Pide with Seasoned Lamb Meat

FOR 8 pieces
PREP 10 min.
BAKE 8 to 10 min.

lactose-free
refined sugar–free

1 recipe for pide (see page 137), prepared until the dough has risen for the second time
1 tbsp olive oil
2 onions, diced
3 cloves garlic, minced
9 oz (250 g) lamb meat, ground in the food processor or by hand
1 tbsp ground cumin
1 tbsp za'atar
salt & freshly ground black pepper
2 tbsp tomato puree

Place a pizza stone on the middle rack in the oven. Preheat the oven to the highest temperature.

Heat the olive oil in a skillet. Add the onions and sauté until translucent. Add the garlic and sauté as well. Add the ground lamb, cumin, and za'atar. Season with salt and pepper and cook everything thoroughly. Then add the tomato puree and cook until the puree has a sweetish smell. Deglaze with a splash of water. Let cool a little.

Divide the dough into 8 parts. Roll out each part into a rectangle. Scoop a few spoonfuls of the filling in the middle and squeeze the ends together, shaping it into a little boat. Carefully lift the boats onto the pizza stone. Bake the filled pides for 8 to 10 minutes, until nicely golden brown.

Filled Pide with Spinach, Lemon & Za'atar

FOR 8 pieces
PREP 10 min.
BAKE 8 to 10 min.

refined sugar–free

1 recipe for pide (see page
    137), prepared until the
    dough has risen for the
    second time
1 tbsp olive oil
2 onions, diced
3 cloves garlic, minced
10½ ounces (300 g) spinach,
    rinsed and chopped
2 tbsp raisins, soaked (for
    30 min. to 1 hour) and
    drained
2 tbsp za'atar, plus some
    extra
zest and juice of 1 lemon
3½ oz (100 g) feta, crumbled
1 egg, beaten

Place a pizza stone on the middle rack in the oven. Preheat the oven to the highest temperature.

Heat the olive oil in a skillet. Add the onions and sauté until translucent. Add the garlic and sauté as well. Add the spinach, raisins, and za'atar and cook everything thoroughly.

Stir in the lemon zest and juice and let the mixture cool.

Divide the dough into 8 parts. Roll out each part into a rectangle. Scoop a few spoonfuls of the filling in the middle and squeeze the ends together, shaping it into a little boat. Sprinkle with some feta and extra za'atar. Lift the boats carefully onto the pizza stone and brush the dough with some egg.

Bake the filled breads until golden brown, 8 to 10 minutes.

NEVER THROW OUT OLD BREAD !

MAKE WENTELTEEFJES!

(WENTELTEEFJES ARE A DUTCH VERSION OF FRENCH TOAST)

BEAT TOGETHER: 1 EGG, 1 TBSP VANILLA SUGAR, 1 TSP CINNAMON & 1 CUP (250 ML) MILK. POUR INTO A DEEP PLATE. SOAK 8 SLICES OF BREAD (ONE AT A TIME)

AND BAKE IN A PAN IN BUTTER UNTIL GOLDEN BROWN

MAKE BREAD CRUMBS!

DRY OUT OLD BREAD IN THE OVEN AT 300°F (150°C). DEPENDING ON THE SIZE OF THE BREAD, IT SHOULD BE DONE IN A SEC. GRIND INTO CRUMBS IN A FOOD PROCESSOR

MAKE CROUTONS!

SEASON CUBES OF STALE BREAD WITH OREGANO, ROSEMARY, THYME, OR PAPRIKA TO TASTE. ADD GARLIC, DRIZZLE WITH SOME OLIVE OIL AND SPRINKLE WITH SALT→BAKE AT 350°F (175°C) FOR ABOUT 20 MIN., UNTIL GOLDEN BROWN

MAKE BREAD SOUP!

LET OLD BREAD SIMMER IN A BIG POT OF HOME MADE TOMATO SOUP. ADD KALE, WHITE BEANS & LOTS OF OLIVE OIL →OH!

London, Great Britain

Upstate New York, USA

Mushroom Pie

I don't know about you, but I always have leftover bread. There's tons of things you can make with it, but this is a really cool recipe that isn't so well-known.

The lighter the bread, the better; that way it will become less dense. I like this simple addictive dish so much that I actually keep bread aside for it.

SERVES 3 or 4
PREP 25 min.
BAKE 25 min.

refined sugar–free

1¼ cups (250 g) cubes of old bread (I use pide—see page 137—but anything is possible)
3 tbsp butter, plus extra for greasing
1 large onion, diced
a few sprigs fresh sage or thyme
coarse sea salt & freshly ground black pepper
2¼ lbs (1 kg) mixed wild mushrooms, cleaned and chopped
1 clove garlic, pressed
1 small glass white vermouth, wine, or water or stock (about ½ cup/125 ml)
3 eggs, beaten
¾ cup plus 1 tbsp (200 ml) heavy cream
3 oz (80 g) grated hard, salty cheese, like Parmesan or pecorino or an aged Dutch goat cheese

Preheat the oven to 350°F (170°C).

Arrange the bread cubes on a rimmed baking sheet and toast in the oven until light brown, just a few minutes. Put most of the cubes in a large bowl but set a handful aside.

Butter an 8-inch (20-cm) baking pan.

Melt 1 tablespoon of the butter in a large skillet and add the onion and sage sprigs. Sauté the onion until soft, about 6 minutes, while stirring occasionally. Season with salt and pepper and scoop the sautéed onions into the bowl with the toasted bread.

Melt the remaining 2 tablespoons butter in the same pan and add the chopped mushrooms and garlic. Cook over medium heat until all the moisture released by the mushrooms has evaporated. Add the mushrooms to the bowl with the bread and onions.

Douse the pan with some liquor: Vermouth is nice, and sherry could work, but water or stock are fine too. With a wooden spoon, scrape off all the bits sticking to the bottom of the pan and boil down the liquid to about ⅓ cup (75 ml), give or take.

Pour this liquid into the bowl with the bread. Toss everything through and let stand for 10 minutes, so the bread can soak up the juices. Spoon everything into the greased baking pan.

In another bowl, beat the eggs with the cream, grated cheese, and some salt and pepper.

Pour the egg mixture into the oven dish over the bread-mushroom mixture and sprinkle with the handful of croutons that you kept aside.

Bake for about 25 minutes, until nicely browned. Serve with a green salad as a vegetarian main or lunch dish.

POUND
C A

3 POUND CAKE RECIPES

On the following pages you will find many different versions of cake batter, because the challenge is to make something new each time around.

However, I will also feature some basic recipes for you to improvise on. Give your cakes a personal twist by adding extra lemon zest, instant coffee, green tea, cocoa powder, or ginger. Stack cakes made of biscuit dough or genoise, alternate with layers of whipped cream or mascarpone (or a mixture of both), add homemade jam and seasonal fruits for a supercool birthday cake. Recipes for fillings like lemon curd, meringue icing, and buttercream with herbs can be found in the Mise-en-Place chapter (beginning on page 10). Make a slight variation on the classic pound cake by mixing some finely grated clementine zest and some juice into the batter. Sprinkle with a little orange liqueur after baking and you will have created a fantastic dessert in no time.

As you can see, cakes are very versatile.

Quartre Quart, or Regular Cake

The easiest pound cake to make in the world. The French call it quatre quart, which literally means that all four ingredients are being used in equal proportions. This is, by the way, also an easy way to remember this recipe.

For this cake you don't need anything more, no flavoring, nothing. Use good-quality ingredients and you will taste the difference immediately. If you can't control your urge to add something, just use a drop of vanilla extract or some finely grated lemon zest, but you don't need to.

FOR 1 cake
PREP 30 min.
BAKE 40 min.

1 cup (200 g) sugar
⅞ cup (1¾ sticks / 200 g) (preferably unsalted) farm-fresh butter, at room temperature, plus extra for the pan
4 medium or 3 large eggs, at room temperature (you need about 7 oz/200 g)
1½ cups plus 2 tbsp (200 g) all-purpose flour
1½ tsp baking powder
sea salt

Preheat the oven to 350°F (175°C). Thoroughly grease a 9-inch (22-cm) cake pan or 9-by-5-inch (22-by-12-cm) loaf pan.

Beat the sugar and butter together in a bowl until light and fluffy. For a smooth texture, it's best to use a hand mixer. Separate the eggs. Add the yolks one by one and beat until they are well mixed. Sift together the flour, baking powder, and a pinch of salt (if desired) over a bowl and then add to the butter-sugar mixture.

In a perfectly clean bowl, using a perfectly clean whisk, whisk the egg whites (with a pinch of salt) until stiff. They have the right stiffness if you can turn the bowl upside down without dropping the egg white on the floor. Feeling nervous about trying this usually is a good sign that you should continue beating a little longer.

🕊 With the utmost care, fold the egg whites into the batter and pour the mixture into the greased cake pan.

Bake the cake for about 40 minutes, or until a skewer inserted into the center comes out clean. Allow the cake to cool for 5 minutes, then remove from the pan. Let cool further on a rack.

Biscuit

Biscuit (bis-KWEE) is a pound cake made without butter. This way, you get a wonderfully light crust that can be filled with heavier ingredients like buttercream or whipped cream, without ending up with an impossibly rich cake.

The preparation does require some skill and a bit of patience on your end. The eggs and the sugar should be beaten for a very long time to form a beautiful, stiff white foam—otherwise, you'll end up with a flat crust. A hand mixer or, better, a stand mixer (like a KitchenAid) is essential for this recipe.

When making biscuit batter, it's all about air: Keep as much air as possible in your mixture! Therefore: Do really take the time to sift the flour and the cornstarch. Also be very serious about stirring the flour in with the batter. Be precise and meticulous! For an even better result, simply be prudent and sift the dry ingredients twice. Last piece of advice: Never, ever open the oven door while baking; otherwise the cake will collapse.

Well, hopefully I didn't scare you, because once you have this in your hands, it's a great recipe.

FOR 1 cake
PREP 30 min.
BAKE 35 min.

lactose-free option

6 tbsp (75 g) sifted all-purpose flour, plus extra for the pan
4 eggs, at room temperature
½ cup plus 1 tbsp (125 g) packed light brown sugar
pinch of sea salt
scant ¼ cup (25 g) sifted cornstarch

Preheat the oven to 325°F (170°C). Grease a 9- to 10-inch (22- to 24-cm) round cake pan with butter, oil, or cooking spray and line the bottom with a round of parchment paper cut to fit. Grease the parchment as well. Dust the pan with flour, then shake out any excess.

Thoroughly whisk the eggs, brown sugar, and salt in a stand mixer (or for a really long time using a hand mixer) until they form a frothy mass. The eggs should have tripled in volume and be almost perfectly white. Then gently fold in the flour and cornstarch. Try to retain as much air in the batter as you can.

Pour the batter into the prepared cake pan. Bake for about 35 minutes. During the first 30 minutes, do NOT open the oven.

Allow the cake to cool in the pan for 5 minutes, then remove from the pan. Now, let the cake cool completely before doing anything else. Meaning: You can only begin cutting and filling it after it has cooled off. Carefully wrapped in plastic, it can conveniently be frozen for later use.

Chocolate Genoise

*Genoise is a combination of the two aforementioned cakes (*quatre quart *and* biscuit*). It contains a little bit of butter, which enhances the taste, but not as much as a* quatre quart. *This batter is based on a* sabayon, *or light foamy custard. This means you make it using a bain-marie (double boiler). Although you don't have to add any leavening agent, this batter will result in a wonderfully light cake that, like the biscuit, can be further dressed. I'll give you the recipe for a chocolate genoise; if you want to make a plain genoise, just replace the unsweetened cocoa powder with an equal amount of flour.*

FOR 1 cake
PREP 30 min.
BAKE 30 min.

4 eggs
½ cup plus 2 tbsp (125 g) sugar
3 tbsp butter, melted, plus extra for the pan
1 tsp vanilla extract, or the seeds of 1 vanilla bean
½ tsp sea salt
6 tbsp (75 g) sifted all-purpose flour
5 tbsp (25 g) unsweetened cocoa powder

Preheat the oven to 325°F (170°C). Position a rack in the center. Grease a 9- to 10-inch (22- to 24-cm) round cake pan and line the bottom with a round of parchment paper cut to fit. Grease the parchment as well.

Bring a pot of water to a gentle boil. Set a large metal or glass bowl (i.e., a heatproof one) over the pot, making sure the bottom of the bowl isn't touching the water, and whisk the eggs and sugar in the bowl until tripled in volume and lukewarm to the touch. This takes a while, about 10 minutes, so use a hand mixer. The mixture should look like a thin, very light yellowish-white *sabayon*, or custard.

Drizzle in the butter and vanilla. Remove the bowl from the pot and place it on the counter. Sift together the salt, flour, and cocoa powder over a separate bowl and fold it into the *sabayon* mixture in three batches, a little at a time. Combine carefully, retaining all the air inside the batter. If you overmix, the batter will become runny and you will have to start all over again.

Gently pour the batter into the greased cake pan and bake for 30 to 35 minutes, until a toothpick inserted in the center comes out clean; do NOT open the oven door in the first 30 minutes.

Allow the cake to cool in the pan on the counter for 5 minutes. Then use a knife to loosen the cake from the sides of the pan and turn it out onto a rack. Allow the cake to fully cool before slicing it or topping it with the pistachio cream from page 44, if desired. Carefully wrapped in plastic wrap, it can easily be stored in the freezer for later use.

Good Advice

You can bring a stale cake back to life by dousing it with homemade simple syrup. Here you find the basic recipe:

Simple Syrup

1 cup (200 g) sugar
a flavoring: 1 vanilla bean, sliced open and seeds scraped out, lemon slices, verbena, mint leaves or any other type of herb, Lapsang Souchong tea, lavender blossom, tonka beans, star anise, or bruised lemongrass

Bring ¾ cup plus 1 tbsp (200 ml) water, the sugar, and the flavoring to a gentle boil in a small saucepan and let steep over low heat for 20 minutes. Then strain it over a jug and throw out the flavoring. Drizzle the stale cake with one-third of the syrup and allow it to be absorbed. Keep pouring splashes of the syrup over the cake each time you walk by. Continue doing this until the cake has absorbed everything. Or pass the jug of syrup alongside the cake when serving. Cover the cake with aluminum foil for longer storage.

Light Gooseberry Cake with Custard

SERVES 8
PREP 35 min.
BAKE 40 min.

FOR THE CUSTARD
2 tbsp (30 ml) heavy cream
1 vanilla bean, sliced open
    and seeds scraped out
3 egg yolks (keep the whites)
1 tbsp cornstarch
3 tbsp packed dark brown
    sugar

FOR THE CAKE
⅞ cup (1¾ sticks /
    200 g) butter, at room
    temperature, plus extra
    for the pan
scant 1 cup (200 g) packed
    light brown sugar
3 eggs, separated
2 tsp vanilla extract
1½ cups (200 g) cake flour
1 tsp baking powder
salt
3 egg whites (leftover from
    making the custard)
7 ounces (200 g) goose-
    berries, topped and tailed
3 tbsp coarse sugar

Make the custard: Heat the cream with the vanilla bean pod and seeds in a heavy skillet. Just before it starts boiling, lower the heat and let the cream slowly steep while you prepare the rest.

Whisk the egg yolks, cornstarch, and brown sugar in a bowl until light and foamy. Remove and discard the vanilla bean pod from the hot cream and, while whisking the yolk mixture constantly, slowly pour the hot cream into it. Then pour everything back into the skillet and continue stirring over medium heat until a thick custard begins to form. Remove from the heat and allow to cool.

Make the cake: Preheat the oven to 350°F (180°C). Grease a 9-inch (22-cm) springform pan and line the bottom with a round of parchment paper cut to fit. Grease the parchment as well.

Beat the butter and brown sugar until creamy and light. One by one, add the egg yolks. Also stir in the vanilla. Sift together the flour, baking powder, and pinch of salt over a bowl and fold it into the butter-sugar mixture, creating a smooth batter.

In a perfectly clean bowl, using a perfectly clean whisk, whisk the 6 egg whites (with a pinch of salt) until stiff. At very last moment, gently fold the stiff egg whites into the batter.

Pour half of the batter into the springform pan. Spoon the custard over the top and spread it into an even layer; use the back of a spoon for this. Now pour the rest of the batter on top.

Evenly distribute the gooseberries over the top of the cake and sprinkle with the coarse sugar.

Bake for 40 minutes. Let the cake cool in the pan on a rack for 5 minutes, then you can remove the springform pan sides. Allow to cool completely before cutting it.

HELP!

If the custard curdles because it has become too hot, DO NOT DESPAIR: pour it into a bowl and whisk until it has cooled off. Then it will come together again.

Upside-Down Plum Hazelnut Cake

SERVES 8
PREP 30 min.
BAKE 45 min.

wheat-free

9 tbsp (125 g) butter, plus
    extra for greasing
4 firm, ripe red or purple
    plums, sliced into 8
    wedges each
¾ cup (150 g) coarse sugar
2 eggs
½ cup (125 ml) plain yogurt
1 vanilla bean, sliced open
    and seeds scraped out
⅔ cup (100 g) hazelnuts,
    briefly toasted
2 cups plus 2 tbsp (250 g)
    light spelt flour
1 tbsp baking powder
pinch of salt
½ tsp ground cumin
½ cup (125 ml) crème
    fraîche, for serving
    (optional)

Preheat the oven to 350°F (175°C). Position a rack in the center. Grease a 9-inch (22-cm) round cake pan and line the bottom with a round of parchment paper cut to fit. Grease the parchment as well.

In a skillet, melt 1 tablespoon of the butter. Add the plums and ¼ cup (50 g) of the sugar. Cook over medium heat until the sugar has dissolved and the juices begin running from the fruits, about 5 minutes.

Neatly spread out the plums over the bottom of the cake pan. Pour the juices left in the skillet over the top.

Beat the rest of the butter with the remaining ½ cup (100 g) sugar in a bowl until fluffy. Now beat in the eggs, yogurt, and vanilla bean seeds.

Using a food processor, finely grind the hazelnuts. Transfer to a bowl and add the flour, baking powder, salt, and cumin. Add the hazelnut mixture to the butter mixture and stir into a smooth batter. Pour it over the plums in the cake pan.

Bake the cake for 45 minutes. Let rest for 5 minutes in the pan, then invert onto a plate. Carefully remove the parchment paper from the plums and: voilà! Isn't this a dream cake?

Serve with a dollop of unsweetened crème fraîche, if you want.

Beurre Noisette Madeleines

*The rich flavor of browned, clarified butter (*beurre noisette*) is addictive. In Home Made Summer, I included a recipe for financiers, small French pound cakes made with almond flour, and beurre noisette. They are so addictive that I tried the same trick when making my madeleines. And the result . . . was great. Wow!*

FOR 30 madeleines
PREP 10 min.
INACTIVE 20 min. to 1 night
BAKE 7 min.

⅔ cup (1⅓ sticks / 150 g) butter
3 eggs
¾ cup (150 g) granulated sugar
pinch of salt
1¼ cups (150 g) all-purpose flour, plus extra for the pan
grated zest of ¼ lemon
1 vanilla bean, sliced open and seeds scraped out
confectioners' sugar, for dusting

In a saucepan, melt the butter over medium heat until it begins to smell like caramel and the color turns dark brown, about the color of a cup of tea.

Strain and leave the residue (those black particles at the bottom) in the pan—if some particles sneak through, that's fine. Set aside to cool somewhat.

Beat the eggs and granulated sugar in a bowl until light and foamy. This works best with a hand mixer. Spoon in the browned butter (reserving a bit for greasing the pan later), salt, flour, lemon zest, and vanilla bean seeds. Transfer the batter to a pastry bag or a jug. Set aside in the fridge for at least 20 minutes, although overnight would be even better.

Preheat the oven to 425°F (220°C).

Grease a scallop-shell madeleine pan with the reserved browned butter and sprinkle with some flour. Tap out the excess flour. Fill the cups of the pan three-quarters of the way with batter.

Bake the little cakes for 7 minutes, until golden brown.

Let cool for 1 minute, then immediately turn them out onto a rack. Allow them to further cool, but do, however, eat them while they're still warm. Sprinkle with some confectioners' sugar from a tiny strainer before serving.

Chocolate Olive Oil Cake with Grapefruit

SERVES 10   **PREP** 20 min.   **BAKE** 35 min.   *gluten-free* *lactose-free*

7 ounces (200 g) good-quality dark chocolate
7 tbsp (100 ml) extra-virgin olive oil, plus more for greasing
5 eggs, separated
scant ⅔ cup (70 g) almond flour
grated zest of 2 grapefruits
salt
1 cup (200 g) granulated sugar
unsweetened cocoa powder, for dusting

Preheat the oven to 350°F (175°C). Grease a 9-inch (23-cm) springform pan and line the bottom with a round of parchment paper cut to fit. Grease the parchment as well.

Melt the chocolate *au bain-marie*. As soon as the water begins to boil, turn off the heat and let the chocolate finish melting gently.

Now stir in the olive oil and mix it into an even sauce.

In a bowl, using a hand mixer, combine the egg yolks, almond flour, grapefruit zest, pinch of salt, and ½ cup (100 g) of the sugar.

In a perfectly clean bowl, using a perfectly clean whisk, whisk the egg whites (with a pinch of salt) until almost stiff. Keep beating while gradually adding the rest of the sugar until everything has been absorbed. Gently fold a bit of the egg white mixture into the almond meal mixture, then add the rest in three additions, a little at a time, combining everything into a smooth mixture.

Pour into the prepared pan and bake for 35 to 40 minutes, until a toothpick inserted in the center comes out with a few wet crumbs attached.

Allow the cake to cool completely in the pan. It will sink a little, but that's normal. Just before serving you can dust the cake with some cocoa powder.

Olive Oil Cake with Clementine & Rosemary

SERVES 8
PREP 20 min.
BAKE 45 min.

lactose-free

FOR THE CAKE
⅔ cup (160 ml) extra-virgin olive oil, plus extra for greasing
¾ cup plus 1 tbsp (160 g) sugar
4 eggs
2 tbsp fresh rosemary, finely chopped
grated zest and juice of 2 clementines
1¼ cups (160 g) cake flour
1 tbsp baking powder
pinch of salt

FOR THE GLAZE
2½ cups (250 g) confectioners' sugar
juice of 1 clementine
juice of 1 lemon

FOR THE TOPPING
some dried citrus fruits (see box!)
a few sprigs fresh rosemary

Make the cake: Preheat the oven to 325°F (170°C). Grease a 9-inch (22-cm) springform pan and line the bottom with a circle of parchment paper cut to fit. Grease the parchment as well.

Using a hand mixer, whisk the oil and the sugar in a bowl until foamy. One by one, beat in the eggs. Add the rosemary, clementine zest, and clementine juice and once again beat thoroughly. Sift together the flour, baking powder, and salt over a bowl and fold the flour mixture into the batter.

Pour the batter into the prepared pan and bake the cake for about 45 minutes. It should bounce back if you softly press down on it with your finger.

Let the cake cool in the pan for about 5 minutes, then carefully remove the sides of the springform pan. Allow to cool completely.

Make the glaze: Stir together the confectioners' sugar with the clementine juice and lemon juice until it has the consistency of thin yogurt.

Pour the glaze over the cake and further dress the top with slices of dried citrus fruit and sprigs of fresh rosemary. Now, let the cake dry for at least an hour before cutting it.

DRYING CITRUS FRUITS!

Preheat your oven to the lowest temperature.

Cut the citrus fruits into slices of about ¼ inch (0.5 cm). Spread them out on a parchment paper–lined baking sheet in a single layer. Let them dry in the oven for the entire night, flipping the slices over toward the end so the bottoms dry out fully. To ensure the moisture can escape, leave the door ajar—stick a ladle in the oven door to hold it open. The fruits have to be bone dry—otherwise, they will mold over time. Store in an airtight container in a dark place. The fruits will keep for a couple of months.

Raspberry Coconut Cakes

This little sponge cake is a much healthier version of those terrible cupcakes, which seem to be omnipresent these days. If you use spelt flour instead of regular wheat flour, these cakes will be wheat-free to boot. This way sinning isn't that bad now, is it?

FOR 12 cakes
PREP 10 min.
BAKE 25 min.

wheat-free option
refined sugar–free

2 eggs
3 tbsp coconut oil or butter, melted and slightly cooled, plus extra for greasing
½ cup plus 2 tbsp (150 ml) buttermilk
7 tbsp (100 ml) honey
zest of 1 orange
1½ cups (175 g) light spelt flour or all-purpose flour
1 tsp baking powder
1 cup (100 g) grated unsweetened coconut
generous ½ cup (50 g) rolled oats (not instant) from the natural foods store (see page 18)
pinch of salt
1 tsp *speculaas* spices (see page 245) or pumpkin pie spice
1¼ cups (150 g) fresh raspberries or blueberries (or use frozen fruits, defrosted)

Preheat the oven to 350°F (180°C). Grease a 12-cup muffin pan.

Beat the eggs in a bowl and add the coconut oil, buttermilk, honey, and orange zest.

In another bowl, combine the flour with the baking powder, grated coconut, oatmeal, salt, and *speculaas* spices. Pour the egg mixture into the flour mixture and, using a wooden spatula, stir until it is just about mixed together well. Don't stir too long!

Fold in the raspberries and pour the mixture into the muffin pan until the cups are two-thirds full.

Bake the little sponge cakes until golden brown, 25 minutes.

Lemon Polenta Cakes

For these cakes, I sometimes use fine polenta; other times I'll use corn flour, which isn't the same as cornstarch. It's a type of flour, produced by sifting cornmeal and grinding it even finer (see page 18). My Parisian organic food store sells it. And I love it since it gives my cakes a softer, finer texture.

When using polenta, however, the cakes become wonderfully crumbly, which is delicious too. Try both and see which one you prefer. While you're at it, you can also replace the lemon juice with elderflower syrup. Very tasty as well.

FOR 9 cakes **PREP** 15 min. **BAKE** 25 min. *gluten-free*

⅞ cup (1¾ sticks / 200 g) butter, at room temperature, plus extra for the pan
scant 1 cup (200 g) packed dark brown sugar
3 eggs
zest and juice of 2 lemons
1¾ cups (200 g) almond flour
¾ cup (100 g) fine polenta or corn flour
1½ tsp baking powder
pinch of salt

FOR THE GLAZE
1 cup (100 g) confectioners' sugar
finely grated zest and juice of 1 lemon

Preheat the oven to 350°F (180°C).
Grease 9 wells of a muffin pan or 9 individual baking cups.

Using a hand mixer, beat the butter and brown sugar together until nicely white, light, and fluffy. One by one, beat in the eggs, then the lemon zest and juice. In another bowl, combine the almond meal with the polenta, baking powder, and salt. Using a spatula, carefully fold this mixture into the butter and sugar mixture, adding small amounts at a time. Spoon the batter into the prepared muffin pan or baking cups. Bake the cakes for 25 minutes, until nicely brown. Take out of the oven and leave to cool in the pan or cups on a rack for 5 minutes. Remove from the pan or cups and allow to cool further.

Meanwhile, make the glaze: Stir the confectioners' sugar into the lemon juice until it becomes a glaze of medium consistency.

Pour the glaze over the cakes, sprinkle with the zest, and let them dry a bit before serving.

Carrot Banana Cake

Oh, delicious. Look, I figured: I love carrot cake, I love banana bread, why don't I throw the two together and combine them into a single thing I love?

The cake doesn't contain any sugar, butter, or wheat, so it's pretty healthy. But by adding the apricots, banana, apple juice, and carrot, it ends up being pretty sweet anyhow.

If you can't get spelt flour, you can of course simply use wheat flour, I won't stop you. Bake this cake and bring a thick slice to work. It's the perfect snack.

FOR 1 cake
PREP 25 min.
INACTIVE 30 min.
BAKE 50 min.

wheat-free
lactose-free
refined sugar–free

1 cup (250 ml) unsweetened organic apple juice
1¼ cups (150 g) grated carrot
⅔ cup (100 g) unsulphured dried apricots, halved
2 to 3 tbsp honey or agave syrup
2 cups plus 2 tbsp (250 g) light spelt flour
½ cup (50 g) grated unsweetened coconut
2 tsp baking powder
1 tbsp ground ginger (cinnamon is nice too)
pinch of salt
3 eggs, beaten
2 bananas, sliced

Preheat the oven to 350°F (180°C). Position a rack in the center. Thoroughly grease a 1½-qt (1.5-L) loaf pan, or any other pan with approximately the same volume. I use some melted coconut oil, but baking spray or olive oil also works fine.

In a saucepan, bring the apple juice, carrot, apricots, and honey to a boil. Turn off the heat and allow to rest for 30 minutes. Let cool until the mixture is nearly at room temperature. I usually spoon the mixture into a large dish to make sure it cools faster.

Meanwhile, combine the flour with the coconut, baking powder, ginger, and salt. Then spoon in the carrot mixture. Stir in the beaten eggs and finally the banana slices. Pour the batter into the prepared pan. Bake the cake for 50 minutes or so. The cake is done when a skewer inserted into the center comes out clean. Let it cool in the pan, then turn out onto a rack. Once cooled off, the cake will be slightly firmer.

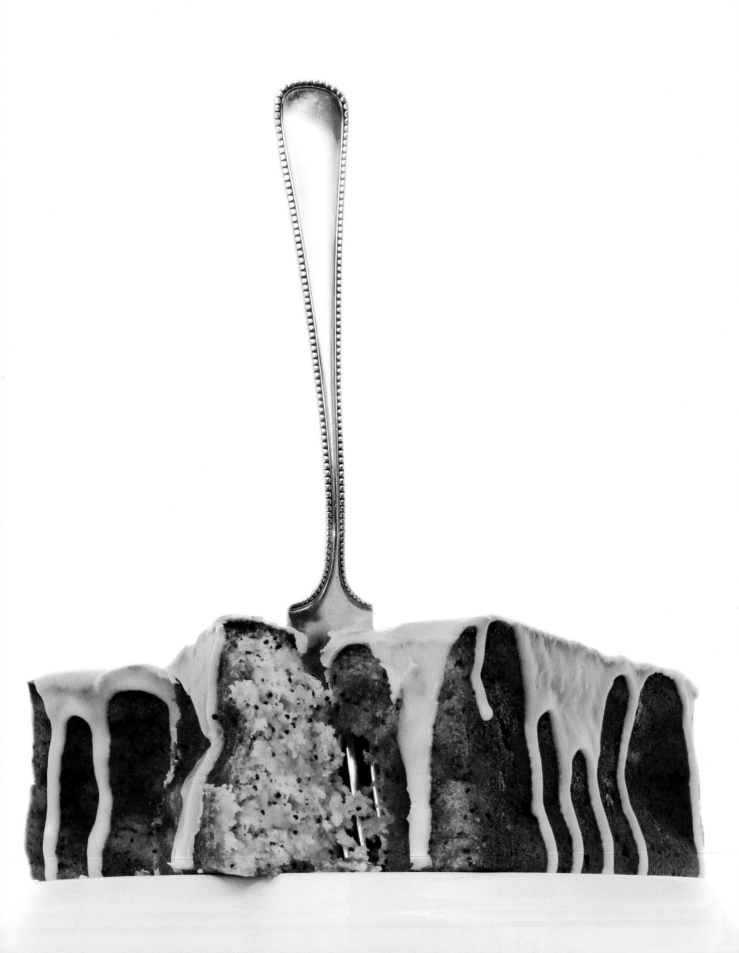

Super-Light Lemon Poppy Seed Cake

Once my friend Horas ate a cake like this one at London's Borough Market. He took a slice back home with him to the Netherlands and tried to replicate it in his own kitchen, using the ingredients listed on a sticker on the wrapper as the only instructions.

He immediately called me to pass along the recipe, after which I took to the kitchen to try it. This cake is super light and airy and has a wonderful lemon flavor that makes you never want to stop eating. A word-of-mouth recipe, which happens to be one of my favorites.

Here you'll find my own version of his recipe.

FOR 1 cake
PREP 10 min.
BAKE 35 min.

FOR THE CAKE
⅞ cup (1¾ cups / 200 g) butter, at room temperature, plus extra for the pan

scant 1 cup (200 g) packed light brown sugar

2 eggs

1 tsp vanilla extract

finely grated zest and juice of 2 lemons

2 tbsp poppy seeds

1½ cups plus 2 tbsp (200 g) all-purpose flour

1¼ tsp baking powder

salt

4 egg whites (keep the yolks for making lemon curd; see page 30)

FOR THE LEMON GLAZE
juice of 1 lemon

about 2½ cups (250 g) confectioners' sugar, could be a little more

Make the cake: Preheat the oven to 325°F (170°C). Place the rack just below the center of the oven. Grease a 10-inch (24-cm) round cake pan (or a 1½-qt / 1.5-L loaf pan) and line the bottom with a piece of parchment paper cut to fit. Grease the parchment as well.

Using a hand mixer, beat the butter and brown sugar together until the mixture is creamy and soft. One by one, beat in the eggs and continue beating until they're fully incorporated. Add the vanilla, lemon zest, lemon juice, and poppy seeds and mix thoroughly.

Combine the flour with the baking powder and a pinch of salt. Sift the mixture over the bowl with the batter and fold it in until it's nice and smooth.

In a perfectly clean bowl, using a perfectly clean whisk, whisk the egg whites (with a pinch of salt) until stiff. They have the right stiffness if you can turn the bowl upside down without dropping the egg whites on the floor.

Carefully fold one portion of the egg whites into the batter. After that has been incorporated you can fold in the rest. Pour the batter into the prepared pan and bake the cake for about 35 minutes, or until a skewer inserted into the center comes out clean.

Let the cake cool in the pan for 5 minutes. Then turn it out onto a rack to cool further.

Make the lemon glaze: Pour the lemon juice into a bowl and add confectioners' sugar, stirring until the glaze more or less has the consistency of thin yogurt.

Pour the glaze over the cake. Allow the glaze to dry for 1 hour before cutting the cake.

Chocolate Pecan Cake

FOR 1 cake
PREP 35 min.
BAKE 45 min.

FOR THE CAKE

1 cup plus 2 tbsp (2¼ sticks / 250 g) butter, plus extra for the pan
½ cup plus 2 tbsp (50 g) unsweetened cocoa powder
1⅓ cups (300 g) packed dark brown sugar
2 large eggs
7 tbsp (100 ml) buttermilk
1 tbsp vanilla extract
2¼ cups (300 g) all-purpose flour
2 tsp baking powder
2 tsp cinnamon
pinch of salt
½ cup (75 g) dates, pitted and coarsely chopped
1⅓ cups (200 g) raisins
¾ cup (70 g) pecans, plus a handful extra as garnish: briefly toast all the nuts in a dry skillet

FOR THE GLAZE

3 tbsp butter
½ cup (125 ml) milk or cream
5½ ounces (150 g) dark chocolate, finely chopped
pinch of salt

Make the cake: Preheat the oven to 350°F (175°C). Thoroughly grease a 1½-qt (1.5-L) loaf pan and line the bottom with a piece of parchment paper cut to fit. If you leave the short ends a little longer they will fold upward like two handles, making it easy to remove your cake later. Grease the parchment paper as well.

Melt the butter in a saucepan over medium heat. Stir in the cocoa powder and ½ cup (125 ml) water until you have a smooth sauce. Remove the pan from the heat.

In a jug, beat together the brown sugar, eggs, buttermilk, and vanilla until smooth.

Sift together the flour, baking powder, cinnamon, and salt over another bowl. Spoon the flour mixture into the cocoa-butter mixture and stir until there aren't any lumps left.

Then stir in the egg-buttermilk mixture and fold in the dried fruits and the nuts.

Pour the batter into the prepared pan and bake for about 45 minutes, or until a skewer inserted into the center comes out clean.

Let the cake cool in the pan for 5 minutes, then remove from the pan and place the cake on a rack to further cool off.

Meanwhile, make the glaze: Melt the butter in a heavy skillet over medium heat. Then stir in the milk. When the milk is just about to boil, lower the heat. Add the chocolate and allow it to slowly melt without stirring. Wait about 7 minutes, when all chocolate has melted, before gently stirring the glaze. Now stir in the salt.

Spoon the glaze over the cake. Allow to solidify, and as a final touch, press some extra pecans into the glaze to make your cake look even better.

Fruity Almond Cake

Even though this recipe doesn't contain any gluten or any refined sugars, the honey and the fruits do make this cake lightly sweet. But more important: This cake is very healthy, which is something I just crave some days. Eating a thick slice of this cake after you're done exercising is very good, as it contains lots of proteins, which—according to my trainer—is just what I need. "Your muscles will become big and strong," she always tells me.

FOR 1 cake
PREP 10 min.
BAKE 45 min.

gluten-free
refined sugar–free
lactose-free

scant 2¼ cups (250 g)
    almond flour
1 tbsp cinnamon or *speculaas*
    spices (see page 245) or
    pumpkin pie spice
½ tsp baking soda
½ tsp sea salt
1 apple or pear, peeled,
    cored, and cubed
⅔ cup (100 g) unsulphured
    dried apricots
⅔ cup (100 g) dried prunes,
    pitted
½ cup (50 g) walnuts or
    pecans
4 eggs
1 tbsp honey or agave syrup
    (to taste, can also be left out)

Preheat the oven to 325°F (170°C). Thoroughly grease a 1½-qt (1.5-L) loaf pan with extra-virgin olive oil and cut a piece of parchment paper to size to line the bottom. Grease this as well.

First, using a whisk, combine the almond flour, cinnamon, baking soda, and salt in a bowl. Add the cubed apple or pear, apricots, prunes, and nuts.

Beat the eggs and honey or agave (if using) together and stir them into the dry mixture. Add enough water to turn it into a soft and creamy batter. Sometimes 3½ tbsp (50 ml) will be sufficient, sometimes you'll need ⅓ cup (75 ml). It's not important really. The dried fruits will eagerly absorb the water.

Pour the batter into the prepared pan and bake the cake for 40 to 45 minutes. Let cool on a wire rack. Sufficiently wrapped, this cake will keep for an entire week.

APPLE~LEMON YOGURT CAKES

4 CUPS (400 G) LIGHT SPELT FLOUR
OR 3 CUPS (375 G) ALL-PURPOSE FLOUR
2 TSP BAKING POWDER
A PINCH OF SALT
½ CUP (125 G) APPLE SAUCE
7 TBSP (100 ML) HONEY
1 TBSP OLIVE OIL OR MELTED COCONUT OIL, PLUS EXTRA FOR THE PAN
GRATED ZEST & JUICE OF 1 LEMON
1 EGG & ¾ CUP + 1 TBSP (200 ML) FAT-FREE PLAIN YOGURT

PREHEAT THE OVEN TO 350°F (180° C). GREASE 12 SMALL CAKE PANS

COMBINE THE DRY INGREDIENTS

COMBINE THE WET INGREDIENTS & STIR IN THE DRY ONES →

POUR THE BATTER IN ⅔ FULL

BAKE THE CAKES FOR ABOUT 25 MIN. UNTIL GOLDEN.

Date Rum Cakes with Salty Caramel

FOR 8 small cakes
PREP 30 min.
BAKE 30 min.

FOR THE CAKES
1 cup (200 g) sugar
2½ cups (250 g) dates,
    pitted and chopped
¾ cup plus 1 tbsp (200 ml)
    boiling water
1¾ cups (225 g) all-purpose
    flour
1 tsp baking powder
¾ tsp salt
1 egg
1 tsp vanilla extract

FOR THE GLAZE
3 tbsp butter
⅓ cup (75 g) packed dark
    brown sugar
¼ cup (60 ml) good-quality
    rum
¼ tsp flaky sea salt, such as
    Maldon, to garnish

Preheat the oven to 350°F (175°C). Grease 8 (4-inch / 10-cm) mini pie pans. (You can also use a 9-by-5½-inch / 22-by-14-cm) loaf pan and cut the cake into pieces afterward. In that case, you'll need to bake the cake slightly longer.)

Make the cakes: Melt the sugar in a heavy saucepan over medium heat, until the caramel is tea-colored. This will take a while—say, 15 minutes. Try not to stir, but use a wet pastry brush to brush down the edges of the pan where the sugar crystals form. Shake the pan occasionally.

Add the dates and the boiling water. Be careful! It can splatter a lot!!!

Remove from the heat and let the pan stand for 15 minutes. When the caramel hardens, you can heat it up again to melt it.

Combine the flour with the baking powder and salt. Stir in the warm caramel mixture and then the egg and vanilla.

Pour the batter into the mini pie pans and bake for 30 minutes.

Meanwhile, make the glaze: Melt the butter and brown sugar in that same saucepan until the sugar has dissolved. Remove from the heat and carefully stir in the rum.

Remove the warm cakes from their pans and place them on a rack. Pour the warm glaze over the tops and sprinkle with salt flakes.

Let cool or eat immediately, when they're still a little warm. With crème fraîche. Oy!

Parsnip Apple Cake

Ohhhh, this cake is divine . . .

The nutmeg, the parsnip, the apples—you'll taste them all in this cake.

For the fearful ones: The cake doesn't taste healthy—more like carrot cake, but much better! This cake has made a lot of my friends happy. Now it's your turn.

SERVES 12
PREP 20 min.
BAKE 45 min.

wheat-free option

scant 1 cup (80 g) rolled oats (not instant) from the natural foods store (see page 18)

¾ cup plus 1 tbsp (200 ml) boiling water

¾ cup (1½ sticks / 175 g) butter, at room temperature

1⅓ cups (300 g) packed light brown sugar or granulated sugar

4 eggs

1 tsp vanilla extract

2½ cups (250 g) light spelt flour or 2 cups (250 g) all-purpose flour

2 tsp baking powder

1 tsp salt

2 tsp cinnamon

1 tsp ground nutmeg

½ cup (50 g) grated unsweetened coconut

2 apples, peeled, cored, and cubed

1¼ cups (150 g) peeled and coarsely grated parsnip

TO GARNISH
confectioners' sugar, for dusting
nutmeg, ideally freshly grated, for garnish

Preheat the oven to 350°F (175°C). Grease a Bundt pan or a 10-inch (24-cm) round cake pan with butter or oil (and line the bottom with a sheet of parchment paper cut to fit, if using a round pan). Grease the parchment as well.

Mix the rolled oats with the boiling water and set aside for 15 minutes.

With a hand mixer, beat the butter with the brown sugar until nicely fluffy. One by one, add the eggs.

Stir the vanilla into the oat mixture.

Combine the flour, baking powder, salt, cinnamon, and nutmeg and stir the dry mixture into the butter mixture.

With a spatula, mix the oats into the batter as well.

Finally, fold in the coconut, apples, and parsnip.

Pour the batter into the prepared pan and bake for 45 minutes, or until the cake is golden brown and a skewer or toothpick inserted into the center comes out clean. The cake should spring back if you press it lightly. If that's not the case, bake for a little while longer.

Let the cake cool for 5 minutes, then remove from the pan and let the cake cool completely on a rack.

Dust with confectioners' sugar and some nutmeg. Serve with gallons of tea.

Upside-Down Polenta Cakes with Salty Caramel and Apples

FOR 1 large or 6 small cakes
PREP 35 min.
BAKE 50 min.

gluten-free

FOR THE CARAMEL
½ cup plus 2 tbsp (120 g)
    sugar
¼ tsp sea salt
¼ tsp ground nutmeg
2 tbsp salted butter

FOR THE CAKES
1 cup plus 2 tbsp (2¼ sticks /
    250 g) butter, at room
    temperature, plus extra for
    the pan
2 large or 3 small apples
    (they should be a bit tart,
    like the Dutch Elstar, for
    example, or Jonagold),
    peeled, cored, and sliced
1 cup plus 2 tbsp (225 g)
    sugar
zest and juice of 1 lemon
1 tsp vanilla extract
3 eggs, separated
generous 1¼ cups (150 g)
    almond flour
1¾ cups (225 g) fine polenta
    (buy gluten-free, if you like)

unsweetened whipped
    cream or crème fraîche,
    for serving

Make the caramel: Heat the sugar with ⅓ cup (75 ml) water, the sea salt, and the nutmeg in a saucepan until the sugar has dissolved. Slowly bring to a boil and boil the caramel down until it's amber colored. This takes about 10 minutes. Try not to stir, but gently shake the pan occasionally. With a wet brush, wipe the inside edge of the pan to remove the sugar crystals. Remove from the heat and carefully stir in the butter until you have a smooth caramel.

Make the cakes: Preheat the oven to 325°F (160°C). Butter a 9-inch (22-cm) round cake pan and cover the bottom with a piece of parchment paper cut to fit. Grease the parchment as well. (Alternatively, you can use a baking pan with 6 cups and place two strips of parchment paper across each cup. This makes it easier to lift the cakes out once they're ready.)

Pour the caramel in the bottom of the pan. Press the apple slices clockwise on the caramel (or if using individual cups, push two slices into each cup). Set aside until ready to use.

Beat the butter with the sugar until light and fluffy. Add the lemon zest, lemon juice, and vanilla and beat once more. Then beat in the egg yolks.

Spoon in the almond flour and polenta and whisk to make a smooth batter.

In a perfectly clean bowl, using a perfectly clean whisk, whisk the egg whites until they form soft peaks. Fold the egg whites into the batter very carefully, so as not to let too much air escape.

Pour the batter over the apples in the baking pan.

Bake for 50 minutes, or until the cake bounces back when you press down lightly. If baking the small cakes, bake for 40 minutes. Let stand for 10 minutes in the pan on a rack on the counter.

Run a knife along the edge of the cake to detach it from the wall of the baking pan. Place a large plate on top of the cake and carefully invert the plate and pan together so the cake ends up on the plate. Lift off the pan.

Let the cake cool and serve warm with unsweetened cream or crème fraîche.

Our bakery, Paris

Sticky Gingerbread

The batter for this gingerbread is almost liquid, and you'll probably think it's going all wrong, but it's perfectly fine! Because the batter is so wet, the consistency of the breakfast bread becomes so soft and sticky. Ah, insanely, addictively delicious. My mother used to always serve us a slice of gingerbread, thickly covered with salted butter, and a cup of tea when we got home from school. Yes . . . this tastes like the good old days.

FOR 1 loaf
PREP 25 min.
BAKE 50 min.

wheat-free
refined sugar–free option

2 cups plus 2 tbsp (250 g)
    light spelt flour
2 tsp baking powder
1 tsp sea salt
1 tsp ground ginger
2 tsp cinnamon
1 tsp ground allspice
7 tbsp (100 g) cold butter,
    cubed
½ cup (100 g) chopped
    candied ginger
¼ cup (50 g) chopped
    candied orange or
    candied lemon peel
1¼ cups (300 ml) milk
scant ½ cup (100 g) packed
    light or dark brown sugar
    (or ideally: palm sugar)
¾ cup plus 1 tbsp (200 ml)
    agave or maple syrup
2 eggs

Preheat the oven to 350°F (180°C). Butter a 1½ qt. (1.5-L) loaf pan, line it with parchment paper cut to fit, and butter the parchment paper.

Combine the flour, baking powder, salt, and spices and rub in the butter until it looks like fine bread crumbs. Add the candied ginger and orange pieces and mix well.

In a saucepan, warm up the milk, brown sugar, and syrup over low heat and stir until the sugar has dissolved. Add to the flour mixture and stir until everything just about comes together—don't stir too long!

One by one, beat the eggs and pour on top. Stir them in with the batter so that everything is smooth. Pour the batter into the prepared pan.

Bake the cake for 50 minutes, or until a skewer inserted into the middle comes out clean.

Let the cake cool for 5 minutes and gently invert onto a rack. Let cool completely.

I like to eat this with just salted butter and some golden syrup, but if that makes your teeth hurt, you can just leave that out.

Chocolate Fudge with Melted Marshmallows

FOR 4 mason jars
(about 2 cups / 450 ml each)
PREP 25 min.
BAKE 32 min.

FOR THE CRUST
8 gingerbread cookies (see
    page 215) or Bastogne or
    Biscoff cookies
3 tbsp butter, at room
    temperature
pinch of salt

FOR THE CHOCOLATE
    FUDGE
1 egg
½ cup plus 1 tbsp (125 g)
    packed light brown sugar
½ cup (125 ml) milk
½ cup (125 ml) heavy cream
3 tbsp butter, melted
2 heaped tbsp (50 ml) sour
    cream
1 tsp vanilla extract
1¼ cups (150 g) all-purpose
    flour
¼ cup(25 g) unsweetened
    cocoa powder
1¼ tsp baking powder
pinch of salt
1 bag marshmallows

Preheat the oven to 350°F (175°C).

Make the crust: In a food processor, grind the cookies into a fine crumble. Mix in the butter and salt and press the crumble into the bottom of 4 ovenproof mason jars. Press firmly with the end of a spatula or a rolling pin.

Make the chocolate fudge: In a bowl, beat the egg with the brown sugar until completely smooth. Add the milk, cream, melted butter, sour cream, and vanilla and mix until you have a cohesive consistency.

Sift the dry ingredients over a bowl and fold them into the wet mixture. Mix by hand or with a spatula into a smooth batter.

Spoon the fudge into the jars. Tap the jars on the counter to allow the batter to spread out evenly.

Place an oven dish (which fits the jars) just below the middle of the oven.

Place the jars in the dish and pour boiling water into it until it reaches the rim of the dish.

Bake for about 30 minutes.

Remove the jars carefully (the water is boiling hot!) and turn on the broiler.

Top the jars with marshmallows; though be careful, as the glass is hot. Press firmly so that you fit in as many as possible.

Place the jars under the broiler and broil for about 2 minutes until the marshmallows are nicely browned. This goes quickly: stay on it!

Eat immediately, with a long spoon: Whoaaaa, yummy!

Currant Cake with Sweet Potato & Ginger

FOR 1 cake
GETTING READY 20 min. plus cooling
PREP 15 min.
BAKE 35 min.

FOR THE CAKE
9 ounces (250 g) sweet potato (approximately 1 large), peeled and cubed
⅔ cup (150 g) packed light brown sugar
½ cup (125 ml) vegetable oil
3 eggs
2½ cups (300 g) whole-wheat flour
2 tsp baking powder
1 tsp *speculaas* spices (see page 245) or pumpkin pie spice, or even Chinese five spice powder (star anise, black pepper, fennel, cloves, and cinnamon)
½ tsp salt
1 cup (150 g) currants
about ½ cup (75 g) candied ginger in syrup, cubed, plus some extra to garnish

FOR THE CARAMEL GINGER GLAZE
¼ cup (½ stick / 60 g) butter
4 tbsp (60 ml) ginger syrup from a jar
2 tsp ground ginger
1½ to 2½ cups (150 to 250 g) confectioners' sugar, depending on the amount of liquid

Make the cake: Boil the sweet potato for about 10 minutes or until the cubes are tender, then drain and mash them as finely as possible, ideally with a hand masher. Let cool.

Preheat the oven to 325°F (170°C). Butter a 1-qt (1-L) loaf pan or Bundt pan. If using a loaf pan, line the pan with a piece of parchment paper cut to fit, and butter the parchment paper.

In a large bowl, mix the mashed sweet potatoes, brown sugar, oil, eggs, and ¼ cup (60 ml) water into a smooth batter. Sift the flour, baking powder, spices, and salt over the bowl and stir them into the batter. Fold in the currants and ginger pieces. Stir just long enough to create a smooth batter.

Pour the batter into the prepared pan and bake for about 35 minutes, or until a bamboo skewer inserted into the middle comes out dry.

Let the cake cool for 5 minutes, then remove from the pan and let cool completely on a rack.

Meanwhile, make the caramel ginger glaze: Over low heat, brown the butter in a saucepan until it's tea-colored. Pour the clear part (the clarified butter) into a small bowl and leave the brown bits at the bottom (these are the burned proteins) in the pan. Pour the ginger syrup, ground ginger, and confectioners' sugar into the clarified butter and stir until smooth. The mixture should be the consistency of thin yogurt.

Pour the glaze over the cooled cake and let dry.

Garnish, if you wish, with pieces of candied ginger.

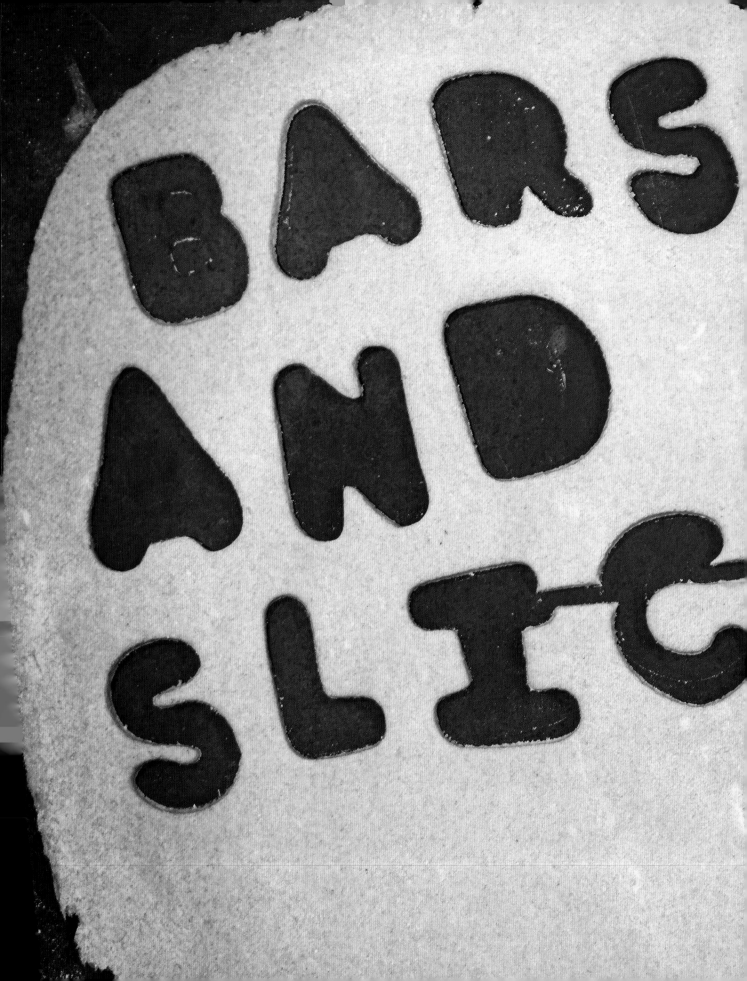

My Millionaire's Shortbread with Salty Caramel & Coconut

FOR 20 small pieces, as it's rich
PREP 60 min.
BAKE 25 min.
INACTIVE about 7 hours altogether

FOR THE COCONUT SHORTBREAD
1 cup (2 sticks / 225 g) butter, at room temperature, plus extra for the pan
⅓ cup (75 g) packed light brown sugar
1 tsp vanilla extract
pinch of salt
1¾ cups (225 g) all-purpose flour, plus extra for dusting
½ cup (50 g) grated unsweetened coconut

FOR THE SALTY CARAMEL
⅞ cup (1¾ sticks / 200 g) butter
1 tsp salt
1 (14-oz/396-g) can sweetened condensed milk
6 tbsp (90 ml) maple syrup (or more)

14 ounces (400 g) dark chocolate, chopped

Make the coconut shortbread: In a bowl, whisk the butter and brown sugar with a hand mixer until light and airy. Whisk in the vanilla and salt. With a spatula, fold in the flour and coconut and stop immediately once the mixture is nicely combined. Shape into a rectangle and wrap in plastic wrap.

Refrigerate for at least 1 hour.

Make the salty caramel: Melt the butter and salt in the condensed milk in a saucepan over low heat. Keep stirring with a whisk. Once the butter has melted, it will likely curdle, but that's okay—add the syrup; it will turn into a smooth sauce again. Cook for at least 15 minutes while stirring continuously. The sauce should become caramel-colored. If the sauce keeps curdling, you can add some more syrup.

Let cool.

Preheat the oven to 350°F (180°C). Grease an 8-by-12-inch (20-by-30-cm) baking pan and line the bottom with parchment paper cut to fit. Grease the parchment paper, too.

Roll out the dough on a flour-dusted countertop and shape it into a rectangle. Set the dough rectangle in the prepared pan and press the dough firmly into the corners so it evenly covers the bottom of the pan. Using a fork, prick the dough all over. Bake for 5 minutes, then lower the heat to 300°F (150°C) and bake for another 20 minutes.

Let the shortbread cool on a rack, but don't remove it from the pan. Pour the caramel on top, and gently tilt the pan so the caramel reaches all the corners.

Let cool to room temperature. Place the pan in the fridge for 2 hours to allow the caramel to set completely. 🐁

🐿 Melt the chocolate *au bain marie*. Once the chocolate has melted about two-thirds of the way, remove from the heat. The rest will melt because the pan is still warm, and this way the chocolate won't break and crystallize.

Pour the chocolate over the solidified caramel and place the pan back in the fridge for another 2 hours.

If you'd like to cut the shortbread into nice, professional-looking squares, do the following: Let the shortbread warm up to room temperature. This prevents the cold and hard chocolate from breaking, as the caramel beneath it is softer. Use the biggest sharp knife you have: Hold it under hot running water, dry it, and, using firm pressure all the way down, cut nice squares. Rinse the knife under the hot water between each cut. This way the slices remain clean and sharp.

Keep the shortbreads in an airtight container in the fridge, separating the pieces with parchment paper. You can keep them for at least a week.

Street in our village, Ireland

Triple-Chocolate Chunky Brownies

This is by far the most delicious recipe from this book.

I may have said that before, but this time I mean it.

FOR about 24 pieces
PREP 20 min.
BAKE 20 min.

7 ounces (200 g) dark
    chocolate, chopped
3 tbsp butter, cubed, plus
    extra for the pan
½ cup plus 1 tbsp (125 g)
    packed light brown sugar
1 tsp vanilla extract
½ cup (60 g) all-purpose
    flour
1 tsp baking powder
1 tsp unsweetened cocoa
    powder
pinch of salt
1½ ounces (50 g) white
    chocolate, chopped
½ cup (50 g) walnuts,
    coarsely chopped
2 eggs, beaten

Preheat the oven to 350°F (175°C). Grease a 7-by-11-inch (18-by-28 cm) baking pan and line the bottom with parchment paper that extends over two edges of the pan. Grease the parchment paper, too.

Melt 3½ ounces (100 g) of the chocolate with the butter *au bain marie*. Turn off the heat when it's nearly completely melted and let stand for a bit while you prepare the rest.

In a bowl, mix the brown sugar with the vanilla, flour, baking powder, cocoa powder, and salt into an even-colored powder.

Stir in the remaining dark chocolate, the white chocolate, and the walnuts.

Pour the beaten eggs into the slightly cooled chocolate-butter mixture. Add the dry ingredients, mix well with a spatula, and spoon the mixture into the prepared pan. Spread the batter with a spatula so that it reaches all corners.

Bake the brownies for 20 to 25 minutes, until just firm and a toothpick inserted in the center comes out with wet crumbs attached.

Let cool in the pan for 5 minutes, then lift the brownies out of the pan, and let cool until the brownies have firmed up a bit before cutting into squares. Eat when still warm, as that's when the chocolate chunks are still a bit melty . . . mmm!

Date Cake with Pecans

FOR about 12 pieces
PREP 20 min.
BAKE about 30 min.

wheat-free

FOR THE BOTTOM

1 cup (150 g) fine rolled oats
    (not instant!) from the
    natural foods store (see
    page 18)
⅓ cup (70 g) granulated
    sugar or packed light
    brown sugar
¼ tsp salt
¼ cup (½ stick / 60 g) cold
    butter, cubed, plus extra
    for the pan

FOR THE FILLING

½ cup (120 ml) molasses or
    maple syrup
5 tbsp (60 g) granulated
    sugar
1 egg
⅓ cup (50 g) fine rolled oats
1 tsp vanilla extract
¼ tsp salt
1 cup (150 g) dates, pitted
    and chopped
scant 1 cup (100 g) pecans
5 oz (150 g) dark chocolate,
    chopped

Preheat the oven to 350°F (175°C). Grease an 8½-by-5½-inch (22-by-14-cm) baking pan and line the bottom with parchment paper cut to fit. Grease the parchment paper, too.

Make the bottom: In a bowl, combine all the ingredients and mix until it resembles coarse sand. Press the crumble evenly over the entire bottom of the prepared pan, flattening it out with the back of a spoon.

Prebake the crust for 8 minutes.

Make the filling: Thoroughly mix the molasses, sugar, egg, oats, vanilla, and salt in a bowl. Stir in the dates, nuts, and 2½ oz (75 g) of the chocolate chunks and pour over the prebaked crust. Slide the pan into the oven and bake the cake for about 30 minutes, until it's nearly solidified. Make sure it doesn't burn, which could happen quickly with all those sugars and dates.

Let the cake cool completely, then run a knife along the edge to make it come loose from the pan. Turn the cake out onto a plate. Slice into bars.

Melt the rest of the chocolate *au bain marie* and drizzle thin lines of the chocolate over the bars. Let the chocolate set and store the bars between layers of parchment paper in an airtight container.

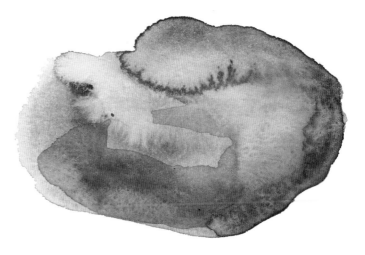

Bounty Brownies

Oh god, stop me. These brownies are everything you ever wanted: squishy cakes with lots of chocolate, a cookie layer with chocolate chunks, topped with a crispy coconut crust. Let's say: a kind of Bounty bar inside a brownie. This recipe is for a huge pan, so it's a good dish to share.

Cut them as big or small as you wish.

FOR about 16 pieces
PREP 20 min.
BAKE 35 min.

FOR THE BROWNIE LAYER
7 tbsp (100 g) butter, plus
    extra for the pan
1¾ oz (50 g) dark chocolate,
    chopped
½ cup (125 ml) coconut milk
2 eggs
6 tbsp (75 g) sugar
1¼ cups (150 g) all-purpose
    flour
pinch of sea salt

FOR THE COOKIE LAYER
7 tbsp (100 g) butter, at
    room temperature
½ cup (100 g) sugar
1 egg
¾ cup plus 1 tbsp (100 g)
    all-purpose flour
1½ tsp baking powder
pinch of sea salt
½ cup (50 g) grated
    unsweetened coconut
3½ oz (100 g) dark
    chocolate, chopped

Preheat the oven to 350°F (180°C). Grease a 9-by-13-inch (23-by-33-cm) baking pan and line it with parchment paper cut to fit. Grease the parchment paper, too.

Make the brownie layer: Melt the butter with the chocolate and coconut milk *au bain marie*.

Beat the eggs with the sugar until foamy, then add the melted butter mixture and steadily stir with a whisk until everything is mixed well. Next stir in the flour and salt and keep stirring until all flour lumps have been broken up and incorporated.

Pour the batter into the prepared pan.

Make the cookie dough: Beat the butter with the sugar until it's nicely soft, then add the egg.

Stir in the flour, baking powder, salt, coconut, and chocolate. Drop dots of the cookie dough on top of the brownie batter, until they cover the entire brownie layer. They will expand in the oven, so no need to be terribly precise.

Bake for 35 minutes. Let cool a little, then slice.

Toffee Nut Bar with Chocolate

FOR about 16 bars
PREP 25 min.
BAKE 10 min.
COOL 4 hours

5¼ oz (150 g) crispy cookies, such as Gingerbread Pepper Cookies (page 215) or Flawless Flourless Hazelnut Cookies (page 229)
1 cup (100 g) pecans, coarsely chopped, or peanuts
6 tbsp (75 g) granulated sugar
⅓ cup (75 g) packed dark brown sugar
pinch of salt
⅔ cup (1⅓ sticks / 150 g) butter, plus extra for the pan
3½ oz (100 g) dark chocolate, chopped
3½ oz (100 g) milk chocolate, chopped
1¾ oz (50 g) white chocolate, chopped

Preheat the oven to 175°F (75°C). Grease a 6-by-10-inch (15-by-25-cm) rimmed baking sheet, line it with parchment paper, and grease the parchment paper.

Put the cookies in a resealable plastic bag and crush them into crumbs with a rolling pin or something.

Scatter the crumbs all over the prepared baking sheet, creating an even layer. Sprinkle with the chopped nuts.

Melt both sugars and the salt with 3 to 4 tbsp water in a heavy saucepan. Don't stir, just swirl the pan occasionally. When the sugar has dissolved, add the butter and leave it to melt in the hot syrup. Gently stir with a spatula until you get a smooth caramel.

Pour the caramel over the nuts and the cookie crumbs on the baking sheet.

Bake for about 10 minutes, or until the caramel begins to boil. Take the sheet out of the oven.

Sprinkle immediately with the chopped dark, milk, and white chocolates, let stand for 2 minutes to allow them to melt, then swirl the chocolate with the tip of your knife to create a marble effect.

Let cool for 4 hours, then break or cut the cookie into pieces. (The recipe for My Millionaire's Shortbread on page 193 describes how you can make very professional, clean cuts.)

Lemon Slices with Almond Crust

FOR 20 pieces
PREP 10 min.
BAKE 30 min.

gluten-free
lactose-free
refined sugar–free

FOR THE CAKE
¾ cup (125 g) white or
  brown rice flour
4 eggs
juice of 2 lemons and zest of
  1 lemon
¾ cup plus 1 tbsp (200 ml)
  honey (or to taste)
1 cup (100 g) grated
  unsweetened coconut
1 vanilla bean, sliced open
  and seeds scraped out

7 tbsp (100 ml) almond
  milk (see page 40 for
  homemade)
3 tbsp coconut oil, melted,
  plus more for the pan

FOR THE ALMOND CRUST
2 egg whites, beaten
1 cup (100 g) sliced almonds
3 tbsp honey

Preheat the oven to 350°F (°C). Grease a 10-inch (24-cm) round cake pan or an 8-by-12-inch (20-by-30-cm) baking pan with coconut oil and line it with parchment paper cut to fit. Grease the parchment paper, too.

Make the cake: Process all the ingredients for the cake in a blender or food processor.

Pour the batter into the prepared pan and bake the cake for about 30 minutes.

Meanwhile, make the almond crust: Combine all the ingredients for the almond crust in a bowl. About 15 minutes before the end of the baking time, spread the almond crust mixture over the cake, and bake for the remaining 15 minutes.

Let the cake cool completely in the pan, and only then cut it into pieces.

Keep the slices in an airtight container. Great sweets for your everyday tea.

Peach & Apricot Almond Slice

FOR 10 pieces
PREP 30 min.
BAKE 25 min.

gluten-free
refined sugar–free

FOR THE BOTTOM
7 tbsp (100 g) butter, plus
    more for the pan
7 tbsp (100 ml) agave syrup
1 egg
1 tsp vanilla extract
1¼ cups (200 g) brown rice
    flour
1 tsp baking powder
1 tsp thyme
pinch of salt

FOR THE FILLING
7 tbsp (50 g) almond flour
2 egg yolks
1 egg
2 tbsp agave syrup
1 tsp fresh thyme
pinch of salt
a drop of real almond oil
    (optional)
4 apricots, pitted and sliced
    into 8 pieces
2 peaches, pitted and sliced
    into 8 pieces

FOR GARNISH
some fresh thyme leaves

Preheat the oven to 350°F (180°C).

Grease a shallow 9-by-13-inch (23-by-33-cm) rectangular baking pan (ideally with a removable bottom) or a 10-inch (26-cm) round one and line the bottom with parchment paper cut to fit. Grease the parchment paper, too.

Make the bottom: Beat the butter with the agave syrup until it's mixed well. Then beat in the egg and the vanilla. Combine the dry ingredients in a separate bowl and stir them into the wet mixture until all comes together.

Press the batter in the bottom of the prepared pan and flatten with a fork.

Prebake the bottom for 15 minutes. Remove from the oven but leave the oven on.

Meanwhile, make the filling: Beat together the almond flour, egg yolks, whole egg, agave syrup, thyme, salt, and almond oil (if using) with a whisk until smooth. Spread over the prebaked crust and arrange the apricot and peach pieces on top.

Bake for about 25 minutes more, until golden brown.

Let cool until you slice it. Garnish with fresh thyme leaves.

Pumpkin Cheesecake

These slices are wonderful for a winter evening, with some tea or coffee and with the fire going.

You'll need mashed pumpkin for this recipe. I chop my pumpkin into large chunks, remove the seeds, and cook for 20 minutes. I let them sit for a while, and then hold them under running cold water and peel the skin. Then I puree the pumpkin in a blender or in a bowl with an immersion blender.

FOR 8 slices
PREP 20 min.
BAKE 25 min.

wheat-free option

scant ½ cup (50 g) all-purpose flour (or light spelt flour)
¾ cup (150 g) granulated sugar
scant ½ cup (100 g) packed light brown sugar
⅔ cup (1⅓ sticks / 150 g) cold butter, plus more for the pan
1⅔ cups (150 g) rolled oats (not instant) from the natural foods store (see page 18)
pinch of salt
½ cup plus 2 tbsp (60 g) walnuts, coarsely chopped
1 cup (250 g) cream cheese, at room temperature
3 eggs
2 cups (500 g) mashed pumpkin
1 tsp pumpkin pie spice, or Chinese five-spice powder (star anise, black pepper, fennel, cloves, and cinnamon), or *speculaas* spices (see page 245)
1 tsp vanilla extract
some cinnamon, to garnish

Preheat the oven to 350°F (175°C). Grease a 12-by-8-inch (30-by-20-cm) baking sheet and line it with parchment paper; let it stick out a little on the short ends as this will make it easier to lift the cake off the tray. Grease the parchment paper as well.

In a stand mixer with the paddle attachment, combine the flour with ¼ cup (50 g) of the granulated sugar and all of the brown sugar. Add the butter and pulse a few times until you have a crumbly dough. (You can do this with your hands if you work quickly and have cold hands.)

With a spatula, stir in the oats, salt, and walnuts. Divide the dough into two parts of two-thirds and one-third. Press out the larger portion over the bottom of the prepared baking sheet and bake for 15 minutes.

With a hand mixer, whip the cream cheese, the remaining ½ cup (100 g) sugar, the eggs, pumpkin, spices, and vanilla until all is mixed well.

Pour the cream cheese mixture over the prebaked bottom and drop the remaining one-third oat mix in little dots on top.

Bake for 25 minutes. Let cool on the baking sheet for 15 minutes, then lift the bars up, using the parchment paper at the sides as handles, and let cool on a rack.

Slice when completely cool. Sprinkle with cinnamon.

Rhubarb Honey Pie
with Meringue and Coconut

FOR 12 slices
PREP 20 min.
BAKE 25 min.

lactose-free
wheat-free option
refined sugar–free

FOR THE CRUST
2¼ cups (200 g) rolled oats (not instant) from the natural foods store (see page 18)
½ cup (50 g) grated unsweetened coconut
⅓ cup (80 ml) honey
1 egg white
7 tbsp (100 g) coconut oil, melted

FOR THE FILLING
juice of 1 orange
⅓ cup (80 ml) honey
1 tsp cinnamon
14 oz (400 g) rhubarb, chopped into 1- to 1½-inch (3- to 4-cm) pieces

FOR THE MERINGUE
3 egg whites
pinch of salt
2 tbsp honey
½ cup (50 g) unsweetened grated coconut, plus extra for garnish (if you can find flaked coconut, that would make it very pretty)

Preheat the oven to 350°F (180°C). Grease a 9-by-13-inch (22-by-33-cm) baking pan, line it with parchment paper, then grease the parchment paper.

Make the crust: Combine all the ingredients for the crust. Press the dough out in an even layer over the prepared pan. Prebake for 20 minutes. Remove from the oven but leave the oven on.

Meanwhile, make the filling: Bring the orange juice, honey, and cinnamon to a boil in a saucepan. Add the rhubarb and cook for 15 minutes, until the rhubarb is soft.

Scoop the rhubarb out of its juices with a slotted spoon and arrange the pieces over the prebaked crust.

Bake for 15 minutes.

Meanwhile, make the meringue: In a perfectly clean bowl with a perfectly clean whisk, beat the egg whites with a pinch of salt until stiff. Beat in the honey at the last moment. Carefully stir in the coconut and spread the mixture out over the rhubarb. Sprinkle with extra coconut and bake for another 10 minutes.

Gingerbread Pepper Cookies

These cookies are very similar to classic Dutch sugar-candy Bastogne cookies. Although these are many times more delicious, naturally. That is to say: They are divine! And, yes . . . the recipe is correct: It really requires that much pepper.

FOR 24 cookies
PREP 12 min.
BAKE 12 min.

wheat-free option

scant 1 cup (100 g) wheat
(or light spelt) flour
generous ¾ cup (75 g) rolled
oats or quick oats (not
instant) from the natural
foods store (see page 18)
½ tsp baking powder
½ tsp salt
1 tsp freshly ground black
pepper
1 tsp ground cinnamon
½ tsp ground allspice or
cloves
½ tsp grated nutmeg
scant 1 cup (200 g) packed
dark brown sugar
5 tbsp (75 g) butter, at room
temperature, plus more
for the pan
1 vanilla bean, sliced open
and seeds scraped out
1 egg

Preheat the oven to 350°F (175°C). Grease a baking sheet.

Combine the flour, oats, baking powder, salt, pepper, and spices. In another bowl, beat the brown sugar with the butter and vanilla seeds into a light and fluffy mixture. For a good result, use a hand mixer and beat for at least 3 minutes. Beat in the egg and continue beating until it has been completely incorporated. Then stir in the flour mixture.

Using two tablespoons or an ice cream scoop, divide the batter into balls the size of walnuts and place them on the prepared baking sheet. They don't need to be perfect. They will spread out anyway.

Bake the cookies for 12 minutes, or until they are crispy (you'll most likely need to bake in batches). Leave to cool on the baking sheet for 5 minutes. Then, using either a spatula or your heat-resistant fingers, transfer them to a rack for further cooling.

Nutella Cream–Filled Mini Meringues

FOR 48 single shells
(24 complete meringues)
PREP 20 min.
BAKE 1 hour and 30 min.

FOR THE SHELLS

3 egg whites, at room
temperature
½ cup plus 2 tbsp (120 g)
superfine sugar
¾ cup (75 g) sifted
confectioners' sugar
1 to 2 tbsp homemade
Nutella (page 46), at
room temperature

FOR THE FILLING

1 tbsp homemade Nutella
(page 46)
¾ cup plus 1 tbsp (200 g)
cream cheese

Preheat the oven to 215°F (100°C). Line two baking sheets with parchment paper.

In a perfectly clean bowl using a perfectly clean whisk, beat the egg whites until stiff and frothy. Gradually add the superfine sugar, beating for 3 to 4 minutes in between each addition, until thick peaks form and the mixture has a glossy sheen.

Now fold one-third of the sifted confectioners' sugar into the egg white, followed by the other two-thirds. In two or three additions, spoon in the Nutella. The mixture shouldn't become too even—those stripes actually make your batter look great. Fill up a pastry bag with the mixture and shape small dollops about 1½ inches (4 cm) apart on the prepared baking sheets.

Bake for about 1 hour and 30 minutes, or until the cookies have become nicely dry. Let cool completely.

Meanwhile, make the filling: Mix the Nutella with the cream cheese. Apply a generous dab of filling onto the bottom of 1 meringue, then press on a second meringue. Place on a large dish and serve.

TiP: If you would like to save them for later use, store the filling and the meringues separately. The filling should be stored in the fridge, the shells in an airtight container at room temperature. All you have to do before serving your meringues is press them together with some filling.

SHORTBREAD CARDAMOM COOKIES
That Will Melt in Your Mouth

This shortbread recipe is so creamy—or rather, velvety—it's truly mouthwatering. Wow! One thing, though: Never use ground cardamom from a jar. It tends to have lost all its flavor. Freshly ground cardamom, straight from the mortar, frankly is a totally different spice. Conduct a little test yourself; you'll be shocked by the contrast.

FOR 50 cookies   **GETTING READY** 10 min.   **INACTIVE** 1 hour   **PREP** 15 min.   **BAKE** 12 min.

1½ cups plus 2 tbsp (200 g) all-purpose flour
½ cup (60 g) cornstarch
¼ tsp salt
1 cup (2 sticks / 225 g) butter, at room temperature
½ cup (50 g) sifted confectioners' sugar, plus a little extra for dusting
1 vanilla bean, sliced open and seeds scraped out
seeds from about 8 cardamom pods, ground in a mortar

Sift the flour, cornstarch, and salt over a bowl and set aside.

Using your hand mixer, beat the butter with the confectioners' sugar until light and airy—it really takes a minute or three. Add the vanilla bean seeds and cardamom. Then, using a spatula, fold in the flour mixture until the dough just starts to come together, no longer. (Once baked, the dough should remain crisp. The secret to this is keeping your kneading and whisking brief.)

Wrap the dough in plastic wrap and let rest in the fridge for 1 hour.

Preheat the oven to 350°F (175°C). Position a rack in the center of the oven. Line a baking sheet with parchment paper.

When making these cookies I use a melon baller. That way, I won't knead the dough too much while still being able to form perfect balls. If you don't have one of these, you can do the following: Divide the dough into three or four portions, roll them into sausages, and quickly cut them into pieces crosswise and roll these into small balls. Slightly press down on the balls when placing them on the prepared baking sheet.

Bake the cookies for 12 to 14 minutes, until the edges of the cookies begin to brown (you may need to bake these in batches). Allow to cool on the baking sheet, then let them continue cooling on a rack. Dust with confectioners' sugar. Repeat until you have used all the dough.

Pinwheel Cookies
with Cardamom, Orange & Walnut

FOR 16 cookies
GETTING READY 25 min.
INACTIVE 15 min.
PREP 10 min.
BAKE 25 min.

1 cup (100 g) walnuts, briefly
　　toasted in a dry skillet
⅔ cup (150 g) packed light
　　brown sugar
¼ tsp ground cardamom
　　seeds (grind in a mortar—
　　you'll need 6 to 7
　　cardamom pods)
grated zest of 1 orange
½ tsp salt
21 oz (600 g) homemade
　　puff pastry (page 256) or
　　store-bought puff pastry
flour, for dusting your
　　kitchen counter
1 egg, beaten
ample granulated sugar, say
　　about 2½ cups (500 g)

Using a food processor, grind the walnuts with the brown sugar, cardamom, orange zest, and salt into crumbs.

Quickly roll out the puff pastry dough on a flour-dusted counter-top until you have a sheet of 10 by 20 inches (25 by 50 cm). (When using store-bought puff pastry dough, remove the protective pieces of paper between the dough sheets. Stack the sheets and roll out.) Lift the dough slab onto a large sheet of parchment paper.

Brush the dough with the egg and sprinkle with the crumb mixture. Now, roll up the dough as tightly as possible, starting at the short edge. Use the parchment paper to pull up the dough like you would when rolling sushi with the use of a sushi mat. Tightly pack the roll in the parchment paper and place in it the freezer for 15 minutes, allowing the dough to stiffen up nicely. If you plan on storing the dough for a little longer before baking it, transfer it to the fridge.

Preheat the oven to 400°F (200°C). Line large baking sheets with parchment paper.

Sprinkle a heap of granulated sugar in the middle of your work surface. Remove the dough from the freezer and place it on a cutting board. Cut off one ⅜-inch- (1-cm-) thick slice. Place it on top of the sugar, gently pressing a loose end of your roll. Sprinkle the top with sugar as well. Using a rolling pin, roll out the slice into a round disc of about 6 inches (15 cm) in diameter. Lift it onto a prepared baking sheet with a spatula. Depending on the size of your baking sheet, you may be able to fit a few cookies on at a time.

Bake until crispy golden brown, about 25 minutes. Continue doing so until all the dough has been baked. Depending on the size of your oven, you may be able to bake several cookie sheets at once. In the meantime, make sure the dough roll doesn't get too warm. Wrap it and put it back in the fridge each time you wait for the oven. (You can also freeze part of the roll for later.)

Leave the cookies on the baking sheet for 3 minutes before using a spatula to lift them onto a rack to further cool off. Be sure not to touch them with your fingers! Hot sugar is SCORCHING.

Whole-Wheat Almond Cookies with Cinnamon-Sugar

FOR 20 cookies
PREP 15 min.
BAKE 12 min.

scant 1 cup (200 g) packed
  light brown sugar
7 tbsp (100 g) cream cheese,
  at room temperature
7 tbsp (100 g) butter, at
  room temperature
finely grated zest of
  ½ lemon
1 vanilla bean, sliced open
  and seeds scraped out
2 egg yolks
1¼ cups (150 g) all-purpose
  flour
6 tbsp (50 g) whole-wheat
  flour
7 tablespoons (50 g) almond
  flour
1 tsp baking powder
½ tsp salt
1½ tsp cinnamon
2 tbsp granulated sugar

Preheat the oven to 325°F (170°C). Line a baking sheet with parchment paper.

Thoroughly beat the brown sugar, cream cheese, butter, lemon zest, and vanilla bean seeds for at least a minute or three, until light and airy. Then add the egg yolks and beat some more until all the egg has been absorbed.

Combine the all-purpose flour, whole-wheat flour, and almond flour with the baking powder, salt, and ½ teaspoon of the cinnamon. Then beat the flour mixture into the butter mixture.

Mix the granulated sugar with the rest of the cinnamon and set aside.

Using two tablespoons, form heaps of batter on the prepared baking sheet, placing them a little apart because the cookies will spread out.

Sprinkle with some cinnamon-sugar and bake for about 12 minutes (you may need to bake these in batches).

Let the cookies cool on the baking sheet before transferring them to a rack for further cooling while you bake the next batch.

Kletskoppen—Spicy Almond Snaps

FOR about 25 cookies   **PREP** 10 min.   **BAKE** 8 to 10 min.

1 cup plus 2 tbsp (250 g) packed light brown sugar
½ cup (75 g) almonds, chopped
1 cup (125 g) all-purpose flour
9 tbsp (125 g) butter
1 tsp Chinese five-spice powder (star anise, black pepper, fennel, cloves, and cinnamon)
½ tsp salt

Preheat the oven to 400°F (200°C). Grease a baking sheet.

In a bowl, swiftly work all the ingredients into a firm ball. Divide the ball into
equal portions and roll those into about 25 small balls each the size of a marble.

Arrange 6 to 8 of the dough balls on the prepared baking sheet, leaving ample space
between them. Gently press down on the balls so they won't start rolling around the oven.

Bake them a notch higher than the middle position of the oven until they've spread and
nicely browned; this will take 8 to 10 minutes but, depending on your oven, sometimes
less, so keep a close eye on them. Leave them to cool on the baking sheet, then transfer to
a rack with a spatula. Allow the cookies to fully cool while baking the next batches.

Store these *Kletskoppen* in an airtight container.

Lightning-Fast Banana Balls

Made in a jiffy and über-healthy. Throw a couple into your bag before you leave the house. Oof doesn't think they are sweet enough, but that's exactly what I like about them. Things don't always have to be super sweet.

FOR 12 balls
PREP 7 min.
BAKE 15 min.

wheat-free
sugar-free
lactose-free

1 egg white
1 banana
1⅔ cups (150 g) rolled oats
  (not instant) from the
  natural foods store (see
  page 18)
½ cup (50 g) pistachios and
  pecans, chopped

Preheat the oven to 350°F (180°C). Line a baking sheet with a piece of parchment paper cut to fit.

Thoroughly beat the egg white until light, frothy, and white. Just use a whisk for this. Then, using a fork, mash the banana and use that same fork to stir it into the egg whites to make a thick batter with tiny chunks of banana in it.

Add the oats and stir in the nuts.

Using a small ice-cream scoop or two tablespoons, form little dollops of the batter and dot them out on the prepared baking sheet.

Bake the banana dollops for 15 minutes, until light brown.

Eat them immediately or keep them in an airtight (resealable) bag or container. They will keep for about 4 days. Handy as a snack and super-duper healthy to boot.

Flawless Flourless Hazelnut Cookies

FOR 24 cookies
PREP 20 min.
BAKE 14 min.

lactose-free
gluten-free

9 oz (250 g) hazelnut paste
  (without chocolate—no
  Nutella—go pure and
  natural!)
¾ cup (150 g) granulated
  sugar
1 egg, beaten
½ tsp baking powder (check
  the package to see
  whether it's gluten-free,
  or make it yourself:
  recipe on page 23)
¼ tsp sea salt
3½ oz (100 g) dark chocolate
  (at least 70% cacao),
  chopped
½ cup plus 1 tbsp (75 g)
  whole hazelnuts
cocoa powder, for dusting
  (optional)

Preheat the oven to 350°F (175°C). Line a large baking sheet with parchment paper, or if you have two baking sheets, line both. If you use two sheets, configure the oven racks to divide the oven in thirds. If you have only one baking sheet, set the rack in the middle.

Combine the hazelnut paste with the sugar, egg, baking powder, and salt and stir into a smooth batter. Stir in the chocolate and whole hazelnuts.

Using a small ice-cream scoop or two tablespoons, form about 24 little balls and spread them out on the prepared baking sheet(s).

Bake the cookies until they puff up, which should be after about 14 minutes. If you work with two sheets, switch their positions about halfway through the baking time.

Leave the cookies to cool for 5 minutes and then transfer them to a rack to further cool.

Bake the next batch, and, well . . . continue baking until all the cookies are done. Dust with the cocoa powder, if desired.

Butter Galettes

Hey, why don't you just start out by doubling all the amounts in this recipe? Because in our house, these cookies usually are gone by the time we're finished cooking. Terribly addictive stuff indeed.

FOR 24 cookies
INACTIVE 30 min.
PREP 25 min.
BAKE 15 min.

1 cup (2 sticks / 225 g) butter, at room temperature
1½ cups (150 g) confectioners' sugar
1½ cups plus 2 tbsp (200 g) all-purpose flour
½ cup (60 g) cornstarch
pinch of sea salt
grated zest of 1 lemon
1 tsp vanilla extract

Preheat the oven to 325°F (160°C). Line a baking sheet with parchment paper.

Beat the butter and confectioners' sugar until creamy and light. Sift the flour with the cornstarch and salt, then stir in the lemon zest. Stir the flour mixture into the butter mixture. Briefly knead with clean hands. The dough might be a bit dry, but that's fine. Shape into a ball, wrap in plastic wrap, and set aside in the refrigerator for 30 minutes.

Roll out the dough on a flour-dusted countertop and cut out cookies using a cookie cutter with a diameter of about 2¾ inches (7 cm), or a large glass. Scrape together the dough scraps, roll them out again, and cut out more cookies. Use a spatula to place the cut-out cookies on the prepared baking sheet. I often only bake six at a time because they really spread during baking.

Bake for 15 minutes, or until nicely golden brown. Allow them to cool a bit on the baking sheet before using your spatula to transfer them to a rack to cool off completely.

Bake the next batch and keep on baking until all are done.

Chocolate-Coconut Macaroon Eggs

FOR 20 cookies
PREP 15 min.
BAKE 12 min.

gluten-free

1¾ oz (50 g) dark chocolate, chopped
2¼ cups (200 g) grated unsweetened coconut
1 cup (200 g) sugar
pinch of sea salt
2 tbsp unsweetened cocoa powder
3 egg whites
1 tsp vanilla extract

Preheat the oven to 325°F (170°C). Grease a baking sheet, line it with parchment paper, and grease the parchment paper.

Melt the chocolate *au bain marie*—this goes really fast if you simply put a bowl with the chocolate on top of a pan of boiling water, with the heat turned off. The chocolate will melt in a few minutes. Meanwhile, combine the dry ingredients and stir in the egg whites and vanilla until you have a thick, smooth batter.

Pour in the melted chocolate and mix thoroughly.

With two spoons and wet hands, create egg shapes from the batter.

Place the shapes on the prepared baking sheet and bake for 12 to 14 minutes—they should still be a little soft inside.

Let them cool off completely.

Innocent Country Cookies

Look, you can eat these cookies when you're watching your diet but are still ravenous for something sweet. I cater to everyone.

FOR 8 cookies
PREP 15 min.
BAKE 12 min.

wheat-free
refined sugar–free
lactose-free

1 cup plus 2 tbsp (100 g)
  rolled oats (not instant)
  from the natural foods
  store (see page 18)
1 tsp cinnamon
pinch of salt
½ cup (65 g) dried
  cranberries
1 tbsp coconut oil, melted,
  plus more for the pan
1 egg
3 tbsp good honey or other
  natural sweetener
½ tsp vanilla extract

Preheat the oven to 400°F (200°C). Grease a baking sheet.

Mix the oats, cinnamon, salt, cranberries, and coconut oil in a bowl.

Beat the egg with the honey, vanilla, and 2 tbsp water. With a spatula, stir the egg mixture into the oat mixture to make a firm dough. If it's too dry, you can add a few drops of water.

With two spoons, create 8 little heaps on the prepared baking sheet. Flatten them into larger cookies with a fork.

Bake until golden brown, 10 to 12 minutes.

Let the cookies rest on the baking sheet for 5 minutes before transferring them to a rack to cool completely.

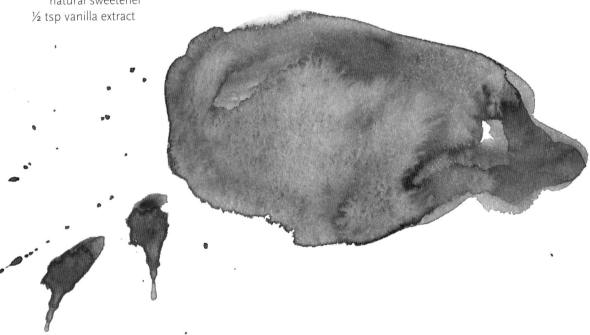

Orange Florentines

FOR 24 cookies
PREP 45 min.
BAKE 8 min.

FOR THE CANDIED ORANGE
3 oranges
½ cup plus 2 tbsp (125 g) granulated sugar

FOR THE COOKIES
⅓ cup (75 ml) crème fraîche
generous ½ cup (125 g) packed light brown sugar
3 tbsp butter, plus some extra
2 cups plus 2 tbsp (200 g) sliced almonds, briefly toasted in a dry skillet
scant ½ cup (50 g) all-purpose flour
about 7 oz (200 g) dark chocolate, chopped

Make the candied orange: Peel the oranges, making sure to only catch the orange part, no pith, with the peeler. Slice 1 tablespoon of the orange peel into fine strips and set aside; blanch the rest of the peel for 2 minutes in boiling water. Drain. Return them to the pan with ½ cup (125 ml) water and the sugar and bring to a boil. Boil for 5 minutes, then strain over a bowl (keep the syrup, as it's lovely in yogurt).

Let the candied orange peel cool on a sheet of parchment paper, then chop it.

Make the cookies: Preheat the oven to 350°F (180°C). Grease a baking sheet, line it with parchment paper, and grease the parchment paper.

Heat the crème fraîche, brown sugar, and butter in a heavy saucepan. Stir until the sugar has dissolved. Then add the non-candied strips of orange peel and 2 tbsp of the candied orange peel, the almonds, and the flour. Bring to a boil while stirring continuously.

Take the pan off the heat. Place a spoonful of the mixture on the prepared baking sheet and continue until the tray is full. Allow the mixture room to spread a little, leaving 2 inches (5 cm) between each cookie.

Bake until golden brown, about 8 minutes. Let cool for 2 minutes, and use a round cookie cutter to cut out the cookies. Remove carefully from the baking sheet and let the cookies harden on a rack. Repeat until you've used all your dough.

Place a large sheet of parchment paper on the counter. Melt the chocolate *au bain marie*.

Dip the cookies halfway into the chocolate and place them on the parchment paper.

Let them set completely. Store between sheets of parchment paper in an airtight container.

Oof

Sesame Nougatine & Chocolate Chip Cookies

FOR 22 cookies
PREP 10 min.
BAKE 12 min.

wheat-free

⅔ cup (1⅓ sticks / 150 g)
    butter, at room
    temperature
¾ cup (150 g) sugar
1½ tsp vanilla extract
1 egg
2 cups (200 g) spelt flour
1 tsp baking powder
pinch of sea salt
3½ oz (100 g) dark
    chocolate, coarsely
    chopped
1 batch Sesame Nougatine
    (page 30), coarsely
    chopped

Preheat the oven to 350°F (180°C). Grease a baking sheet.

Whip the butter with the sugar and vanilla until light and creamy.

Beat in the egg.

Combine the flour with the baking powder and salt. Stir that into the butter mixture and mix until you have a smooth dough. Fold in the chocolate and sesame nougatine.

Make 22 little heaps from the dough and place them on the prepared baking sheet, leaving plenty of space between them as they'll spread considerably. I use a small ice-cream scoop, so all cookies have the same size.

Bake the cookies for 10 to 12 minutes, until they are light brown. Bake in batches until you've used up all the dough.

Keep them in an airtight container.

OLIVE OIL ALMOND
COOKIES

FOR 15 COOKIES · PREP: 10 MIN. · BAKE: 15 MIN.
Lactose-free · gluten free · refined sugar-free

COOKIES
FOR PEOPLE
WHO ARE ALLERGIC
TO EVERYTHING,
COOL!

PREHEAT
THE OVEN TO
300°F (150°C).

1 TBSP OLIVE OIL, 3 TBSP MAPLE
SYRUP, ½ CUP (75 G) ALMOND FLOUR
SCANT ½ CUP (75G) WHITE (OR BROWN)
RICE FLOUR, GRATED ZEST OF 1 ORANGE
& 1 PINCH OF SALT.
→ MIX INTO A SMOOTH DOUGH,
ADDING MORE OLIVE OIL IF ITS
TOO DRY.

DIVIDE THE DOUGH INTO SMALL
BALLS. FLATTEN THEM ON A
GREASED BAKING SHEET WITH A
COOKIE STAMP OR A FORK.
BAKE FOR 15 MIN. UNTIL GOLDEN.
(ROTATE THE BAKING SHEET HALFWAY
THROUGH THE BAKING TIME SO THE
COOKIES BROWN EQUALLY.)

Meringue Snow Stars

FOR, SAY 12 snowflakes, depending on the size
PREP 20 min.
BAKE 1 hour, plus drying time

gluten-free

2 egg whites
pinch of sea salt
2 cups (200 g) confectioners' sugar, plus some extra
a few drops of lemon juice or vinegar
1 tbsp cornstarch
5 tbsp (30 g) sliced almonds (optional)

A MUST
1 pastry bag, with a small round tip (or a different shape—up to you)

In a perfectly clean bowl with a perfectly clean whisk, whip the egg whites with a tiny pinch of salt, and gradually add the confectioners' sugar and lemon juice. Once the sugar has dissolved, add the cornstarch. Continue whipping until you have very stiff peaks. Fill the pastry bag with the batter.

Preheat the oven to 215°F (100°C). Line a baking sheet with parchment paper and glue the paper to the tray by squirting some batter in each corner.

With your pastry bag, draw large, pretty, detailed snowflakes on the parchment paper. Sprinkle with almonds, if you wish. Bake for 1 hour, then turn off the oven and let cool completely in the warm oven, ideally overnight.

Sprinkle with some extra sugar, if you wish, and hang them on your Christmas tree with a ribbon.

Speculaas

This recipe is for all my friends in Ireland who keep asking me to bring them "those spicy windmill cookies." You can of course mix the necessary speculaas *spices yourself, whether you live in the Netherlands, Ireland, or wherever. Store-bought* speculaas *spices are never as good and strong in flavor as your own, freshly ground stuff, so you can bake windmill cookies anywhere.*

FOR 10 cookies
PREP 25 min.
INACTIVE 1 hour to 1 day
BAKE 10 min.

5 tbsp (75 g) butter, at room temperature
scant ½ cup (100 g) packed dark brown sugar
1 tbsp milk, ideally buttermilk
finely grated zest of ¼ lemon
1½ cups (150 g) superfine flour (type 00)
1 tsp baking powder
pinch of salt
1½ tsp *speculaas* spices (see illustration)
a generous handful of fine rice flour (from the organic or gluten-free section!) or cornstarch
1 egg, beaten
sliced almonds

good to have: a *speculaas* board, but you can also use cookie cutters

Beat the butter with the brown sugar until soft and airy. Whisk in the buttermilk and lemon zest and sift the flour, baking powder, salt, and *speculaas* spices over the top. Mix with a spatula until everything just comes together and you have a smooth dough.

Shape the dough into a flat ball, wrap it in plastic wrap, and let rest for 1 hour to 1 day in the fridge. The longer you wait, the better the flavors will be.

Preheat the oven to 350°F (180°C). Line a baking sheet with parchment paper.

Dust a *speculaas* board with some sifted rice flour and press a ball of dough into each shape. Cut off the excess dough with a knife and tap the board on the counter to remove the cookies. (If you don't have a board, just roll out the dough and use a cookie cutter.) Divide the cookies evenly over the prepared baking sheet. Brush with some egg and decorate with almonds.

Bake for 10 to 15 minutes (depending on size and form). In my case, the wings brown very fast, so stay close to the oven to keep an eye on how things are going.

Let them cool completely on a rack.

IDEALLY GRIND WHOLE SEEDS IN A MORTAR (OR COFFEE GRINDER!) INTO POWDER FOR MORE INTENSE FLAVOR

SPECULAAS SPICES
2 TBSP. CINNAMON
1 TSP. GROUND NUTMEG
½ TSP. GROUND CLOVES
½ TSP. GROUND CARDAMOM
½ TSP. GROUND WHITE PEPPER
½ TSP. GROUND GINGER
½ TSP. GROUND CORIANDER

Wellingtons

This recipe requires a short introduction.

My friend Bianca called me when she heard I was working on a baking book.

A very long time ago, her grandfather was an apprentice pastry chef, and Bianca has always kept his notebook. One afternoon she came by to bring it. A beautiful, handwritten notebook from 1915. We carefully leafed through the vellum pages. Bianca's grandfather had added small drawings, of various pastries, and of how to decorate a cake. Awfully lovely.

I tried out a few recipes. They had a sweet tooth in 1915, I noticed. Take the recipe for these chewy almond cookies, for example: yikes—so sweet, they hurt my teeth. I tried again, with less sugar, and then another time with even less. Until the recipe was good. Perfect. And really very delicious.

Thank you, Grandpa!

FOR 40 cookies
PREP 10 min.
BAKE 10 min.

lactose-free
gluten-free

1¾ cups (200 g) almond
    flour
2 cups (400 g) sugar
1 tsp vanilla extract
3 egg whites
1 drop real almond oil
    (optional)
3 tbsp sliced almonds

Preheat the oven to 375°F (190°C).

Combine everything except the almonds, and stir into a thick paste. Scoop the batter into a pastry bag.

Line a baking sheet with parchment paper and glue it to the tray by squirting a bit of the batter underneath each corner and pressing gently.

Pipe nice oval cookies 2½ inches (6 cm) long on the prepared baking sheet. Make sure to space them apart, as they will spread. If tips stick up, round them off with a wet finger. If you don't have a pastry bag, you can make small heaps the size of a walnut with two spoons.

Sprinkle the cookies with almonds and bake them briefly, just 10 minutes, until they are light brown. Let them cool. They should be soft and chewy.

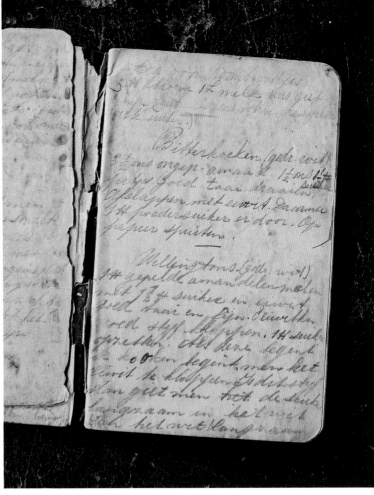

Crinkle Cookies
with Lemon & Fennel Seed

These cookies are deliciously lemony. Their core is soft and the edges crispy. Real binge-eat biscuits. You've been warned.

FOR 40 cookies
PREP 20 min.
BAKE 8 min.

1 cup (2 sticks / 225 g) butter,
   at room temperature,
   plus extra for the pan
1 cup plus 2 tbsp (225 g)
   granulated sugar
1 tsp vanilla extract
zest and juice of 1 lemon
1 tbsp fennel seed (ground
   in the mortar)
1 egg
pinch of salt
¾ tsp baking powder
2¼ cups (300 g) all-purpose
   flour
about 2 cups (200 g)
   confectioners' sugar

Preheat the oven to 350°F (175°C). Grease the largest possible baking sheet.

Beat the butter with the granulated sugar using a hand mixer until light and airy. Add the vanilla, lemon zest, lemon juice, and fennel seed and whip the batter once more. Then beat in the egg.

Combine the salt and baking powder with the flour and stir that mixture with a spatula into the butter mixture to form a dough.

Pour the confectioners' sugar over a deep plate.

With wet hands, form small balls the size of large grapes from the dough. Roll them through the confectioners' sugar and space them generously (2 inches / 5 cm apart) on the prepared baking sheet.

Bake briefly, about 8 minutes. Keep an eye on the oven.

You can bake them in batches, as it's unlikely they'll fit on one baking sheet. Continue until you've used all the dough.

Keep the cookies in a large airtight container, where they'll stay fresh for at least a week.

BASIC PIE CRUST RECIPES

Unless mentioned otherwise, the amounts given in all these recipes will make 1 average-size, single-crust pie, say, 9 inches (24 cm) in diameter. For each recipe on the following pages I'll let you know whether you'll need more or less of the amounts stated in the basic recipes.

Of course you can add flavorings to taste. Spices, for instance, or finely chopped fresh herbs (thyme, rosemary, oregano) or sesame seeds, to give the dough some extra punch. If you're craving chocolate, replace 3½ tbsp (25 g) all-purpose flour with 5 tbsp (25 g) unsweetened cocoa powder in a shortcrust or sweet dough to turn it into a chocolate crust dough. Simple.

Shortcrust Dough

A multipurpose dough. Be swift when you make it, for the longer you knead, the more gluten strands will be formed, causing the dough to become compact and tough instead of light and crisp. Although that can be wonderful for some doughs, for shortcrust dough it certainly isn't. Sometimes I'll add an egg yolk to strengthen the dough. This can be useful when I'm making a large pie and don't want my crust to be so crumbly that it breaks apart when I'm cutting it.

pinch of sea salt
2¼ cups (300 g) all-purpose
    flour
⅔ cup (1⅓ sticks / 150 g)
    butter, cubed
1 egg yolk (optional)
a few drops of ice water

Mix the sea salt with the flour. Use your cold hands, or two knives, to mix in the butter cubes until the mixture looks like coarse sand. Another way of doing this without having to touch the butter is pulsing it in a food processor. If a firmer dough is desired, add the egg, then just enough liquid for the dough to come together. Do so sparingly—usually just a tiny drop or two will suffice.

Swiftly work the dough into a flattened ball. Wrap it in plastic and let rest in the fridge for at least 1 hour. Remove the dough from the fridge and allow it to come back to room temperature. After about 25 minutes, it will be easier to roll out on a flour-dusted countertop.

Sweet Dough / Pâte Brisée

This is a lightly sweetened and crumbly dough that can be used as a basic crust for just about any type of sweet pastry. Sometimes I even like to use a sweet crust for savory fillings. Something containing salt, like strong-flavored cheeses, bacon, or stewlike fillings, combines really well with a lightly sweetened crust. To create a contrast with the filling, feel free to add other flavorings, like cinnamon, minced rosemary, or ground ginger.

2 cups (250 g) all-purpose flour, plus some extra if needed
3 tbsp confectioners' sugar
pinch of sea salt
¾ cup (1½ sticks / 175 g) cold butter, finely cubed
1 egg, beaten
about 3 tbsp cold milk or water, as needed

Sift the flour with the confectioners' sugar and salt over a bowl. Quickly, using cold hands, work in the butter until the dough has the appearance of coarse crumbs. Swiftly add the egg and knead until you have a consistent dough. If the dough is too dry, add a few drops of milk or water. You can use a food processor as well. Make sure you work fast. Overkneading will result in tough dough. You want crumbly dough.

Shape into a ball, slightly flatten, and wrap in plastic. Set aside to rest in the fridge for 1 hour.

After removing the dough from the fridge, leave it out on the kitchen counter for about 15 minutes before using it.

Almond Shortcrust Dough

gluten-free

generous 2½ cups (300 g) almond flour, plus some extra if needed
½ tsp sea salt
1 tbsp good-quality agave syrup, maple syrup, or honey
1 egg
2 to 3 tbsp coconut oil or cold butter

Quickly combine everything (as you would when making regular shortcrust dough) into a firm ball. This can be done by hand or in a stand mixer. If the dough is too wet, add some more almond flour. The dough shouldn't be sticky to the touch, but it should form a firm ball if you press everything together. Shape into a ball, wrap in plastic, and leave in the fridge for at least 30 minutes before using it.

Rice Flour Shortcrust Dough

gluten-free

2 eggs, beaten
7 tbsp (100 g) coconut oil or butter (no margarine!), melted
1½ cups (250 g) white or brown rice flour
½ tsp baking powder
⅛ tsp sea salt
2 tbsp granulated sugar or confectioners' sugar (optional)

In a bowl, beat the eggs with the coconut oil. Over another bowl, sift the rice flour, baking powder, and salt. If you plan on making a pie with a sweet filling, also sift the sugar. Stir in the egg-butter mixture. It will turn into a soft, crumbly mixture. This is normal. If it turns out too powdery, add a few drops of cold water.

Scrape the dough into your pie pan and use your palms or the flat bottom of a measuring cup or drinking glass to pat the dough evenly all over the bottom and up the sides of the pan. Fill the pie with your favorite filling or, for particularly wet fillings, first blind bake the crust for 15 minutes in an oven that has been preheated to 400°F (200°C).

Open-Face Pie (Vlaai) Dough

For an open-face pie with a classic crosshatch lattice top, you need to prepare a little more dough than the recipe below; use: ½ cup plus 2 tbsp (150 ml) milk, 2½ tsp (10 g) instant yeast, 3¼ cups (400 g) all-purpose flour, sea salt, 5 tbsp (75 g) butter, 3 tbsp sugar, and 1 egg.

7 tbsp (100 ml) milk
scant 2 tsp (7 g) instant
    yeast
2¼ cups (300 g) all-purpose
    flour, plus extra for dusting
pinch of sea salt
3 tbsp butter, plus extra for
    the pan
3 tbsp packed light brown
    sugar
1 egg, beaten

Heat the milk until lukewarm, add the yeast, and leave for 20 minutes until the yeast has dissolved.

Sift the flour with the salt over a bowl. Add the butter, brown sugar, and egg. Make an indentation at the center and pour in the lukewarm milk. Stir with a spoon until all the flour has been incorporated. Then, with flour-dusted hands, work into a smooth dough. If necessary, add a little flour or milk. Knead for about 10 minutes, then put the ball back into the bowl. Cover with plastic wrap and leave to rise for 1 hour.

Roll out the dough into a disc the size of your vlaai pie pan (these tend to be rather large: about 12 inches / 30 cm). Grease the pan with some butter and press the dough into the pan. Neatly trim the edges and, using a fork, prick the bottom a couple of times.

Savory Pasty Dough

Because this dough is cooked, it becomes wonderfully pliable and it will also retain its shape when you pour in hot filling. It's enough for a pasty of 8 inches (20 cm) with a top. If you like to make a larger pasty just multiply the recipe, which in this case should be very easy.

2 tsp sea salt
3½ cups (450 g) all-purpose
    flour, plus extra for
    dusting
7 tbsp (100 g) butter, plus
    extra for greasing
¾ cup plus 1 tbsp (200 ml)
    milk

Add the salt to the flour. Combine the butter and milk in a saucepan with ½ cup plus 2 tbsp (150 ml) water. Heat until all the butter has melted. Add the flour and stir the mixture into a firm ball. Remove from the pan and knead on a flour-dusted counter until you have a cohesive dough. Let rest for a while, then proceed as described in the pasty recipe (see page 312, for example).

Provence, France

Puff Pastry Dough

Making puff pastry is a lot of fun, and although time consuming, it's easy to do. That's why you should make a lot at once. It can be easily frozen so you can have a little backup supply for those days when you really don't have time. Once in a while, I make my own puff pastry, and I have to say that really is VERY delicious. And like with all cooking: Use good-quality ingredients. Use organic butter from the farmers' market, for instance, and you will really taste the difference.

When working with dough containing a lot of butter it is important to KEEP IT COOL. Butter should never get too warm—otherwise, the dough will become impossible to work with and your pastry won't get those desired flaky layers. So, work fast and refrigerate the dough in between steps.

Also keep in mind that while the oven is preheating, the kitchen tends to get warm fast.

Also good to know: Always put your puff pastry–lined pie pan back in the fridge while preparing the filling. That way, the pie will retain its shape as much as possible when you bake it.

Puff Pastry: Official Version

3⅓ cups (6⅔ sticks / 750 g) cold butter
6 cups (750 g) all-purpose flour
1 tsp sea salt
about 2 tbsp ice water

Slice three-quarters of the butter (2½ cups / 560 g) into flat strips. Then form a rectangle by placing the strips side by side on a large sheet of parchment paper. Cover with a second sheet of parchment paper and use a rolling pin to roll out the butter into a smooth rectangle of about 4¾ by 12 inches (12 by 30 cm). Refrigerate for at least 4 hours, until firm.

Cube the remaining butter. Sift the flour with the salt and then combine with the butter cubes in a food processor, gently pulsing into a coarse crumb—you can also swiftly rub the butter in with your cold hands. Add just enough water for the dough to come together (about 2 tbsp). Shape into a ball, wrap in plastic wrap, and let rest in the fridge for about 1 hour.

Roll out the dough into a rectangle almost twice the size of the butter slab. Place the butter at the center and fold the dough edges over the butter so it is completely covered.

Now roll out the dough to its original size again.

Fold the slab into thirds. Fold the left third inward, then fold the right third on top of it, as if you were folding a letter. Wrap the block in plastic wrap and put it back in the fridge. Leave it there for 1 to 2 hours. ✑

🐦 Then roll out the dough again to 4¾ by 12 inches (12 by 30 cm) and fold it like you did in the previous step. Using your finger, make two indentations at the center. This way you know how many times you have rolled out and folded the dough. This, by the way, is called "turning," and you should repeat this process four to six times. The more turns, the better your puff pastry will turn out.

After the final turn, allow the dough to rest in the fridge for at least 1 night. Then divide the dough into practical portions (about 10½ oz / 300 g). Wrap them well before freezing. Or use the fresh dough right away to make a wonderful pastry.

Puff Pastry: The Quick Version

If you are pressed for time, but still want to make a fine dough from scratch, one that comes really close to that authentic buttery puff pastry, you can also follow this recipe. Unlike the version described above, this recipe is for one portion because it doesn't take much work.

2 cups (250 g) all-purpose flour
1 tsp sea salt
1 cup plus 2 tbsp (2¼ sticks / 250 g) butter, at room temperature though not too soft
about ½ cup plus 2 tbsp (150 ml) ice water, plus more as needed

Sift the flour and salt over a large bowl. Break up the butter into small chunks with your hands and quickly rub these into the flour. Don't try to be too meticulous; the chunks should remain visible. They will melt in the oven, giving the pastry its characteristic layers.

Make an indentation at the center of the dough and pour in half of the ice water. Mix the ice water and the dough, but don't over-knead, and if you think the dough needs more water, just add a few drops. Wrap the dough in plastic wrap and refrigerate for 30 minutes. Afterward, on a flour-dusted counter, knead the dough again briefly—remember, the lumps of butter shouldn't melt but should remain visible—and shape it into a rectangular slab. Then roll it out into a sheet of about 8 by 20 inches (20 by 50 cm).

Fold this sheet in thirds like a letter. Rotate the dough block 90 degrees and roll it out again into a rectangle of the same size as before. Repeat these steps twice more. Now put the dough back in the fridge to allow it to stiffen for 30 minutes before using it as you'd like.

County Dublin, Ireland

Strawberry-Thyme Pie

SERVES 8

PREP 30 min.

INACTIVE more than 1 hour and 30 min., all in all

BAKE 15 min.

sugar-free

FOR THE DOUGH

1 cup (125 g) all-purpose flour, plus some extra

1¼ cups (125 g) almond flour (or use 2 cups / 250 g all-purpose flour in total)

9 tbsp (125 g) butter

pinch of salt

1½ tsp (7.5 g) stevia (100% pure), or 6 tbsp (30 g) confectioners' sugar

cold water, as needed

FOR THE THYME CUSTARD

¾ cup plus 1 tbsp (200 ml) milk

1 vanilla bean, sliced open and seeds scraped out

a few sprigs fresh thyme

2 egg yolks

1½ tsp (7.5 g) stevia (100% pure), or 6 tbsp (30 g) confectioners' sugar

½ cup plus 2 tbsp (150 g) cream cheese

FOR THE TOPPING

17 to 21 oz (500 to 600 g) delicious fresh strawberries

some fresh thyme leaves

Make the dough: Quickly work together both flours, the butter, salt, and stevia into a smooth dough. If the dough is too dry, add a few drops of cold water. Shape into a flat disc and wrap in some plastic wrap. Let rest in the fridge for 1 hour.

Meanwhile, start the thyme custard: Bring the milk to a near boil with the vanilla and thyme. Turn off the heat and let steep until ready to use.

Preheat the oven to 350°F (180°C).

Dust the countertop with flour and pat the dough into a thin slab that fits an 8½-inch (22-cm) pie plate or a pie pan with a removable bottom. Grease the pan and line it with the dough. Leave some overhanging the edge. Carefully press a sheet of parchment paper onto the dough and fill up the pan with baking beans or regular beans. Blind bake the bean-filled crust for 15 minutes. Use the parchment paper to lift out the beans. Now bake the crust for 10 minutes more.

Leave your pie crust out on the counter to cool for a while. Then neatly trim the edges with a small knife. Keep the oven on.

In the meantime, back to the custard: Beat the yolks and stevia until light and frothy. Pour in the warm milk through a strainer. Thoroughly whisk everything and pour it back into the pan. While stirring, bring the mixture to a near boil and reduce it slightly over low heat. Turn off the heat and beat in the cream cheese. Pour the mixture into the blind-baked crust and put the pie back in the oven for 15 minutes.

Allow the pie to cool on a rack for at least 30 minutes.

Quarter the strawberries and use them to dress the pie.

Serve the pie garnished with some thyme.

Eccles Cakes

The taste of Eccles cakes reminds me of my younger years. One bite and I'm transported back to Ireland. The combination of the crunchy dough and the warm buttery filling, teeming with currants and spices: stupendously delicious.

Recently I had one in an upscale New York City restaurant. Not long after that, during a visit to London, I ordered another one. Both restaurants served them with cheese; an excellent idea, as it turned out.

Which is why I want you to try one as well.

Eccles cakes (named after the English town of Eccles) pair really well with almost any type of cheese, as long as it has a pronounced flavor and offers a hint of saltiness to offset the cake's sweetness. A robust blue cheese could work, for instance, or an aged crumbly cheese, or a sheep's-milk cheese like pecorino. Anyway, you'll figure it out.

Oh, and while you're at it: Make a whole bunch at once; they can be stored in the freezer.

FOR 22 cakes
PREP 45 min.
INACTIVE 15 min.
MORE INACTIVE 24 hours
BAKE 20 min.

FOR THE FILLING
7 tbsp (100 g) butter
1 bay leaf, crushed (throw out the hard stem)
1 star anise

½ nutmeg, grated (grate away . . .)
2 whole cloves
1½ cups (250 g) currants
scant ½ cup (75 g) sultanas (golden raisins)
grated zest of 2 lemons
juice of 1 lemon
grated zest of 2 oranges
⅓ cup (75 g) packed light brown sugar or granulated sugar
2 tbsp brandy

AND FURTHER
26 oz (750 g) puff pastry, homemade (see page 256) or store-bought frozen puff pastry, defrosted
2 eggs, beaten
several tbsp granulated sugar, for sprinkling

Make the filling: Melt the butter in a saucepan and add the bay leaf, star anise, nutmeg, and cloves. Allow to steep for 5 minutes or so. Add the currants, raisins, lemon zest, lemon juice, orange zest, and brown sugar and allow everything to steep over very low heat for about 15 minutes. Stir occasionally. Remove from the heat. Stir in the brandy and let cool. Preferably leave the mixture in the fridge overnight so that all the flavors will really be absorbed.

Preheat the oven to 400°F (200°C). Line a baking sheet with parchment paper.

If you use store-bought puff pastry, stack the separate defrosted sheets and roll them out into one slab.

Divide the dough into three portions. Leave two in the fridge while you roll out one portion to ⅛-inch (3-mm) thickness on a flour-dusted counter.

Using a 3-inch (8-cm) round cookie cutter, cut out circles. Place a small heap of filling, about ½ tablespoon, in the middle of a dough circle and fold the edges around the filling. I do this by pulling two halves to the center and sealing them together with my fingers. Then I fold the two tips inward as well and press down to secure them.

Now turn the pasty over, with the seam facing down and the smooth side facing up. Gently roll over the pasty with your rolling pin, until a flat, even, and nicely round pasty lies on the counter in front of you. Don't press down too hard or the filling will burst out.

Using a pointy knife, make three parallel cuts across the top. These are for letting out the steam during baking to ensure you get a crispy dough.

Do all of this quickly (don't worry—you'll get the hang of it). The dough shouldn't get too warm. To be sure, immediately place the finished cakes back into the fridge while working on the other ones.

Set the finished pasties a little apart on the baking sheet. Brush with the egg and sprinkle with the sugar.

Bake for about 20 minutes, until crisp and golden brown.

Wait a little before tasting them; the filling will be pretty hot.

Preferably serve them with a nice chunk of cheese. Although naturally, a dab of crème fraîche is lovely too.

TiP: Eccles cakes are best eaten warm. If you don't plan to eat them right away, you can bake them for only 15 minutes, until just light brown. Then you can freeze them for later use. Just finish them in a preheated oven at 350°F (180°C) for 10 to 12 more minutes.

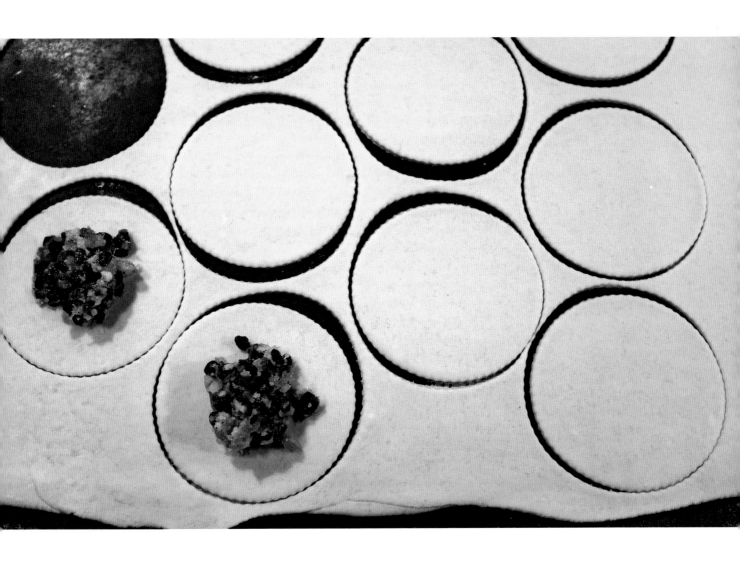

Almond Custard Tarts

Once, when I had dinner guests who were lactose intolerant, I tried to make custard without using any milk or cream. It became a huge success. Wow! Well, sometimes you're just unabashedly proud of your own inventions. Making your own almond milk isn't difficult, by the way. For my recipe, see page 40.

FOR 12 small tarts
PREP about 1 hour
BAKE 25 min.

lactose-free option

FOR THE DOUGH
1 recipe shortcrust dough
   (page 252), made without
   the egg yolk (you will
   have some leftover
   dough, which you can
   freeze for later or use to
   bake some cookies)
If you choose to make
   this dough completely
   lactose-free you can
   replace the butter with
   a hard (nonspreadable)
   plant-based organic
   margarine, or with chilled
   coconut oil

FOR THE ALMOND
   CUSTARD FILLING
about 3 cups (700 ml) sugar-
   free almond milk, from
   the health food store or
   homemade (page 40)
1 vanilla bean, sliced open
   and seeds scraped out
7 egg yolks
7 tbsp (90 g) packed dark
   brown sugar
freshly grated nutmeg

Make the dough as described and refrigerate until ready to use.

Allow it to come back to room temperature while you prepare the filling.

Preheat the oven to 400°F (200°C). Grease 12 mini pie pans or a 12-cup muffin pan.

Roll out the dough on a work surface that has been lightly dusted with flour.

Using a 4½-inch (11-cm) cookie cutter, cut out 12 circles and press them into the pie pans or the cups of the muffin pan. The edges of the dough discs should stick out a little, but they will shrink in the oven.

Make the almond custard filling: Heat the almond milk with the vanilla bean pod and seeds in a saucepan over medium heat. Bring to a near boil, then reduce the heat and let steep for about 15 minutes.

In a large bowl, beat the egg yolks with the brown sugar into a pale, foamy mass. Remove the vanilla bean pod from the almond milk and pour the almond milk into the bowl with the egg mixture. Thoroughly beat into a thin, smooth batter. Pour the batter into a large jug so filling the cups will be easier later on.

Place the pie pans or muffin pan on a rack in the middle of the oven. Pull out the rack a little so you have easy access and fill up the cups with the almond custard. Grate some nutmeg over each cup. Then slide the rack back into the oven with the utmost care and bake for about 25 minutes. If the dough looks too brown or puffs up too much, you can lower the oven temperature to 350°F (175°C) for the last 10 minutes.

The dough should be light brown and the filling just set: not puffed up. That would indicate that the tarts have baked too fast. While the tarts are cooling off, the custard should slightly tremble, like a firm pudding.

Leave the tarts in the pan to cool slightly, then remove them using a knife. Allow them to fully cool on a rack.

Apple Pie, The Only Right Way

Yes, I really think that this is how an apple pie should be made. Large, robust, and generously filled. This pie recipe really requires about a bushel of various apples. It's these different apple varieties that give this pie its punch. In addition, I've used all of my favorite ingredients: blackberries, ginger, lemon, and Chinese five-spice powder, and voilà—a winner.

Everybody loves a pie like this, especially when served with some whipped cream. Mmmm . . .

SERVES 10 to 12
PREP 30 min.
REST 1 hour
BAKE 1 hour and 30 min.

FOR THE DOUGH
2 recipes sweet dough (page 252)

FOR THE FILLING
about 1½ pounds (750 g)
    cooking apples like Rome
    Beauty, washed and
    sliced
about 1½ pounds (750 g)
    tart fresh apples like
    Granny Smith, washed
    and sliced
5 oz (150 g) blackberries
1 (2-inch / 5-cm) piece fresh
    ginger, peeled and chopped
¾ cup plus 2 tbsp (175 g) sugar
juice of 1 lemon (or the juice
    of 2 limes)
1 tsp Chinese five-spice powder
    (or a mixture of cinnamon,
    ground ginger, and allspice)
pinch of salt
1 tbsp vanilla extract
2 tbsp all-purpose flour

AND THEN ALSO
3 tbsp butter, cut into small
    cubes
1 tbsp milk
1 tbsp sugar
1 tsp ground ginger

First, swiftly make the dough. It's best to use a stand mixer, fast and easy. Don't knead for too long! Wrap the dough in plastic wrap and set aside in the fridge for at least 1 hour.

Preheat the oven to 400°F (200°C). Grease a 9-inch (24-cm) (or 10-inch / 26-cm is fine as well) springform pan or pie pan.

Combine all the ingredients for the filling minus the flour in a large bowl. Let rest for 15 minutes, then drain the excess liquid. Stir in the flour.

Divide the dough into two parts: two-thirds for the bottom crust and one-third for the lattice top. Roll out the dough for the crust on a flour-dusted countertop. Press the dough into the prepared springform pan or pie pan, allowing some overhang. Fill the pie with the apple filling and spread the small butter cubes on top. Now roll out the dough for the top and slice it into strips or punch out shapes with a cookie cutter. Stars always look nice. Carefully arrange the dough strips on top of the filling. Weave a classic lattice pattern if you can.

It's important that the top has enough openings. The fruits contain a lot of liquid, which needs to partly evaporate. You don't want a soggy bottom.

You can press the edges together using a fork, although if you are handy, you can also try to skillfully fold the top under. Whichever you prefer.

Brush the top with the milk and sprinkle it with the sugar and ground ginger.

Put the pie into the oven. Lower the heat to 350°F (180°C) and bake the pie for about 1 hour and 30 minutes, until done. Allow to cool and serve at room temperature.

Raspberry Cream Pie

SERVES 10
PREP 20 min.
BAKE 40 min.

⅔ cup (1⅓ sticks / 150 g)
    butter, at room
    temperature
scant 1 cup (200 g) packed
    light brown sugar
2 eggs
grated zest of ½ lemon
1½ cups plus 2 tbsp (200 g)
    all-purpose flour
2 tsp (10 g) baking powder
pinch of salt
10½ oz (300 g) raspberries
    (can be frozen)
1 cup (250 ml) sour cream
1 tsp vanilla extract

Preheat the oven to 400°F (200°C). Grease a 9-inch (24-cm) pie pan (or tart pan with removable bottom).

Beat the butter with ¾ cup (150 g) of the brown sugar until light, creamy, and nearly white. Beat in 1 egg and the lemon zest. Now sift the flour, baking powder, and salt over it. Combine everything into a smooth batter.

Spoon the batter into the pie pan. Make sure the bottom and the walls of the pan are covered in an even layer of batter. Prebake the crust for 10 minutes, then return it to the kitchen counter.

Lower the heat to 350°F (180°C). Spread the raspberries over the crust. Whip the sour cream with the rest of the brown sugar, the other egg, and the vanilla into an even, smooth mixture. Pour the cream over the raspberries.

Bake the pie for another 30 minutes and then turn off the oven. Allow the pie to cool inside the oven until the top feels firm (this should be after about 15 minutes).

Remove from the pan (if using a pan with a removable bottom) and leave the pie on a rack to further cool off.

Tarte au Vin Rouge

Each year, during the month of August, we live in the south of France. We build an outdoor kitchen in the orchard and we cook. All our visiting friends bring something: One brings a record player and his collection of French 45s. Another builds a BBQ out of rocks found in the river. It's been our home away from home for as long as I can remember, this apple and pear orchard in Provence.

When I wake up, I find fresh flowers from the field on the breakfast table, picked by Georges and his brother Charles, two retired fruit farmers who live on the farm down the road. Sometimes when we return from a long hike through the mountains or a day at the beach, we'll find our table covered with apples. Or pears. Or artichokes.

Together the family decides which days we will all eat together. On those days everybody prepares something so nobody has to spend too much time cooking.

For dessert, I prepared this pie in the farmhouse kitchen, using the apples I found lying on my table after a day of swimming in the river. This tarte au vin rouge *is my version of an old, similarly named Provençal recipe. And it's just mouthwatering.*

SERVES 10 to 12
PREP 30 min.
INACTIVE 1 hour and 15 min.
BAKE 40 min.

FOR THE DOUGH
1 recipe sweet dough (page 252)

FOR THE FILLING
1½ cups plus 2 tbsp (400 ml) red wine from Provence
½ tsp cinnamon
pinch of nutmeg
3 eggs
½ cup plus 3 tbsp (130 g) fine sugar
1 large or 2 small apples, washed and very thinly sliced (use a mandoline)

FOR THE GLAZE
½ cup plus 2 tbsp (150 ml) red wine
1½ tsp unflavored powdered gelatin
3 tbsp granulated sugar

Make the sweet dough as described and refrigerate for 1 hour. Then roll it out on a flour-dusted counter and fit it into a greased 9- to 10-inch (24- to 26-cm) pie pan. Allow some overhang around the edges. They will be trimmed after baking. Use a fork to pierce the bottom of the crust and place the pan in the freezer for 15 minutes.

Preheat the oven to 350°F (180°C). Blind bake your crust for 15 minutes (see page 25).

In the meantime, you can prepare the filling: Bring the wine to a gentle boil in a saucepan, then add the cinnamon and the nutmeg. Beat the eggs and sugar in a bowl until light and almost yellowish white. While stirring continuously, pour in the hot wine in a thin stream. Then pour everything back into the saucepan and cook over medium heat, stirring constantly, until the custard has the consistency of runny yogurt, about 10 minutes.

Remove the crust from the oven and fill it with the wine custard and then carefully cover with the apples in a clockwise spiral of overlapping slices. Bake the pie for another 25 minutes, until its center is just about done. The filling will remain soft (later it will stiffen up a little). Leave the pie to cool off on a rack and trim the crust edges, if desired.

Make the glaze: Put the wine in a small saucepan and sprinkle the gelatin over it. Let soak for 5 minutes, then add the sugar and place over low heat and stir until the sugar and gelatin are dissolved. Carefully brush the top of the pie with glaze; you won't need all of the glaze.

La Durance, Provence

Provence, France

Peach & Berry Tarts with Buttermilk Custard

If you like to bake with less gluten, you can easily make this recipe with just an almond shortcrust dough or the rice flour shortcrust dough (page 253). I, however, really like the combination of almond flour with wheat flour: This results in a delicious dough that also has a very nice texture. Try it sometime.

FOR 4 to 6 tarts or 1 large
(8- to 9-inch / 22- to 24-cm) pie
PREP 30 min.
INACTIVE 4 hours
BAKE 30 min.

FOR THE CUSTARD
½ cup plus 2 tbsp (125 g)
　　sugar
¼ cup (30 g) all-purpose flour
1¼ cup plus 2 tbsp (350 ml)
　　buttermilk
3 large eggs, thoroughly beaten
2 tsp vanilla extract
1 vanilla bean, sliced open
　　and seeds scraped out

FOR THE DOUGH
¾ cup plus 2 tbsp (100 g)
　　almond flour
¾ cup plus 1 tbsp (100 g)
　　all-purpose flour, plus
　　some extra
scant ¼ cup (50 g) packed
　　light brown sugar
pinch of sea salt
7 tbsp (100 g) butter
a few drops of ice water

FOR ON TOP
2 peaches, some red berries,
　　1 handful of cherries and
　　strawberries, or about
　　10½ oz (300 g) washed
　　and sliced fresh fruits of
　　your choice
some leaves of fresh basil,
　　mint, or lemon verbena
　　(optional)

Make the custard: Combine the sugar and flour in a heavy saucepan. Add the buttermilk, eggs, vanilla extract, and vanilla bean seeds and pod and bring to a boil while beating continuously with a whisk. Lower the heat somewhat and stir into a thick custard. Allow to softly boil for another 7 minutes while stirring continuously. Then take the custard off the heat and allow it to cool. Remove the vanilla bean pod, if using. First leave it on the counter until room temperature, then cover and refrigerate to solidify for at least 4 hours.

Make the dough: Combine the almond flour, all-purpose flour, brown sugar, and salt. Using cold hands, or two knives, rub in the butter until the dough resembles coarse sand. Of course you can also pulse in the butter with a stand mixer. If needed, add just enough drops of ice water until the dough starts coming together.

Swiftly shape it into a flattened ball. Wrap in plastic wrap and refrigerate for at least 1 hour.

Preheat the oven to 350°F (180°C).

Roll out the dough on a flour-dusted countertop and cut out circles the size of your small pie pans (or make 1 large pie crust). Grease the cups and fit in the dough. Scrape together the dough scraps and roll them out again to fill all of your pie pans. Cover each of them with fitted sheets of parchment paper and fill up with dried beans (or special baking beans from the cookware store).

Blind bake the pie crusts for 15 minutes, then remove the parchment paper with the beans and bake the crust for another 6 minutes or so, until golden brown. Allow to cool down. Fill them with the custard right before serving. Dress with the fresh fruit and garnish each with a leaf of basil, mint, or lemon verbena (if using) and serve right away.

Cherry Almond Pie

FOR 1 large or 6 to 8 smaller pies
PREP 25 min.
INACTIVE 1 hour
BAKE 35 min.

FOR THE DOUGH

1 recipe sweet dough
    (page 252)
some extra flour, for dusting

FOR THE ALMOND
FILLING

⅞ cup (1¾ sticks / 200 g)
    butter
scant 1 cup (200 g) packed
    light brown sugar
2 eggs
1¾ cups (200 g) almond
    flour

AND FURTHER

3 handfuls of cherries, halved
    and pitted, or 5 or 6
    pieces of other kinds of
    stone fruit
confectioners' sugar
whipped cream, crème
    fraîche, or vanilla ice
    cream, for serving

Make the dough as described and set aside in the fridge.

Make the almond filling: Beat the butter and brown sugar in a bowl until light and airy. This works best with a hand mixer. Beat in the eggs one by one. Fold in the almond flour with a spatula and stir into a smooth batter. Set aside for later use.

Preheat the oven to 350°F (180°C). Grease a 9- or 10-inch (24- or 26-cm) pie pan, an 8½-by-11-inch (21.5-by-27.5-cm) tart pan, or 6 to 8 individual smaller pans of about 3 inches (8 cm) in diameter with some butter. Then dust them with flour. Hold the pan (or pans) upside down and lightly tap to shed any excess flour.

Dust your work surface with flour and roll the dough into a thin disc the size of the pie pan. Press the dough into the pan and neatly trim the edges. Spoon the almond filling into the crust, filling it up about halfway. Spread the filling evenly. Scatter the cherries or other fresh fruits on top.

Bake the pie, or pies, until nicely golden brown, about 35 minutes for a large pie or about 20 minutes for the smaller ones. Let rest for 5 minutes on a rack and dust with a little confectioners' sugar before serving.

Serve warm or cold, with some whipped cream, crème fraîche, or vanilla ice cream on the side.

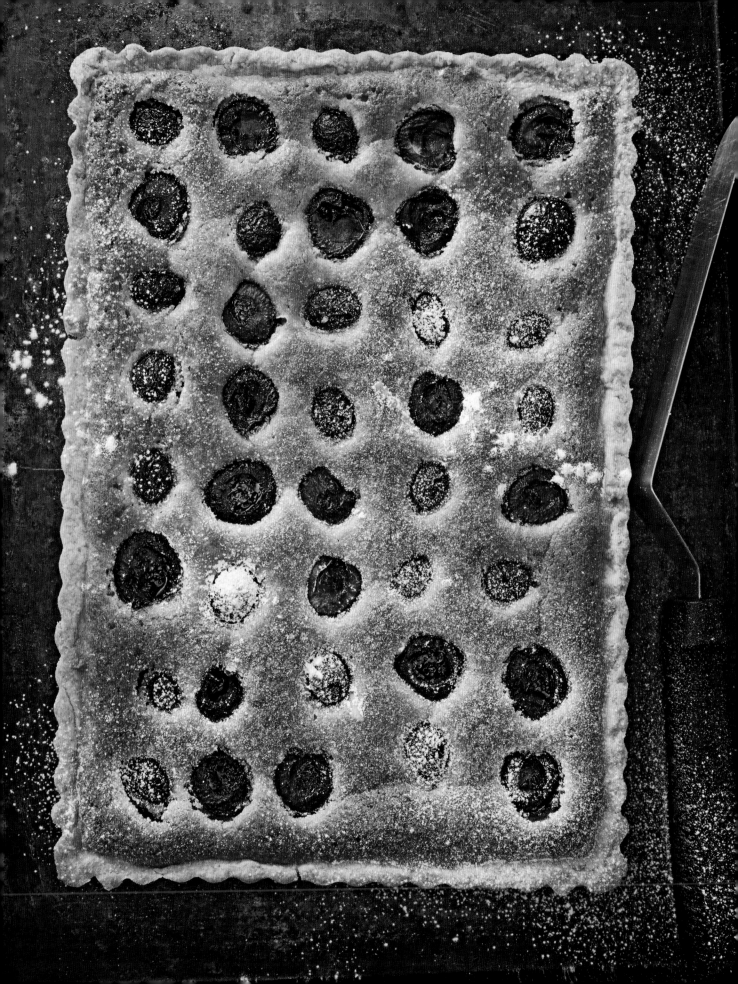

Cherry Cream Pie
with Raspberry-Campari Sauce

SERVES 8
PREP 15 min.
BAKE 12 min.
INACTIVE 1 hour and 30 min.

11½ oz (325 g) biscotti or
    Butter Galettes (page
    230), or gingerbread
    cookies (see page 215)
1 tbsp ground ginger
½ tsp sea salt
7 tbsp (100 g) butter, melted
1 cup (250 g) cream cheese
3 tbsp confectioners' sugar,
    sifted, plus extra for
    dusting
½ tsp vanilla extract
finely grated zest of ¼
    lemon
¾ cup plus 1 tbsp (200 ml)
    heavy cream
3 heaping tbsp raspberry jam
1 tbsp Campari
10½ oz (300 g) cherries,
    halved and pitted
    (raspberries, strawberries,
    peaches, or apricots,
    however, are delicious for
    this as well)

Preheat the oven to 350°F (180°C).

Grind the cookies with the ginger and salt in a food processor into fine crumbs. Add the butter and grind until the mixture starts to come together.

Spread the cookie crumb mixture out over the bottom and up the sides of a 10-inch (24-cm) tart pan with a removable bottom (if you like, you can line it with some parchment paper first). Bake the crust for 12 minutes. Allow it to completely cool off on a rack.

Using a hand mixer, beat the cream cheese with the sugar, vanilla, and lemon zest until smooth. Beat in the heavy cream.

Fill the pie crust with the cream cheese mixture and place it in the fridge for at least 1 hour and 30 minutes to set the filling.

Briefly heat the raspberry jam in a saucepan over medium heat. As the jam begins to boil, lower the heat and swiftly stir in the Campari. Press the jam through a strainer over a little bowl.

Spread the halved cherries over the pie. Pour over the raspberry-Campari sauce and serve straightaway.

Chocolate Truffle Pie with Sea Salt Flakes

FOR 12 slices
PREP 45 min.
BAKE 22 min.
INACTIVE 5 hours and 30 min.

FOR THE DOUGH
1½ cups plus 2 tbsp (200 g) all-purpose flour, plus more for dusting
½ cup plus 2 tbsp (60 g) confectioners' sugar, sifted
6 tbsp (30 g) unsweetened cocoa powder
7 tbsp (100 g) cold butter, cubed
2 egg yolks
cold water, as needed

FOR THE FILLING
1 cup plus 2 tbsp (150 g) hazelnuts
¾ cup plus 2 tbsp (175 g) packed light brown sugar
½ cup plus 2 tbsp (150 ml) heavy cream
9 oz (250 g) dark chocolate, finely chopped
4 tbsp (60 ml) amaretto or coffee liqueur
pinch of salt flakes, such as Maldon

Also delicious with small bits of candied orange or tangerine mixed in.

Make the dough: Sift the flour, confectioners' sugar, and cocoa powder over the bowl of your food processor. Then add the butter and egg yolks. Combine into a cohesive, smooth dough in a few pulses. If it's too dry, you can add a few drops of cold water. Once the dough has become nicely smooth and no longer feels sticky, shape it into a flattened disc, wrap it in plastic wrap, and refrigerate for 1 hour. By the way, if you want to do all of the above by hand, that's fine too.

Roll out the dough on a flour-dusted countertop into a slab of about ⅛ inch (3 mm) thick. Grease an 11-inch (28-cm)—or thereabouts—pie pan with a little butter and line with parchment paper. Line with the dough slab and neatly trim the edges with a knife. Use a fork to prick holes in the bottom and then set the pie pan aside in the fridge for 30 minutes.

Preheat the oven to 350°F (180°C).

Line the chilled dough in the pan with baking beans or pie weights. Blind bake the crust for 12 minutes (see page 25), then remove the baking beans and bake the empty crust for another 10 minutes, until crisp. Let cool on a rack.

Meanwhile, make the filling: Spread the hazelnuts out on a baking sheet lined with parchment paper.

Bring the brown sugar and ⅓ cup (75 ml) water to a boil in a saucepan over medium heat and cook until all the sugar has dissolved. Gently shake the pan now and then and allow the caramel to softly boil for about 6 minutes, or until it attains a tea-like, golden-brown color.

Pour the hot caramel over the nuts on the baking sheet and leave to solidify for 15 minutes. Break the hazelnut praline into coarse chunks, then finely grind it in the cleaned food processor. Set aside.

Bring the cream to a near boil in a saucepan over medium heat. Add the chocolate and remove from the heat. Allow to cool for 5 minutes, then stir until smooth. Add two-thirds of the praline along with the liqueur and stir thoroughly.

Pour the chocolate filling into the crust, spread it evenly, and sprinkle with the remaining praline mixture and the sea salt flakes.

Let the pie rest in the fridge for at least 4 hours so it can set properly.

Serve with some unsweetened crème fraîche on the side.

Pistachio Cream Tarts with Raspberries

This is the easiest recipe in the book. I make eight mini tarts here, but making a large one or four single-serving tarts is just as simple. I fill these with the Pistachio Cream featured on page 44, but you can also use Orange Pastry Cream (page 36). You'll come up with something.

On top we put fruit. Whatever is in season: just raspberries, a mix of red fruits, cherries, mangoes, or apricots—it's all good!

You can also prepare this pie some time in advance and put it together at the very last moment before serving. This recipe is so versatile, you can use it for any occasion. It's the perfect dessert to top off an elaborate dinner, for instance.

FOR 8 mini tarts, 4 small tarts, or 1 large pie
PREP 20 min.
INACTIVE 30 min.
BAKE 30 min.

10½ oz (300 g) puff pastry (page 256), right out of the fridge, or 7 or 8 sheets of frozen puff pastry, defrosted
some all-purpose flour
half the Pistachio Cream recipe on page 44 (for 1 large pie, you need the full recipe)
about 7 ounces (200 g) raspberries (for 1 large pie I would indulge and use at least 14 ounces / 400 g)

Thoroughly grease the mini pie pans. Cut 8 small pieces out of parchment paper, a little wider than the pans.

Roll out the cold puff pastry into a thin slab on a lightly flour-dusted work surface. The slab should be as thick as a single sheet of puff pastry. If you use store-bought puff pastry, stack the sheets and roll them out. Punch circles out of the pastry using the largest cookie cutter you have: I own a set of cutters ranging from small to large. You can also simply cut out large circles with a sharp knife. Fit them into the pans. Allow some overhang around the edges. Scrape together the dough scraps and roll them out again to line all of your pie pans. Prick a few holes in the bottom with a fork.

Refrigerate the pans for 30 minutes to allow them to really cool down again. Preheat the oven to 400°F (200°C).

Place the parchment-paper squares in the dough-lined pie pans. Fill them with baking beans and place all the pans on a baking sheet (for easy removal from the oven). Blind bake the crusts for 15 minutes (see page 25).

Remove the baking sheet from the oven and take out the beans by lifting up the parchment paper squares. Neatly trim the edges of the pie crusts with a serrated knife. Then bake the empty crusts for another 15 minutes, or until golden brown.

Let cool and remove them from their pans so they can cool off further on a rack. Fill them with the pistachio cream and garnish with the raspberries.

Sweet Goat Cheese
Almond Pie with Grapes

This recipe is enough for a small pie of 7 to 8 inches (18 to 20 cm) in diameter—preferably a deep tart pan with a removeable bottom. If you'd like to bake a larger one—say, in a 9½-inch (24-cm) pie plate—use a full recipe of the dough and double the filling amounts (you may have a bit of filling left over; if so, pour it into a buttered ramekin or custard cup and bake it alongside the pie for a snack). Bake the larger pie for about 50 minutes.

Also keep in mind the capacity of your pie pan: Is the pan deep? Double the recipe. Is it shallow? Halve the amounts. This recipe is pretty forgiving so you can afford to play around with the amounts. You can also omit the goat cheese for a completely lactose-free recipe. Although that savory counterpoint to the almond milk is exactly what I like so much about it. Feel free to replace the grapes with stone fruits or blackberries or something, no strict rules for making this pie.

SERVES 6
PREP 30 min.
BAKE 30 min.

gluten-free
lactose-free option

1 recipe rice flour shortcrust dough (page 253)

3 eggs

½ cup plus 2 tbsp (150 ml) unsweetened almond milk, homemade (see page 40) or store-bought

3 tbsp rice syrup or other sweetener

3 oz (80 g) fresh goat cheese, crumbled (optional)

2 tbsp coconut oil, melted

1 tsp vanilla extract

1 tsp white wine vinegar

1 generous handful of seedless grapes, halved (plus some extra for serving)

2 tbsp sliced almonds

Preheat the oven to 325°F (170°C). Grease a pie pan (or deep tart pan with a removable bottom) with spray, butter, or oil.

Make the shortcrust dough as described and fit it into the pie pan. Refrigerate while you prepare the filling.

Beat the eggs with the almond milk, rice syrup, goat cheese (if using), coconut oil, vanilla, and vinegar into a smooth, liquid batter and set aside.

Use a fork to prick a few holes in the bottom of the dough and then blind bake the pie crust for 10 minutes in the hot oven (see page 25).

Pour the batter into the crust and arrange the grapes on top, then sprinkle with some sliced almonds. Bake the pie until firm in the center, 30 minutes.

Allow the pie to cool to room temperature before removing it from the pan (if you're able) and cutting it. Garnish with some extra fresh grapes. After all, the eyes want something to feast on as well.

Rosemary Pear Pie

You can also make this divine pie using quinces. We loved that version, although quinces are more difficult to peel than pears. Therefore it's best to quarter them after peeling. Boil the wedges and slice them afterward. Depending on their shape and size, you may need four quinces because you'll throw out a considerable part with the peels.

SERVES 6
PREP 45 min.
BAKE 25 min.

lactose-free option
gluten-free
refined sugar–free

1 recipe almond shortcrust dough (page 253)
3 pears, peeled and halved, with the stem
3 cups (750 ml) nice white wine (or water)
¾ cup plus 1 tbsp (200 ml) good-quality honey (or less, if you prefer a less sweet pie)
3 sprigs fresh rosemary
grated zest of 1 lemon
3 eggs
crème fraîche, sour cream, or Stilton cheese, for serving (optional)

Begin by making the dough as described. Refrigerate it.

Core the pears using a sharp knife (or a melon ball scoop). Heat the wine with the pears, honey, rosemary, and lemon zest over medium heat. Bring to a boil and let simmer over low heat for 30 minutes.

Preheat the oven to 350°F (180°C).

Use a skimmer to scoop the pears from the syrup and let them cool on a plate, leaving the syrup in the pan to reduce some more. After reducing it, you should have about 1 cup (250 ml) of syrup left, but it doesn't matter if there's a little more than that.

Meanwhile, grease an 8½-by-11-inch (21.5-by-27.5-cm) tart pan with coconut oil (or butter) and press the dough into the pan, evenly dispersing it. Prick the bottom with a fork and neatly trim the edges of the dough. Line with a large sheet of parchment paper and fill with baking beans or dried beans. Blind bake the pie crust for 15 minutes. Then remove the parchment paper and the beans and bake for another 5 minutes. Allow the pie crust to cool a little.

Remove the syrup from the heat and strain it over a measuring cup. You need 1 cup (250 ml). Slice the pears up to just below their stem (so they stay together) and carefully arrange them in a fan shape in the prebaked pie crust. Beat the eggs in a bowl and pour in ¾ cup plus 1 tbsp (200 ml) of the cooled pear syrup. Pour the egg–pear syrup mixture over the pear-covered pie and place the pie back into the hot oven for 25 minutes. If you feel the edges are getting too dark, cover them with aluminum foil.

Briefly allow the pie to cool and serve it with some crème fraîche, sour cream, or some crumbled Stilton cheese, if you'd like.

Red Currant Meringue Pie

Red Currant Meringue Pie

SERVES 10
PREP 35 min.
INACTIVE 30 to 60 min.
BAKE 40 to 45 min.

FOR THE DOUGH
7 tbsp (100 g) cold butter
1½ cups plus 2 tbsp (200 g)
    all-purpose flour
pinch of sea salt
1 egg, beaten
ice water, as needed

FOR THE FILLING
¾ cup (150 g) fine sugar
4 egg whites
pinch of sea salt
10½ oz (300 g) fresh red
    currants, stemmed
7 tablespoons (50 g) almond
    flour
1 tbsp sliced almonds

Make the dough: Rub the butter into the flour until the mixture has the appearance of coarse crumbs. Add the salt and egg and swiftly work into a cohesive dough. If it's a bit too dry, add a drop of ice water. Wrap in plastic and set aside in the fridge for 30 minutes to 1 hour.

Preheat the oven to 400°F (200°C). Roll the dough into a slab large enough to fit an 8½-inch (22-cm) pie pan (a springform pan would be even better).

Place the dough in the pie pan. Pierce some holes into the bottom with a fork. Cover with a sheet of parchment paper and fill up the pan with dried beans or special blind-baking beans. Whichever you have at hand.

Blind bake the crust for 10 minutes (see page 25), then remove the paper and the beans and bake for another 10 minutes. Allow to cool.

Make the filling: In the meantime, bring the sugar and ⅓ cup (70 ml) water to a boil in a saucepan and continue boiling for, say, 6 minutes, until you have a clear syrup. (If you have a sugar thermometer, the temperature should be 250°F / 121°C.)

In a spic-and-span bowl using a perfectly clean hand mixer, whisk the egg whites with the salt until stiff. While whisking, add the hot sugar syrup in a thin stream. Continue beating until the froth has become tough and stiff and has cooled down to room temperature.

Lower the oven temperature to 350°F (180°C). Divide the currants into two portions. Mix the first half with the almond flour and fold in about three generous spoonfuls of the egg white mixture. Stir into a smooth mixture and fill the pie crust with it.

Put the pie back into the oven for another 15 minutes, allowing the filling to cook. Remove from the oven and put the pie on a rack.

Now spoon the other half of the red currants into the rest of the egg white mixture. Spread over the pie and sprinkle with the sliced almonds. Put the pie back into the oven for 7½ minutes. Remove when the meringue is golden.

Patissier

Aix-en-Provence, France

Pear & Caramel Pies with Walnuts

FOR 4 pies
INACTIVE 5 hours
PREP 20 min.
BAKE 25 min.

1 (14-ounce/396-g) can
sweetened condensed
milk
5½ oz (160 g) puff pastry
(see page 256), or 4
individual sheets store-
bought frozen puff pastry,
defrosted
2 ripe pears, halved
lengthwise
a couple tbsp milk
12 to 15 walnuts, coarsely
chopped
½ cup plus 2 tbsp (150 ml)
crème fraîche, for serving

Place the unopened can of condensed milk in a large pan filled
with ample water. Cover with a lid and boil gently for 3 hours,
making sure the can stays submerged in water at all times. If you
don't, the can may explode—I kid you not! If needed, pour in
some extra water now and then.

Afterward, allow the can to cool off completely.

By now the milk inside the can will have transformed into a thick
caramel. I usually cook 3 or 4 cans simultaneously. Unopened,
they will keep for quite a long time so they'll be ready for use if
you suddenly need them.

Preheat the oven to 400°F (200°C). Line a baking sheet with
parchment paper.

Roll out the puff pastry, cut it into four equal portions and—if
you enjoy this as much as I do—cut these into the contour of a
pear. You don't have to, by the way—you can also make squares.

Place the 4 sheets of puff pastry on the prepared baking sheet.

Spoon 2 generous tablespoons' worth of caramel on top of each
pastry sheet. Remove the hard parts from the pears and slice
them up until the stem. Carefully place the pear halves on the
caramel. Heat the rest of the caramel with a few tablespoons of
milk in a saucepan and stir with a whisk into a thick, smooth
sauce. Use a brush to glaze the pears with a layer of caramel and
sprinkle them with the chopped walnuts.

Bake the pastries to a golden brown crisp, 20 to 25 minutes.

Serve with a little jug of caramel and some crème fraîche on the side.

Buckwheat Blueberry Pies with Coriander

Instead of a large pie, you could make four miniature 3- to 4-inch (8- to 10-cm) pies; reduce the baking time to about 25 minutes.

FOR 1 large pie
PREP 30 min.
INACTIVE 1 hour
BAKE 40 min.

wheat-free

FOR THE DOUGH

2 cups plus 2 tbsp (250 g)
    light spelt flour, plus
    some extra for dusting
7 tbsp (50 g) light buckwheat
    flour
½ tsp ground coriander
pinch of salt
2 tbsp honey
¾ cup (1½ sticks / 175 g)
    cold butter or coconut oil,
    cubed
4 to 5 tbsp (60 to 75 ml) ice
    water

FOR THE FILLING

24 oz (680 g) blueberries
about 6 leaves fresh basil
    torn
¼ cup (60 ml) honey
1 tbsp cornstarch
1 tbsp ground coriander
pinch of salt

AND

1 egg, beaten

Make the dough: Stir together both the flours, the coriander, and the salt, then drizzle in the honey and swiftly cut in the butter or coconut oil until the mixture resembles coarse meal. Sprinkle in ice water and quickly gather the mass into a ball. Shape the ball into a flattened disc, wrap it in plastic wrap, and refrigerate for at least 1 hour.

Make the filling: Put all ingredients for the jam filling (so not the egg!) in a heavy saucepan. Slowly bring to a boil while stirring continuously. Cook until the berries start to burst and the filling is thick and jamlike, 5 to 7 minutes. Turn off the heat and allow the jam to cool.

Preheat the oven to 350°F (180°C). Grease a 9½-inch (24-cm) pie plate.

Dust your work surface with some spelt flour and roll out the dough. Cut out a circle a little larger than the pie pan and press it into the pan, allowing some overhang around the edges. Scrape together the dough scraps so you'll have enough for the top crust later on. Line the dough with parchment paper and fill with baking beans or dry beans. Blind bake the crusts for 10 minutes (for more information on blind baking, see page 25). Then remove the parchment paper and the beans—be careful so the edges won't tear.

Fill the crust with the blueberry filling and roll out the remainder of the dough. Punch a few holes in the top with a cookie cutter. This way the hot air will be able to escape during baking, resulting in a wonderfully crunchy crust.

Brush the edges of the filled pie crust with the beaten egg and set the top crusts over the filling. Thoroughly seal the edges by crimping with a fork. Brush the top with the remaining egg and bake the pie to a golden brown crisp, about 40 minutes. Keep an eye on the pie. Larger pies take a little longer, smaller ones a little shorter.

VLAAi

Open-Faced Pie

For a while after my family moved from Ireland to the Netherlands, I spoke Dutch with an English accent and a Limburg accent. The reason: My mother tongue is English but my parents hail from the southern Dutch province of Limburg. My personal blend of mellow southern Dutch and Irish English really stood out in North Holland (Amsterdam area), where people pride themselves on speaking Standard Dutch. Neighborhood kids sometimes teased me with my accent, calling me "Limburgian Vlaai."

That didn't bother me much, though, for I adored Limburg vlaai. On each family visit to the south, we were treated to one of these traditional open-faced pies. Crumble vlaai (greumelkesvlaai), cherry vlaai, rice vlaai . . . I had no preference, really, all of them are great. Or perhaps the one filled with gooseberries, or sjtaekbaere, as they like to call them in the town of Roermond.

A vlaai is the only open-faced pie I know that's made using yeast dough. This is what makes a vlaai so wonderfully light. Try it yourself.

And make sure to serve generous Limburg-style portions, instead of those uptight northern micro wedges!

Note that it's important to bake a vlaai in a special wide and shallow baking pan. If you don't have one, buy one. If you put too much filling on top, your crust stays soggy. You can also prevent this by making a smaller pie (or two).

Crumble Vlaai (*Greumelkesvlaai*)

FOR 1 large pie
PREP 50 min.
RISE 1 hour and 30 min.
BAKE 30 min.

1 recipe open-face pie (vlaai)
   dough (page 254)

FOR THE PASTRY CUSTARD FILLING

2½ cups (600 ml) milk
¼ cup (50 g) sugar, or to
   taste
1 vanilla bean, sliced open
   and seeds scraped out
6 egg yolks
2 tbsp cornstarch or all-
   purpose flour
2 tbsp butter

FOR THE CRUMBLE CRUST TOP

generous ½ cup (125 g)
   packed light brown sugar
9 tbsp (125 g) butter
1¼ cups (150 g) all-purpose
   flour
pinch of salt

AND ALSO

confectioners' sugar

First make the dough as described. While it is rising, make the filling and the crumble crust top.

Make the pastry custard filling: Heat the milk with half of the sugar and the vanilla bean pod and seeds in a saucepan. Bring to a near boil, then let it steep for 15 minutes over low heat.

Beat the egg yolks with the rest of the sugar in a bowl until frothy, add the cornstarch (or flour), and stir into a smooth batter.

Strain the hot milk and pour it into the batter while stirring continuously. Pour this mixture back into the saucepan and keep stirring until has a nice consistency, then stir in the butter.

Transfer the custard to a wide bowl and place a layer of plastic wrap directly against the surface of the custard (to prevent a skin from forming). Allow the custard to cool. Once the custard has cooled off, spoon it into a pastry bag so it'll be ready for use. Store in the fridge.

Make the crumble crust top: Combine all the ingredients in a bowl using a hand mixer, or pulse into coarse crumbs with a food processor. Cover and refrigerate until ready to use; the butter should remain hard.

Roll out the dough into a slab of about the size of your pie pan (about 12 inches / 30 cm in diameter). Grease an 11- to 12-inch (28- to 30-cm) pan with some butter and press in the dough. Neatly trim the edges and use a fork to prick the bottom several times. Now allow the dough to rise for another 30 minutes underneath a dish towel.

Preheat the oven to 350°F (180°C).

Fill the crust with the custard and sprinkle the top evenly with the crumb, making sure it's completely covered. Bake the pie for 25 to 30 minutes. Rotate the pie halfway through the baking time to ensure even browning. The pie is ready as soon as the crust starts to come away from the sides of the pan. Allow it to completely cool so the custard can set.

Dust with some confectioners' sugar and serve, sliced into large wedges, with a cup of coffee.

Apricot Vlaai

In the Netherlands, you can buy nifty cookie cutter grates for cutting a perfect crosshatch pattern in one motion. But don't stress if you can't find one. Weaving a lattice top yourself is just as good. I often use the smallest cookie cutter I have to make a nice pattern of holes. An apple corer is great for doing this as well.

FOR 1 large pie
PREP about 1 hour
RISE 1 hour and 30 min.
BAKE 25 min.

1½ recipes open-face pie
   (vlaai) dough (page 254)
   (you need the extra ½
   because this pie has a
   dough "rooftop")

FOR THE FILLING
¼ cup (30 g) cornstarch
6 tbsp (80 g) sugar
3 star anise
26 oz (750 g) fresh apricots,
   halved and pitted
   (cherries work really well
   too!)
½ tsp cinnamon
pinch of salt

OPTIONAL
1 small handful bread
   crumbs if the filling is
   too wet

AND ALSO
1 egg, beaten
2 to 3 tbsp coarse sugar

First make the dough as described. Divide it into two portions: one of two-thirds and one of one-third. Allow to rise.

Meanwhile, make the filling: In a small saucepan, dissolve the cornstarch in ¾ cup plus 1 tbsp (200 ml) cold water and add the sugar, star anise, and apricots. Bring to a boil and stir with a ladle until the sugar has dissolved and the fruits have softened a little. Season with the cinnamon and salt. Let the mixture steep for 10 minutes over low heat, then turn off the heat, allowing the filling to completely cool off.

Grease an 11- to 12-inch (28- to 30-cm) pie pan with some butter. Roll the larger portion of the dough into a round slab the size of the pie pan and press the dough slab into the pan. Neatly trim the edges and use a fork to prick some holes into the bottom. Cover the dough with a dish towel and allow it to rise for another 30 minutes.

Preheat the oven to 350°F (180°C).

If needed, dust the crust with some bread crumbs. I do this when the fruits are too juicy (cherries have this tendency). Usually it isn't necessary, but it's still a useful trick. Remove the star anise from the filling and pour it into the dough-lined pie pan. Set aside.

Roll the other one-third of the dough into a circle about ⅜ inch (1 cm) wider than the rim of the pie pan. Cut out a nice pattern of holes using a small cookie cutter or an apple corer. (You can also easily cut the dough into strips and weave a lattice top.)

Carefully roll up the dough in about three turns, then swiftly lay it on top of the pie. This shouldn't be too difficult, as this elastic dough is very forgiving. Brush the dough with the egg and sprinkle with the coarse sugar.

Bake the pie for 20 to 30 minutes. Rotate the pie halfway through to make sure it will brown evenly.

Your pie is ready as soon as you can easily loosen the crust from the pan. Before cutting it, first allow the pie to fully cool off on a rack.

Gooseberry Vlaai with Meringue
(Sjtaekbaerevlaai mit sjoem)

Gooseberries have a sweet and sour flavor so the meringue top works as a nice counterpoint. Goose-berries may very well be my favorite fruit. Or did I already bestow this honor on rhubarb . . . which, by the way, also works really well in this pie? If you decide to use rhubarb instead of gooseberries, you may need to put in a little extra sugar.

FOR 1 large pie
PREP 1 hour
RISE 1 hour
BAKE about 40 min.

1 recipe open-face pie (vlaai)
    dough (page 254)

FOR THE FILLING
2 to 4 tbsp cornstarch
¾ cup plus 1 tbsp (200 ml)
    organic, unfiltered pear
    (or apple) juice
26 oz (750 g) gooseberries,
    topped and tailed
about 2 tbsp sugar, or to
    taste
very finely grated zest of ½
    lemon
¼ cup (60 ml) elderflower
    syrup

FOR THE MERINGUE
3 egg whites
pinch of salt
½ cup (100 g) superfine
    sugar

First make the dough as described.

While the dough is rising, make the filling: Dissolve the cornstarch in the pear juice, stirring until there are no more lumps. Put the gooseberries in a saucepan and pour in the thickened pear juice. Add the sugar, lemon zest, and elderflower syrup and stir until the compote is softly boiling. Cook for 10 minutes over low heat, until the berries begin to burst. The compote should thicken consider-ably. By the time the pie has cooled off completely, you should be able to slice it. If in doubt about the consistency, you can add a few drops of cornstarch dissolved in pear juice or water.

Grease a 12-inch (30-cm) pie plate with some butter. Roll out the dough to a slab the size of your pie pan and press the dough into the pan. Neatly trim the edges and prick some holes in the bottom with a fork. Cover the dough with a dish towel and let it rise for another 30 minutes. Meanwhile, preheat the oven to 350°F (180°C).

Pour the filling into the pan and bake the pie for about 20 to 25 minutes, until the dough is almost set.

Meanwhile, make the meringue: In a perfectly clean bowl using a perfectly clean whisk, beat the egg whites and salt until stiff. Gradually pour in the sugar, only adding more after the previ-ous dash has been fully absorbed. Beat the egg whites into a silky, smooth, firm froth, then—if you have one—transfer the meringue to a pastry bag. Set aside in the fridge until ready to use.

Remove the pie from the oven and reduce the oven temperature to 325°F (160°C). Pipe or spoon the meringue on top of the pie.

Put the pie back into the oven, a little below the center, and bake for another 15 to 20 minutes, allowing the meringue to brown nicely. You can also brown the meringue with a crème brûlée torch. Let cool completely before serving.

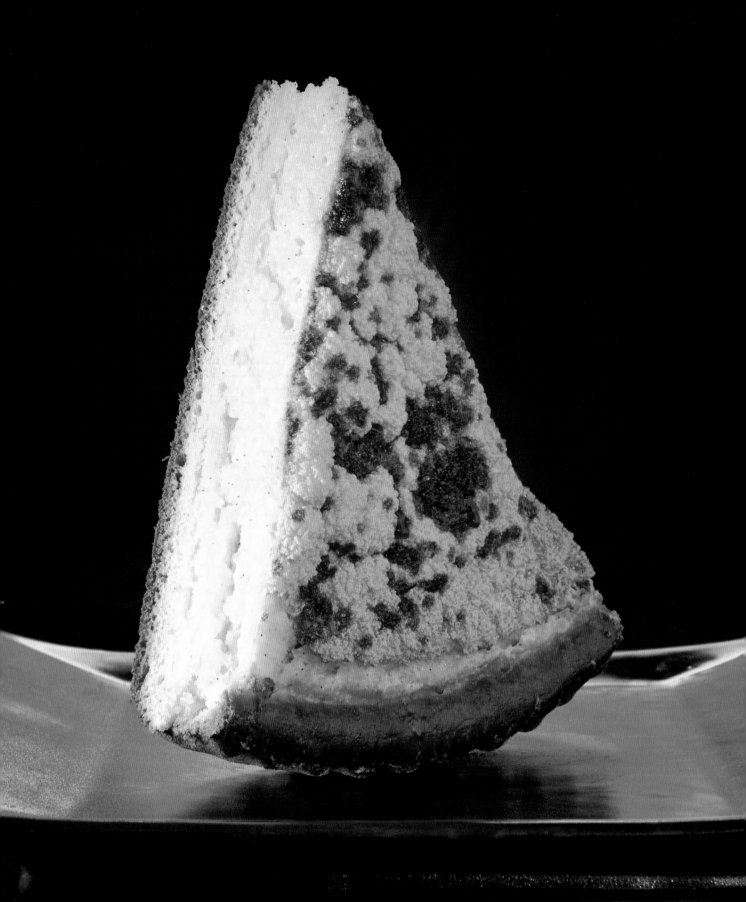

Cardamom Rice Vlaai

FOR 1 large pie
PREP 1 hour
RISE 1 hour
BAKE 25 min.

1 recipe open-face pie (vlaai)
    dough (page 254)

FOR THE FILLING
4¼ cups (1 L) whole milk
1 vanilla bean, sliced open
    and seeds scraped out
5 to 6 tbsp (about 75 g)
    packed light brown sugar,
    or to taste (you can
    also use fine granulated
    sugar)
4 cardamom pods, slightly
    crushed
1 cup (200 g) sticky white
    rice (uncooked)
salt
2 eggs, separated

AND ALSO
butter, for the pie pan
1 tbsp packed dark brown
    sugar, for sprinkling
confectioners' sugar and a
    small strainer, for dusting

First make the dough as described.

While the dough is rising, make the filling: In a heavy saucepan, bring the milk, vanilla bean pod and seeds, brown sugar, and cardamom to a boil. Add the rice and a dash of salt and again bring to a boil. Then immediately turn the heat to its lowest position: Rice pudding burns really easily. Cover with a lid and cook the rice for about 12 minutes. Frequently stir the rice with a wooden spoon or rubber spatula. Be sure to scrape off any rice sticking to the sides of the pan.

Remove the pan from the heat and take out the vanilla bean pod and cardamom pods.

In a perfectly clean bowl using a perfectly clean whisk, beat the egg whites and a pinch of salt until stiff. In another bowl, beat the egg yolks until frothy. Stir the yolks into the lukewarm rice pudding. Carefully fold in half the beaten egg whites. Set the rest aside.

Grease an 11- to 12-inch (28- to 30-cm) pie pan with some butter. Roll out the dough into a circle the size of your pie pan and press the dough into the pan. Neatly trim the edges and prick some holes in the bottom with a fork. Cover the dough with a dish towel and let it rise for another 30 minutes.

Preheat the oven to 355°F (180°C).

Spoon the rice pudding into the pie pan and smooth it with the back of a spoon. Evenly spread the remaining beaten egg whites on top, creating a smooth layer that covers the entire pie. Sprinkle with the 1 tbsp brown sugar.

Bake the pie in the middle of the oven for about 30 minutes, until golden brown. The filling really should be sufficiently cooked by then. If it isn't done yet but the top has already browned, place a sheet of parchment paper or aluminum foil on top of the pie and give it another couple of minutes in the hot oven. Dust with confectioners' sugar before serving.

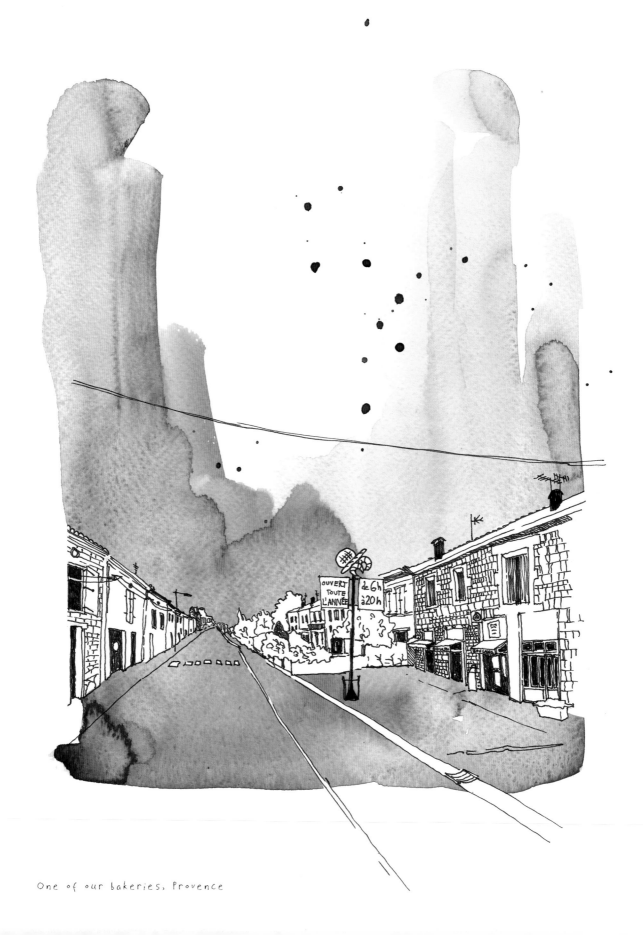

One of our bakeries, Provence

Provence, France

Pork, Chestnut & Cranberry Pie

SERVES 6 to 8
PREP 1 hour
BAKE 1 hour and 30 min.

FOR THE DOUGH
1 recipe open-face (vlaai)
  dough (page 254)
1 tbsp olive oil

FOR THE FILLING
1 tbsp olive oil
small lump of butter
1 onion, minced
about 1 pound (500 g)
  ground pork
about 1 pound (500 g)
  sausage meat
grated zest of 1 lemon
scant 1 cup (100 g) white
  bread crumbs
⅔ cup (100 g) cooked
  chestnuts (canned
  or vacuum-sealed),
  chopped
2 tsp fresh thyme leaves, or
  1 tsp dried thyme leaves
6 fresh sage leaves, finely
  chopped
scant 1 cup (100 g) fresh or
  frozen cranberries
salt & freshly ground black
  pepper
1 egg, beaten

First, make the dough as described.

Preheat the oven to 350°F (180°C). Grease an 8-inch (20-cm pie) pan with the olive oil and line it with parchment paper; leave a bit of paper sticking out above the rim of the pan. Lightly grease the parchment paper as well.

Make the filling: Heat the oil with the lump of butter in a skillet. Add the onion and sauté until tender and translucent. Allow to cool somewhat.

Put the pork and sausage meat in a bowl, add the lemon zest, bread crumbs, chestnuts, sautéed onions, thyme, sage, and cranberries and season with salt and pepper.

Roll out two-thirds of the dough into a disc of about 12 inches (30 cm) in diameter. Use it to line the pie pan so that the edge of the dough is sticking out above the rim. Fill with the meat mixture and thoroughly press down, making sure there are no pockets of air. Roll out the rest of the dough into a slab large enough to completely cover the pie's top. Use an apple corer or a small cookie cutter to make small holes in the top crust. Cover the pie with it. Wet the edges with a brush and some water and seal them securely. If you have a knack for it, you can shape the fold into a decorative fluted pattern, making your pie look even more stylish. Trim the edges and brush the dough with the egg.

Bake the pie for 30 minutes, then turn down the oven temperature to 325°F (160°C) and bake the pie for another 1 hour. Allow it to fully cool and serve with some homemade chutney on the side.

PASTY FILLING ALTERNATIVES

Chicken Pot Pie

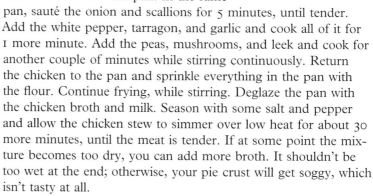

SERVES at least 4
PREP 45 min.
BAKE 45 min.

sugar-free

1 recipe savory pasty dough
(page 254)

FOR THE FILLING
2 tbsp olive oil, plus some
extra for the pan
meat from 1 sizable organic
chicken, bones and
skin removed and meat
chopped into small
chunks (about 1¾ lbs /
800 g or more)
1 onion, minced
3 scallions, finely chopped
1 tsp ground white pepper,
plus more as needed
3 tbsp fresh tarragon, finely
chopped
1 clove garlic, pressed
through a garlic press
2¼ cups (300 g) frozen
green peas
scant 3 cups (200 g)
mushrooms, sliced
1 leek, finely sliced
3 tbsp all-purpose flour
about ½ cup (125 ml)
chicken broth, or a little
more
½ cup (125 ml) milk
coarse sea salt & freshly
ground black pepper
1 egg, beaten

First make the dough
as described.

Heat the olive oil in a
skillet and fry the pieces
of chicken until light brown
all around. Use a spatula to
remove them from the pan. In the same
pan, sauté the onion and scallions for 5 minutes, until tender.
Add the white pepper, tarragon, and garlic and cook all of it for
1 more minute. Add the peas, mushrooms, and leek and cook for
another couple of minutes while stirring continuously. Return
the chicken to the pan and sprinkle everything in the pan with
the flour. Continue frying, while stirring. Deglaze the pan with
the chicken broth and milk. Season with some salt and pepper
and allow the chicken stew to simmer over low heat for about 30
more minutes, until the meat is tender. If at some point the mixture becomes too dry, you can add more broth. It shouldn't be
too wet at the end; otherwise, your pie crust will get soggy, which
isn't tasty at all.

Preheat the oven to 350°F (180°C). Grease an 8-inch (20-cm) pie
pan or springform pan with some olive oil (or soft butter). Roll
out two-thirds of the dough into a round slab 11 to 12 inches (28
to 30 cm) in diameter. Line the pan with the dough so that part of
it will be hanging over the edge. Fill the pie with the chicken stew.
Roll the rest of the dough into a round that will snugly fit over the
pie. Punch some holes in the top crust with an apple corer or a
cookie cutter and cover the filling. Use a brush and some water to
wet the edges of the dough and then squeeze them together, forming a decorative—crimped—fold along the edge of your pie. (Do
this with your thumb and index finger or use a fork.)

Brush the top crust with the egg and bake the pie until golden
brown, 45 minutes.

Delicious as a main course with green salad on the side.

A Very Simple Rabbit Pâté in Shortcrust Dough

You may not use all of the dough called for in this recipe, but using two rabbits instead would be a bit much. Store whatever you have leftover from your dough in the freezer or use it to create elaborate decorations on your pasty's top crust. That always looks great.

SERVES 8
PREP 15 min.
BAKE at least 1 hour

sugar-free

1 recipe short crust dough
    (page 252)

meat of 1 whole rabbit
½ cup (50 g) bread crumbs,
    made from stale bread
3½ tbsp (50 ml) cognac
7 tbsp (100 ml) crème
    fraîche
3 eggs
½ cup plus 2 tbsp (75 g)
    shelled pistachios
1 tbsp whole pink
    peppercorns
pinch of nutmeg, to taste
generous amount of salt
    (about 1 tbsp)
freshly ground black pepper
oil or soft butter, for the pan

Ask your butcher if he can debone the rabbit, but you can also do it yourself. You need about 1½ lbs / 750 g) of meat. Chop the larger parts (the thigh, for instance) into smaller pieces and set those aside (about 9 oz / 250 g).

Mince the rest of the rabbit meat in a food processor. Spoon it into a bowl and add the larger rabbit chunks, the bread crumbs, cognac, crème fraîche, two of the eggs, the pistachios, and peppercorns. Thoroughly combine and season with some nutmeg and a generous dash of salt and black pepper.

Preheat the oven to 325°F (160°C).

Grease an 8-inch (20-cm) pie pan or springform pan with some oil or soft butter. Roll out two-thirds of the dough into a disc of 11 to 12 inches (28 to 30 cm) in diameter. Use it to line the pie pan so that the edge of the dough is sticking out above the rim. Fill up the pan with the rabbit mixture. Roll out the rest of the dough into a slab large enough to completely cover the pie's top. Use an apple corer or a small cookie cutter to make a couple of small holes in the top crust. Cover the pie with it. Use a brush and some water to wet the edges of the dough and then squeeze them together, forming a decorative fold along the edge of your pie. (Do this with your thumb and index finger or use a fork.) Beat the remaining egg and brush the top with it. Bake the pie to a golden-brown crisp, just over 1 hour. If the top still looks a little pale, you can turn up the oven to 350°F (180°C) for the last 10 minutes.

Refrigerate the pasty for at least 1 day before cutting it. That way, the flavors have time to fully settle in.

You can serve slices of this pasty as an appetizer or a lunch dish. Serve with horseradish sauce (see Note) and a small watercress salad.

NOTE: For the horseradish sauce, mix 1 to 2 tbsp horseradish with ½ cup (125 ml) sour cream. Season with salt, pepper, and a few drops of lemon juice and some lemon zest.

Fig, Apricot, Stilton, and Goat Cheese Tart

When my friend Maggie came to visit me in Amsterdam from Boston, we organized a picnic and BBQ in the park for her. At home I baked this pie to bring along. All of us were so enthusiastic about it that I decided to include the recipe in this book. It's sweet and savory at the same time. Perfect, really.

SERVES 6 to 8
PREP 20 min.
INACTIVE 20 min.
BAKE 30 min.

sugar-free

FOR THE DOUGH
1 recipe shortcrust dough
   (page 252) made with
   1 additional egg yolk

FOR THE FILLING
¾ cup plus 1 tbsp (200 ml)
   heavy cream
3 eggs
sea salt & freshly ground
   black pepper
2 apricots, sliced into about
   6 wedges
2 figs, sliced into about
   6 wedges
2½ oz (75 g) soft goat
   cheese
2½ oz (75 g) Stilton cheese
3 or 4 sprigs fresh rosemary,
   coarsely chopped

Preheat the oven to 350°F (180°C). Grease an 8-inch (20-cm) square pan—preferably a tart pan with a removable bottom.

Make the dough as described, adding the additional egg yolk to the dough for a little extra firmness. Roll out the dough into a slab that fits your pie pan and fit in the dough. Neatly trim the edges. Prick the bottom a couple of times with a fork. Refrigerate the dough for about 20 minutes, allowing it to stiffen up nicely. Then blind bake it for 15 minutes (see page 25).

Meanwhile, make the filling: Beat the cream with the eggs and season with salt and pepper. Be careful not to use too much salt—the cheese is salty as well.

Pour the mixture into the prebaked pie crust. Arrange the apricots and figs on top. Crumble the goat cheese and the Stilton and sprinkle them between the fruit wedges. Sprinkle everything with the rosemary and grind some extra pepper over the filling.

Bake the pie for about 30 minutes.

Goat Cheese Soufflé

Just around the beginning of spring, I was staying in Provence all by myself to write. Well, not that I was that alone. I know a lot of people in the small French village I was staying in, so I was being invited to come on more than a few trips to local olive oil producers, bakers, or, in one instance, to visit the best butcher in the region (a one-hour drive). The high point of these excursions was a drive up into the mountains where a distant cousin of my neighbor and friend Norbert runs a goat farm. We entered the semi-open stables to the sight of hundreds of goats of all colors and sizes. We petted them, they nibbled on my coat. We witnessed the birth of a furry brown specimen and I wondered: Can things get any more springlike than this?

In the adjacent farmhouse, we bought fresh cheeses straight from the farmer, and later that night I used the very, very fresh cheese, as well as hazelnuts sourced from the same mountains, to bake this pie. But don't worry—you can buy the ingredients in the supermarket. Just as delicious.

SERVES 6
PREP 25 min.
INACTIVE 1 hour
BAKE 40 min.

sugar-free

FOR THE DOUGH
1¼ cups (150 g) all-purpose flour
¾ cup (75 g) hazelnut meal
9 tbsp (125 g) cold butter, cubed, plus more for greasing
1 egg yolk
some ice water

FOR THE FILLING
2 egg yolks
4½ oz (125 g) fresh goat cheese
1¾ oz (50 g) Parmesan cheese, grated
½ cup (125 ml) crème fraîche
salt and freshly ground black pepper
3 egg whites

Make the dough: Swiftly work all the ingredients into a cohesive dough ball. Wrap in plastic and toss in the fridge to rest for 1 hour.

Grease an 8½- to 9-inch (22- to 24-cm) pie pan. Roll out the dough ball into a thin slab about the size of the pan. Press it in and tidily trim the edges. Prick holes in the bottom using a fork and refrigerate the pie for 20 minutes.

Preheat the oven to 350°F (180°C).

Blind bake the crust for 15 minutes (see page 25).

While the pie crust is baking, make the filling: Thoroughly combine the egg yolks, goat cheese, Parmesan, and crème fraîche in a stand mixer. Season with some salt and ample black pepper.

In a spic-and-span bowl using a spic-and-span whisk, beat the egg whites and a pinch of salt until stiff. Start out by carefully folding a small spoonful of egg white in with the goat cheese mixture and then add the rest (in Dutch, this is called "making family," an expression I really like). Fold with care to keep as much air inside as possible. For the same reason, pour the mixture in from very low above the blind-baked crust. Bake the pie for another 25 minutes.

Allow your pie to rest for a while before cutting it—it will slightly deflate, but that's normal. Serve with salad greens and green asparagus.

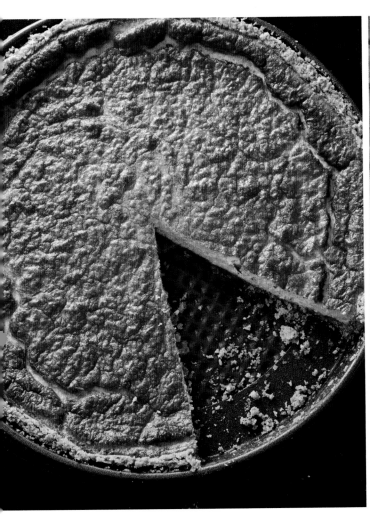

Melted Cheese Pizza

This is a funny recipe, because unlike Italian pizza dough, it requires an egg, causing it to stay softer after you bake it. Please do experiment with different fillings—once you've gotten the hang of it, you can top this pizza with anything. I really love lemon, peppers, and sage. No doubt you'll have your own favorite combination. Perfect as a side dish for when you're serving drinks or as part of a buffet.

SERVES 8
PREP 15 min.
RISE 2 hours and 30 min.
BAKE 15 min.

sugar-free

7 tbsp (100 ml) lukewarm water
2½ tsp (11 g) instant yeast
2 cups (250 g) all-purpose flour, plus extra for dusting
1 tsp sea salt
1 egg, beaten
2 balls mozzarella (not buffalo mozzarella; it's too wet), coarsely grated (14 oz / 400 g)
grated zest of 1 lemon
several sprigs fresh sage (or flat-leaf parsley), chopped
½ red chile pepper, minced (you can remove the seeds, if you like)
sea salt & freshly ground black pepper
1 tbsp olive oil, plus extra for greasing

Pour some of the lukewarm water into a bowl and add the yeast. Leave for about 7 minutes until all of the yeast has dissolved and it starts to foam a little.

Combine the flour and salt in a bowl. Make an indentation in the middle and pour in the egg. Then add the dissolved yeast and maybe also the remaining lukewarm water. Check whether this is necessary (the dough should be pliable and non-sticky). Knead the dough until smooth.

Remove the dough from the bowl and continue kneading on the countertop for about 10 more minutes. Put the dough in a bowl that has been lightly greased with olive oil and cover with plastic wrap. Set aside in a warm spot to rise for 1 hour and 30 min. Press down on the risen dough with your fist to force out the air, then cover and let rise for another hour.

Preheat the oven to 475°F (250°C), or as hot as possible.

On a flour-dusted work surface, press out the dough ball into a large, flat round (a pizza!). Transfer to a large flour-dusted baking sheet.

In a bowl, combine the mozzarella, lemon zest, sage, and red pepper. Generously season with salt and black pepper. With clean hands, shape the cheese mixture into a ball and place it at the center of the dough round.

Gather the edges of the dough, fold them around the filling, and crimp them so they form a rosette. You've now basically made a pizza bag holding a cheese ball inside. Make sure all edges of the rosette have been securely joined together. Then flatten the dough by carefully pressing down on the rosette in a circular motion. Keep doing so until you've got a flat, cheese-filled pizza of, say, 9½ inches (25 cm) in diameter lying in front of you.

Use a knife to make star-shaped slits on top, deep enough to reach the cheese filling. Brush the top with the olive oil.

Slide the pizza into the oven and bake until golden brown and done, 12 to 15 minutes. Cut into slices and serve with drinks.

Beef and Guinness Hand Pies

Because this recipe is about a stew hidden inside bite-size pasties, I won't give you a pie recipe containing precise amounts for the filling. Instead, I'll give you a recipe for the actual four-person stew. Because if you're going make a stew, why not cook a whole lot at once? If you decide not to make individual smaller pies, you could also pour your hot stew into a bowl and cover it with about seven sheets (7½ oz / 210 g) of puff pastry to form a top crust. Make a hole in the dough to let out the steam. Bake until done, about 30 minutes, or until the stew starts to bubble and the crust has turned nicely golden brown. Serve with mashed potatoes and a green salad.

Set a little bit of the stew aside and then make these small pies for a picnic, for when watching a game of soccer, or just for when you suddenly crave a delicious snack. Instant bliss.

FOR 10 small pies; serves 4 to 6 as main course
PREP 30 min.
INACTIVE 2 hours and 30 min.
BAKE 25 min.

sugar-free

FOR THE STEW
(for the individual pies, you need 10 tbsp of this stew)

3½ tbsp (50 g) butter, plus some extra as needed
5 onions, chopped
2 cloves garlic, minced
2¼ lbs (1 kg) marbled beef stew meat, chopped
sea salt & freshly ground black pepper
2 tbsp flour
about 4 sprigs fresh thyme
3 bay leaves
1 large carrot, cubed
½ head celeriac, cubed
2 parsnips, cubed
1 (1-pint / 500-ml) can Guinness

4 cups (1 L) good beef broth (I use fond or I make it myself)
1 bunch fresh flat-leaf parsley, finely chopped
1 to 2 tbsp Worcestershire sauce

FOR THE INDIVIDUAL MINI PIES
12 oz (340 g) puff pastry (page 256), or 10 sheets store-bought frozen puff pastry, thawed
1 egg, beaten

Make the stew: Melt the butter in a large cast-iron pan. Add the onions and fry them over medium heat for 12 to 15 minutes, until light brown, while stirring them frequently. Add the garlic, cook for another minute or so, then remove everything from the pan and put it on a plate for the time being. Meanwhile, generously sprinkle the beef with salt, pepper, and flour and sear it on all sides over high heat (you can do this in two batches). If needed, add more butter to the pan. When the beef has nicely browned, spoon the onions and garlic back in. Add the thyme, bay leaves, and all the vegetables, making sure to thoroughly stir everything. Season with salt and pepper.

Pour in the Guinness. While stirring, bring to a boil and use your wooden spoon to scrape loose any ingredients sticking to the pan's bottom. Now pour in the broth and bring back to a boil. Turn down the heat, cover with a lid, and let the stew simmer for 2 hours and 30 minutes, until the beef has become tender.

If at this point the stew is still too wet, remove the lid and allow the liquid to reduce over high heat until the sauce has reached the right thickness (about as thick as porridge).

Taste and then enhance the flavor a little by adding some Worcestershire sauce. The stew can be prepared a day in advance.

(Stew always tastes better on the second day, but perhaps you don't have the time for that.)

Preheat the oven to 400°F (200°C).

Roll out the dough into a large slab and use your biggest cookie cutter (say, 4¾ inches / 12 cm) to cut out 10 discs. If you don't have enough dough, scrape together the scraps and roll them out again.

Scoop 1 tbsp of the cooled filling into the center of each pie disc and fold one half on top of the other, crimping the edges with a fork. Work fast so the puff pastry doesn't get too warm, or immediately refrigerate the finished pies until ready to bake.

Place the pies on a baking sheet, slightly separated, and brush them with some egg. Bake to a golden brown crisp, 25 minutes.

Eat them right away or, if you want to keep some for later, stick them in the freezer straight out of the oven.

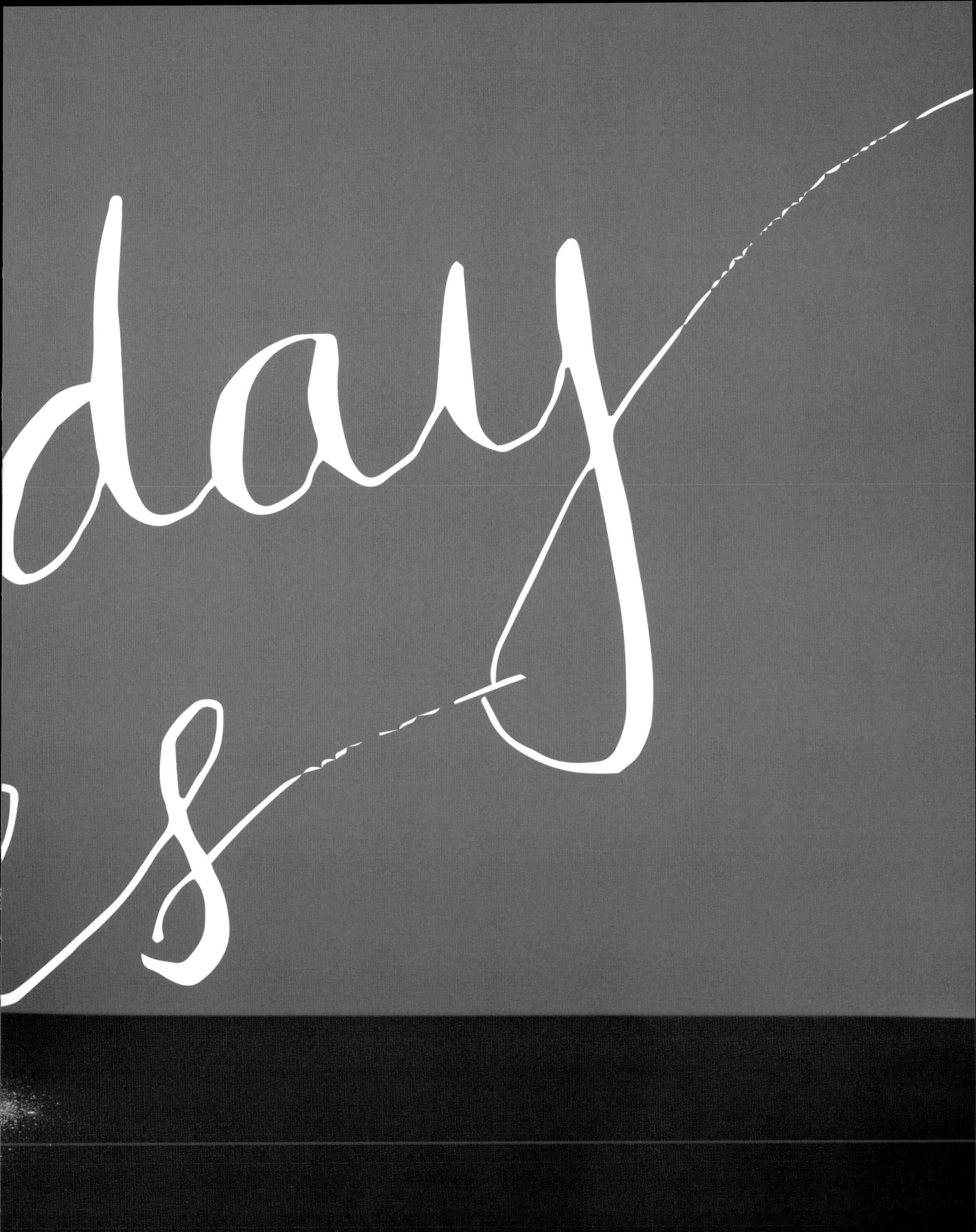
day

Marble Cake with Blackberries & Basil

SERVES 10
PREP 1 hour
BAKE 40 min.

FOR THE CAKE

9 tbsp (125 g) butter, at room temperature, plus extra for greasing the pan
½ cup plus 2 tbsp (125 g) fine sugar or packed light brown sugar
finely grated zest of ½ lemon
2 egg whites
2 whole eggs
1¾ cups (225 g) all-purpose flour
1 tsp baking powder
pinch of salt
½ cup (125 ml) milk
2 heaped tbsp plus ½ jar blackberry basil jam (see the recipe from my book *Home Made*, or use store-bought blackberry or blueberry)

ADDITIONALLY

1 recipe flavored buttercream (page 34), made with 1 large sprig basil
5 oz (150 g) blackberries
a few nice basil leaves, for garnish

Make the cake: Preheat the oven to 325°F (170°C). Grease a 9-inch (23-cm) round baking pan. Line the bottom with a sheet of parchment paper cut to fit. Grease the parchment paper, too.

With a hand mixer, whisk the butter, sugar, and lemon zest in a bowl until airy. First beat in the egg whites one by one and then the whole eggs. Use a spatula to scrape and collect any dough that climbs up the edges of the bowl.

In a separate bowl, mix the flour with the baking powder and salt.

In alternating batches, whisk the flour mixture and the milk into the butter mixture to form a smooth batter.

Pour a ladle of the batter into a small bowl and the rest of the batter into the prepared baking pan. Stir 2 tablespoons of the jam into the batter in the small bowl, until it's all purple. Pour that over the batter in the pan and stir briefly with a knife or the back of a spoon, until it looks marbled.

Bake the cake for 40 minutes, or until a skewer inserted into the middle comes out clean.

Let cool for 5 minutes, then remove from the pan and allow the cake to cool off completely on a rack.

Make the buttercream as described, using basil as the flavoring.

Split the cake in half horizontally to make two layers. Spread buttercream on one half and the rest of the blackberry jam on the other half. Place them on top of each other, with the buttercream and the jam facing each other, sandwiched between the layers.

Spread the rest of the buttercream over the cake and garnish with blackberries and basil leaves.

Super-Duper Choco Cake
with Beets and Hazelnut Filling

This cake consists of two layers, so you'll need to make two cakes. If you don't have two equal-size baking pans, you'll need to bake the two cakes separately.

SERVES 12
PREP about 1 hour
INACTIVE 2 to 3 hours
BAKE 40 min.

FOR THE CAKES
¾ cup plus 3 tbsp (75 g) unsweetened cocoa powder
2¼ cups (300 g) all-purpose flour
2 tsp (10 g) baking powder
pinch of salt
1 cup plus 2 tbsp (250 g) packed light brown sugar
3 tbsp vanilla sugar (see page 32)
9 oz (250 g) cooked beets, peeled and chopped
6 large eggs
1½ cups plus 2 tbsp (400 ml) sunflower oil

FOR THE FILLING AND GANACHE
⅔ cup (100 g) hazelnuts
7 oz (200 g) good-quality dark chocolate
1 heaping tbsp butter
½ cup plus 2 tbsp (150 ml) heavy cream
7 oz (200 g) mascarpone
3 tbsp Cointreau, plus extra for drizzling

ADDITIONALLY
figs or other pretty fruit, for garnish

Preheat the oven to 325°F (170°C). Position a rack in the middle of the oven. Grease two 8½-inch (22-cm) baking pans and line the bottoms with a sheet of parchment paper cut to fit. Grease the parchment paper, too.

Sift the cocoa powder, flour, baking powder, and salt over a bowl and stir in the brown sugar and vanilla sugar. Puree the beets in a blender until smooth. Spoon that into a large bowl. Whisk the eggs in with the beets using a hand mixer and then add the oil. Fold in with the flour mixture. Divide the batter evenly between the two prepared pans.

Bake for 35 to 40 minutes, or until a bamboo skewer inserted into the middle comes out clean.

Allow the cakes to cool for 5 minutes in the pans and then remove from the pans. Let the cakes cool completely on racks.

In the meantime, make the filling and ganache: Increase the oven temperature to 350°F (180°C). Spread the hazelnuts on a rimmed baking sheet and toast in the oven for 8 to 10 minutes. Let them cool for 5 minutes, then grind them in a food processor to a fine flour. Chop 3½ oz (100 g) of the chocolate into small chunks, put it in a bowl, and add the butter. Bring the cream to just under a boil. Pour the warm cream over the chocolate and butter in the bowl. Stir until the chocolate and butter have melted and the mixture is smooth. Cover the ganache so that it doesn't cool off too much. You'll need a fluid ganache that's easy to pour over the cake.

Chop the rest of the chocolate with a sharp knife and put it in another bowl. Add the ground hazelnuts, mascarpone, and Cointreau and stir to combine.

Drizzle some Cointreau over the cake layers and spread the filling over one layer. Stack the second layer on top. Pour the warm ganache over it.

Garnish with pretty fruit and let the ganache set a bit before you serve it.

Meringue Almond Roll with Lemon Curd Cream Filling

SERVES 8 to 10   **PREP** 30 min.   **BAKE** 20 min.   *gluten-free*

FOR THE ALMOND ROLL
4 egg whites (reserve the yolks)
⅔ cup (150 g) superfine sugar
1 tsp cornstarch
1 tsp white wine vinegar
1 tsp vanilla extract
⅔ cup (75 g) almond flour
½ cup (50 g) sliced almonds

FOR THE FILLING
¾ cup plus 1 tbsp (200 ml) mascarpone
a few spoonfuls of heavy cream
½ cup (150 ml) lemon curd (page 30), made with the remaining egg yolks (plus one)
confectioners' sugar, for garnish

Preheat the oven to 325°F (170°C). Line a baking sheet with parchment paper.

Make the almond roll: In a perfectly clean bowl using a perfectly clean whisk, whisk the egg whites until stiff. Add the sugar spoon by spoon, thoroughly whisking after each addition before adding the next spoonful.

With a spatula, carefully fold in the cornstarch, vinegar, and vanilla and finally fold in the almond flour. Spread the meringue mixture evenly over the prepared baking sheet. Sprinkle with the sliced almonds.

Bake the meringue for 20 minutes. It should be a pale light brown color and feel bouncy. Take it out of the oven and let cool on the baking sheet on a rack.

Make the filling: With a whisk, beat the mascarpone with a few spoonfuls of cream. Fold in the lemon curd.

Spread out a clean dish towel over your work surface and carefully place the meringue on top, the almond side facing down. Peel off the parchment paper.

Spread the lemon curd cream mixture all over it and very carefully roll up the meringue, from a short side, using the dish towel to help you roll. It's okay if the meringue cracks a little.

Place on a pretty plate and dust lavishly with confectioners' sugar.

Chocolate, Espresso, and Dark Beer Cake with Chocolate-Hazelnut Frosting

SERVES 12

PREP 45 min.

BAKE 1 hour

FOR THE CAKE

4½ oz (125 g) dark chocolate, chopped

⅞ cup (1¾ sticks / 200 g) butter, at room temperature, plus extra for greasing the pan

¾ cup (150 g) sugar

3 eggs, separated

7 tbsp (100 ml) dark beer, such as Leffe Brune or Guinness

⅓ cup (75 ml) strong brewed espresso, slightly cooled

2 cups plus 2 tbsp (275 g) all-purpose flour

1 tbsp baking powder

pinch of salt

FOR THE FROSTING

1¾ cups plus 2 tbsp (400 g) cream cheese (I use Mon Chou)

1 cup (300 g) homemade Nutella (page 46) or organic chocolate-hazelnut paste

1 shot very strong brewed espresso, slightly cooled

2 tbsp nut liqueur like Frangelico or amaretto

TO GARNISH (OPTIONAL)

unsweetened cocoa powder

mocha beans or camel milk chocolate pebbles like these (see photo) that I brought with me from a trip to Dubai

Make the cake: Preheat the oven to 350°F (175°C). Grease a 9-inch (23-cm) round cake pan. Line the bottom with a sheet of parchment paper cut to fit. Grease the parchment paper as well.

Melt the chocolate *au bain marie* and turn off the heat as soon as the water boils. The chocolate will melt anyway.

Whisk the butter with the sugar in a bowl until airy and pale yellow. One by one, add the egg yolks and beat until each yolk has been completely incorporated before adding the next. With a whisk, stir in the lukewarm chocolate and then the beer and coffee. Whisk until the batter is uniformly brown. Sift the flour with the baking powder in batches over the batter and fold it in.

In a squeaky-clean bowl using a squeaky-clean whisk, whisk the egg whites with the salt until stiff.

Fold one-third of the whipped egg whites into the chocolate batter and continue until all the egg white has been folded in and the mixture is nicely foamy.

Pour the batter into the prepared pan and bake for about 1 hour, or until a bamboo skewer inserted into the middle comes out clean.

Let cool for 5 minutes in the pan, then remove from the pan and let cool completely on a rack.

Make the frosting: Whisk together all the ingredients until fluffy.

Using a long serrated knife, carefully split the cake horizontally into thirds to make three layers. Spread one-third of the frosting over the bottom layer, top with the second layer, spread with another third of the frosting, then top with the third layer and spread the remaining frosting over the top. Dust with cocoa powder or garnish with mocha beans or chocolate pebbles, if you wish. Then serve.

Persimmon Cake

FOR 8 slices
PREP 45 min.
BAKE 30 min.
INACTIVE 4 hours

wheat-free
refined sugar–free

FOR THE CAKE
3 Asian persimmons
juice of ½ lemon
3½ tbsp (50 ml) agave syrup
1 (⅜-inch / 1-cm) piece fresh
    ginger, peeled and finely
    grated, or ½ tsp ground
    ginger
2½ cups (250 g) light spelt
    flour
2 tsp baking powder
pinch of salt

FOR THE BAVAROIS
2 envelopes unflavored
    gelatin powder
¾ cup plus 1 tbsp (200 ml)
    heavy cream
3½ tbsp (50 ml) agave syrup
2 tsp vanilla extract
2 Asian persimmons
juice of ½ lemon
7 tbsp (100 ml) plain yogurt

TO GARNISH
1 persimmon, cut into thin
    slices
2 tbsp apricot jam
edible flowers (such as
    thyme; optional)

Make the cake: Preheat the oven to 350°F (175°C). Grease a 9-inch (23-cm) springform pan and line it with a sheet of parchment paper cut to fit. Grease the parchment paper, too.

In a food processor or blender, puree the persimmons with the lemon juice, agave syrup, and ginger until completely smooth. Transfer the persimmon puree to a bowl. Sift the flour, baking powder, and salt into a separate bowl then fold it into the persimmon puree. Pour the batter into the prepared pan and bake the cake for about 30 minutes, until a bamboo skewer inserted into the middle comes out clean. Let the cake cool, but don't remove the pan.

Make the bavarois: Put ¼ cup (60 ml) cold water in a small saucepan and sprinkle the gelatin over it; let soak for 5 minutes.

Whip the cream with the agave syrup and vanilla until stiff.

Puree the persimmons and lemon juice in a food processor or blender until completely smooth. Transfer to a bowl and stir in the yogurt.

Put the saucepan with the gelatin over low heat and stir until the gelatin has dissolved. Remove from the heat and let cool a little. Stir in 2 tablespoons of the yogurt-persimmon mixture and then stir this at once into the bulk of the yogurt-persimmon mixture. Fold in the whipped cream and pour the bavarois over the cooled persimmon cake. Let the cake set for at least 4 hours in the fridge.

Remove from the baking pan by placing a clean linen towel or paper towel over the surface, inverting the cake onto your palm and lifting off the pan, then swiftly placing the cake upright on a cake platter.

Garnish the cake with thin persimmon slices. Heat the apricot jam in a small saucepan until liquid and then push it through a sieve to make a thin glaze. Brush the apricot glaze over the persimmon slices and garnish with edible flowers.

Almond Crunch

There is no decent way to eat this pastry. But it's so screamingly delicious that no one at the table will notice.

SERVES 4 to 6
PREP 20 min.
BAKE 6 to 7 min.

FOR THE ALMOND FILLING
7 tbsp (100 g) salted butter, at room temperature
½ cup (100 g) granulated sugar
¾ cup plus 2 tbsp (100 g) almond flour or freshly ground blanched almonds
2 tbsp Frangelico, amaretto, brandy, or coffee liqueur
¾ cup plus 1 tbsp (200 ml) crème fraîche

ADDITIONAL
7 tbsp (100 g) butter, for brushing
about 5 sheets of phyllo dough (8½ by 9½ inch / 22 by 25 cm)
granulated sugar, for sprinkling
½ cup (50 g) sliced almonds, briefly toasted in a skillet
confectioners' sugar, for dusting

Make the almond filling: Combine the butter with the sugar and almond flour into a paste. Beat in the liqueur and crème fraîche until you have a nice, light filling. Scoop it into a pastry bag, if you have one. Refrigerate until ready to use.

Preheat the oven to 350°F (180°C). Line a baking sheet with parchment paper. Cut another sheet of parchment paper of the same size and keep a second baking sheet at hand.

Melt the butter. Cut the sheets of phyllo dough into small rectangles. Keep them under a lightly moist cloth, but work fast.

Brush each phyllo sheet with melted butter, then sprinkle with some granulated sugar. The sugar will melt in the oven and that will make the sheets stick together.

Place the sheets stacked two on top of each other on the prepared baking sheet. Cover with the parchment paper and place the second baking sheet on top. (This way, the phyllo dough sheets will remain flat.) Bake for 6 to 7 minutes, until golden brown. Continue until all dough has been baked. Allow the phyllo to cool.

Spread some filling over a sheet of phyllo dough, or pipe it with the pastry bag. Sprinkle it with almonds, reserving some for garnish. Cover with another sheet of phyllo and top with some filling. Cover with a third sheet, garnish with almonds, and dust with confectioners' sugar.

Serve immediately. With spoons.

Matcha Tea Roll
with Lime, Ricotta & Pineberries

This cake is not difficult to make but looks super sophisticated and Parisian. Matcha tea is an expensive green tea available in specialty tea stores. You can replace it with cocoa or leave it out and add some extra vanilla extract. You can also replace those crazy white pineberries with regular strawberries, or with raspberries.

SERVES 8
PREP 1 hour
BAKE 14 min.
INACTIVE about 3 hours

FOR THE FILLING
1 envelope unflavored gelatin
    powder
2 cups (500 g) ricotta
¾ cup plus 2 tbsp (150 g)
    cream cheese, at room
    temperature
½ cup plus 2 tbsp (125 g)
    fine sugar, or to taste
zest and juice of 2 limes
    (about 6 tbsp / 90 ml)

FOR THE CAKE
1 cup (100 g) cake flour
1 tsp matcha tea powder
1 tsp baking powder
5 eggs, separated
¾ cup plus 2 tbsp (180 g)
    fine sugar
¼ cup (60 ml) milk
pinch of salt
9 oz (250 g) pineberries,
    hulled

Make the filling: Put ¼ cup (60 ml) cold water in a small saucepan and sprinkle the gelatin over it; let soak for 5 minutes. With a mixer, beat the ricotta with the cream cheese, sugar, and lime zest into a smooth, thick cream.

Add the lime juice to the softened gelatin and place over low heat, stirring until the gelatin is dissolved. Let cool, then stir the lime-gelatin mixture into the ricotta cream. Scoop the filling into a pastry bag, if you have one. Let solidify in the fridge until ready to use.

Make the cake: Preheat the oven to 350°F (180°C). Grease a 12-by-16-inch (30-by-40-cm) rimmed baking sheet, line it with parchment paper, and grease the parchment paper.

Combine the flour, matcha, and baking powder in a bowl. In another bowl, beat the egg yolks with the sugar and milk into a thick, pale yellow foam. In a third, spic-and-span bowl using clean beaters, whisk the egg whites and salt until stiff. With a spatula, fold the flour mixture in batches into the egg yolk and fold into a smooth batter. Then gently fold in the whipped egg whites, also in batches. Pour the batter into the prepared baking sheet and bake for about 14 minutes, until the roll springs back when you gently press it.

Remove from the oven and run a sharp knife between the cake and the pan to loosen it from the edges. Turn the cake out onto a clean dish towel. Carefully peel off the parchment paper and roll up the cake with the dish towel, as if the towel were the filling. Allow the cake to cool off completely like this.

Gently unroll the cake and remove the dish towel. Spread a thick layer of the filling (keep some aside) over the entire cake, leaving 1¼ inches (3 cm) unfilled on one short end. Arrange nearly all the pineberries over the filling. Keep a few pretty ones for garnish. Carefully roll up the cake from the filled short end, ending with the unfilled short end. Place on a plate with the seam facing down and let the cake set in the fridge for at least 2 hours before serving. Just before serving, pipe a few dollops of the ricotta cream filling on top and press in the remaining pineberries.

Verbena Cake
with Fresh Fruit & Verbena Gin Syrup

FOR a small cake for 6
PREP 50 min.
BAKE 30 min.

FOR THE CAKE
4 eggs, at room temperature
generous ½ cup (120 g)
    packed light brown sugar
pinch of salt
6 tbsp (75 g) sifted all-
    purpose flour
3 tbsp (25 g) cornstarch
2 tbsp loose verbena tea,
    finely ground in a mortar

FOR ON TOP AND IN BETWEEN
2 cups (500 ml) strong
    brewed verbena tea,
    room temperature
2 cups (400 g) granulated
    sugar
2 tbsp white balsamic
    vinegar
¼ cup (60 ml) gin
2 tbsp confectioners' sugar
1 vanilla bean, sliced open
    and seeds scraped out
¾ cup plus 1 tbsp (200 g)
    mascarpone
7 tbsp (100 ml) heavy cream
10½ oz (300 g) red fruit:
    raspberries, strawberries,
    currants, blueberries,
    pomegranate seeds,
    apricots, et cetera
some fresh verbena and/or
    mint leaves

Make the cake: Preheat the oven to 350°F (175°C). Grease an 8½-inch (22-cm) round cake pan. (Or, do as I do and grease two small (6-inch / 15-cm) round cake pans.) Line the bottom with parchment paper cut to fit. Grease the parchment paper, too.

In a perfectly clean bowl using a hand mixer with clean beaters, beat the eggs with the brown sugar and salt until very stiff, until it's almost white and has increased nearly threefold in volume. This takes a while, so be patient.

Sift the flour, cornstarch, and ground verbena tea in small batches over the airy batter and fold it in very carefully. Make sure to keep as much air as possible in the batter.

Pour the batter very carefully into the prepared pan (or pans). Place the cake directly in the middle of the oven and bake for 30 minutes, until light brown. If baking the two smaller cakes, bake for slightly less time, about 25 minutes. Do NOT open the oven door in between. If you can press the cake with your finger without it springing back, it needs another couple of minutes.

Let the cake cool in the pan for a bit, then remove it from the pan and let cool completely on a rack. They will sag a little, but that's okay.

Meanwhile, boil down the brewed verbena tea with the sugar for 20 minutes until it's a syrup (it should reduce to about half its original volume). Pour the syrup into a bottle, let cool, and pour in the vinegar and the gin.

If you make one cake, you can halve it horizontally with a large bread knife to make two layers. Place the cake layers on a rack on top of a plate or tray, cut side up. Pour half of the syrup on top. Let the syrup soak into the cake layers.

With a whisk, stir the confectioners' sugar and vanilla bean seeds into the mascarpone and cream, and spread generously over the bottom cake layer. Top with some of the nice fruit and drizzle some verbena syrup on top. Set the second layer on top and spread some cream over that as well. Decorate with the rest of the fruit. Drizzle some syrup over the fruit.

Serve immediately, garnished with verbena and/or mint leaves.

Walnut Cake with Grilled Fruit and Orange Brandy Cream

SERVES about 12
PREP 1 hour and 30 min.
BAKE 35 min.

FOR THE CAKE
2 recipes Chocolate Genoise
   (page 150; each recipe
   makes one cake), with
   ¾ cup (70 g) finely
   ground walnuts added to
   the flour per cake

FOR THE ORANGE BRANDY CREAM
1 cup (250 ml) heavy cream
1 cup (250 ml) mascarpone
zest of ½ orange
3 tbsp brandy
1 tsp cinnamon
½ tsp ground ginger
2 tbsp confectioners' sugar

FOR THE SYRUP
1 jar apricot jam or
   marmalade
3 to 4 tbsp brandy

ADDITIONALLY
6 apricots, chopped
1 mango, peeled and pitted
5 oz (150 g) Cape
   gooseberries, halved
some edible flowers (I used
   borage)

Make the cakes according to the recipe. Let them cool completely and split them in half horizontally to make two layers each.

Make the orange brandy cream: Whip the cream until nearly stiff, then add the mascarpone, orange zest, brandy, cinnamon, ginger, and confectioners' sugar and whip into a stiff cream. Transfer the cream to a handy pastry bag, if you have one, or keep in a container, and refrigerate until ready to use.

Make the syrup: Heat the apricot jam in a small saucepan until liquid and press it gently through a strainer. Stir in the brandy and set aside.

Grill the apricots and mango pieces on a hot grill pan and let cool.

Place a cake half cut side up on your work space. Generously spread the orange brandy cream over the top of the layer. Drizzle with some syrup and arrange some of the fruit on top. Repeat with the next two layers. Keep some fruit and cream to decorate the very top of the cake.

Place the last cake layer on top. Pipe or spoon on some orange brandy cream and decorate with the rest of the fruit. Drizzle some syrup over it for a shiny effect and garnish with edible flowers.

Serve almost immediately.

Angel Food Cake with
Saffron Meringue Icing & Lemon Curd

SERVES about 10
PREP 45 min.
BAKE 35 min.
INACTIVE 3 hours

FOR THE CAKE

10 egg whites (yolks reserved)
1 tsp baking powder
pinch of salt
1½ cups plus 6 tbsp (425 g) superfine sugar
1 tbsp vanilla sugar (see page 32)
1 tbsp vinegar
1½ cups (175 g) all-purpose flour

ADDITIONALLY

1 jar (about 1½ cups / 350 ml) lemon curd (page 30), made with the leftover egg yolks
1 recipe meringue icing (page 34), with 4 to 5 tbsp (60 to 80 ml) colored water from 1 tsp saffron
2 or 3 passion fruits

Make the cake: Preheat the oven to 350°F (175°C). Very lightly butter a 9- to 10-inch (24- to 26-cm) nonstick angel food baking pan. This pan resembles a smooth Bundt pan; the hole in the middle ensures an even heating of the cake.

In a perfectly clean bowl using a perfectly clean whisk, whip the egg whites until airy. Add the baking powder and salt and continue whipping until the egg whites are nearly stiff. While whisking, add 1½ cups (300 g) of the superfine sugar, the vanilla sugar, and the vinegar in small batches.

Sift the flour with the remaining 6 tbsp (125 g) superfine sugar over the bowl and combine with a spatula. Be very careful—the egg white should stay foamy, so use a spatula and not a whisk. Pour the batter into the pan. Bake the cake for about 35 minutes, until golden brown. !!!Don't open the door while baking!!! When the cake is done, a bamboo skewer inserted into the middle should come out clean.

Let the cake rest in the pan on a rack for 10 minutes. Then invert the cake over the rack and wait until it slides out of the pan. This can take a while, so be patient. Use a sharp knife to cut loose the edges, if you want to give it a hand. Let the cake cool completely and once it's cool, wrap it in plastic wrap until you're ready to decorate.

While the cake is baking, make a lemon curd according to the recipe on page 30, using the leftover egg yolks. Let solidify for at least 3 hours in the fridge.

Make the meringue icing according to the recipe and set everything out on your work surface.

Split the cake horizontally into two or three layers; whatever you dare. Place a cake layer cut side up on your work surface. Spread the lemon curd over the layer. (Place the next layer on top and repeat, if you have three layers.) Place the final layer on top, then cover the entire cake with the saffron meringue icing. Scoop out the pearl-shaped seeds from the passion fruits and loosen the pulp in a bowl until pourable. Pour over the cake and serve immediately.

pâ

Banoffee *Tompouce*

A tompouce *is a common Dutch pastry, a variation on the mille-feuille or Napoleon, as it's known in other cuisines.*

SERVES 6 to 8
INACTIVE 3 hours
PREP 20 min.
BAKE 30 min.

1 (13½-ounce / 397-g) can sweetened condensed milk
12 oz (350 g) homemade puff pastry (page 256), or 8 sheets store-bought puff pastry, thawed
some flour, for dusting
¾ cup plus 1 tbsp (200 ml) heavy cream
6 tbsp (100 g) mascarpone
2 tbsp confectioners' sugar, plus some extra
4 bananas
some white chocolate, for grating (optional)

Place the unopened can of condensed milk in a large pan and cover with water. Boil gently, unopened, for 3 hours. Make sure the can stays submerged, adding more water if necessary. It might explode otherwise—really! But that won't happen to you, since you'll pay attention.

Let the can cool completely before opening. The milk in the can has now transformed into a thick caramel. Set aside until ready to use.

Preheat the oven to 400°F (200°C).

If using store-bought pastry, remove the protective pieces of paper between the dough sheets and stack the sheets on top of one another. Roll out the puff pastry on a flour-dusted counter into a large 9-by-14-inch (24-by-36-cm) rectangle.

Place the pastry on a baking sheet lined with greased parchment paper and, with the blunt side of a knife, score rectangles in the size of a Napoleon (don't cut all the way through). Make two rows of 6 to 8 pieces. Prick the dough with a fork to prevent puffing. I lay another greased parchment sheet and another baking sheet on top of the pastry sheets so they stay flat. Because of the pressure of the baking sheet, the air moves around more evenly so the pastry rises better and more consistently. This improves the taste and makes it crispier!

Bake the puff pastry for 25 minutes, until golden brown and crispy. Let cool on a rack. With a fine bread knife, carefully cut the scored rectangles.

Meanwhile, whip the cream and stir in the mascarpone. Sweeten the cream with the confectioners' sugar and transfer to a pastry bag fitted with a wide tip.

Spread the puff pastry sheets generously with the caramel. Peel the bananas and slice them lengthwise. Arrange the slices over the caramel. Pipe mascarpone cream on top and cover with the puff pastry roofs.

Sprinkle generously with confectioners' sugar and, if you wish, some grated white chocolate.

Cannelés

These small cakes, from Bordeaux in the south of France,
are one of my favorite pastries. I write "cakes" because cannelés look like
that's what they are, but they're actually baked custard.

They are baked in thick-walled, ideally copper, baking molds in a hot oven,
which makes for a crust that turns a solid dark brown—but not quite burned!
The cake will be crunchy when you take a bite, and the filling barely set.

The filling is delicious and creamy, originally made with quality rum,
but you can use any flavoring. The custard is made with vanilla, or star anise,
or tonka beans, or cardamom. Experiment away—that's what makes baking fun.

Traditionally, the molds are greased with a mixture of beeswax and butter,
which gives the cannelés their distinctive sheen, but if you don't have this lying
around, you can make them without the beeswax. (If you do decide to try it,
you can buy food-grade beeswax in natural foods stores.)

Cannelés

FOR 12 cannelés
PREP 30 min.
INACTIVE 24 hours
BAKE 45 min.

2 cups (500 ml) milk
1 vanilla bean, sliced open
    and seeds scraped out
3½ tbsp (50 g) butter, plus
    extra for greasing
2¼ cups (250 g) sugar
1 cup (125 g) all-purpose
    flour
3 egg yolks
1 egg
3½ tbsp (50 ml) rum
    (optional)

In a saucepan, bring the milk, vanilla bean pod and seeds, and butter to a near boil. Let steep over very low heat, possibly with a flame-tamer underneath, for about 30 minutes.

In a bowl, combine the sugar with the flour.

Pour the hot milk through a strainer into the flour-sugar mixture and whisk until all the lumps are gone. Add the egg yolks, whole egg, and rum, if using, and whisk well until you have a thin, smooth batter. Pour it into a measuring cup or jug (this makes for easier pouring tomorrow and fits into your fridge more easily). Let stand for 24 hours in the refrigerator. Really do this—otherwise, you can forget about your *cannelés*.

Preheat the oven to 425°F (220°C). Grease 12 *cannelé* molds with some melted butter. I don't have those fancy copper molds (they are, in fact, better), but stainless steel works very well. Rachel Khoo bakes them in a muffin tin, so that works too. Personally, I'm not a fan of silicone molds, as the *cannelés* don't brown well. Pour the batter until ⅛ inch (5 mm) from the top. Place the molds far apart on a baking sheet, to allow the hot air to circulate everywhere.

Bake the *cannelés* for 45 minutes, until dark brown. Check them after about 30 minutes—how fast the baking goes depends very much on the material of the molds. If the tops turn black, cover with aluminum foil. Remove from the oven. Using oven mitts, turn the *cannelés* out onto a rack immediately, or you'll never get them out of the molds. Let cool.

Guinness & Choco Jars

FOR 6 small jars
PREP 1 hour
INACTIVE 2 hours
BAKE 30 min.

4 egg yolks
scant 1 cup (200 g) plus
    3 tbsp packed light brown
    sugar
1¼ cups (300 ml) Guinness
    (stout)
1¼ cups plus 7 tbsp
    (400 ml) heavy cream
3½ oz (100 g) good-quality
    dark chocolate (about
    72% cacao), chopped

Preheat the oven to 300°F (150°C).

In a bowl, beat the egg yolks with the scant 1 cup (200 g) brown sugar until foamy. Beat for quite a while, so that the mixture contains lots of air and is nicely pale colored and mildly stiff.

Measure the Guinness and wait until the foam has sagged, so that you can be certain you have enough beer. In a heavy saucepan, bring 7 tbsp (100 ml) of the beer and 1¼ cups (300 ml) of the cream to a near boil. Turn off the heat immediately and add the chocolate. Let it stand for 5 minutes so the chocolate melts. Stir until smooth. While whisking, add the beer-chocolate mixture to the egg yolks in the other bowl and whisk into a smooth custard.

Pour the custard into six small ovenproof jars to ⅜ inch (1 cm) from the top and place them in a baking pan. Place the pan in the oven and pour hot water into the dish to come halfway up the sides of the jars. Bake the puddings for 30 minutes. Test by sticking in a knife—if it comes out clean, they are ready. Take them out of the water bath and let cool on the counter. Cover and place in the fridge to set for at least 2 hours.

Meanwhile, boil down the rest of the Guinness with the 3 tablespoons brown sugar into a syrup. This takes about 20 minutes— you'll only need 2 tablespoons of syrup, so let it thicken nicely. Let cool until ready to use.

Before serving, whip the remaining 7 tbsp (100 ml) cream until it just about sticks to a wooden spoon. Pour the cream over the pudding jars and drizzle some Guinness syrup on top. Serve immediately.

Crème Brûlée with Lemongrass

This dessert has long been on the menu in my old restaurant, Aan de Amstel in Amsterdam. The fresh, lightly scented lemongrass is the kicker. It's an adiictively delicious dessert.

SERVES 4
PREP 20 min.
BAKE 1 hour and 15 min.
COOL 2 to 3 hours

gluten-free

butter, for greasing
1 cup (250 ml) milk
1 vanilla bean, sliced open
    and seeds scraped out
finely grated zest of 1 lemon
2 lemongrass stalks, bruised
    and finely chopped
5 egg yolks
¾ cup (150 g) sugar
1 cup (250 ml) heavy cream

Preheat the oven to 260°F (125°C). Grease four small ramekins with some butter and place them inside a large oven dish or roasting pan.

Bring the milk to just under a boil and add the vanilla bean pod and seeds, lemon zest, and lemongrass. Let steep for 15 minutes over very low heat. Strain the milk into a jug.

Beat the egg yolks with half the sugar. Whisk in the cream and then the hot milk. Divide the batter evenly among the prepared ramekins. Pour boiling water into the oven dish to halfway up the sides of the ramekins. Place the pan in the oven and bake for 1 hour 15 min.

Let the custards cool to room temperature on the counter, then cover and refrigerate to cool completely.

Before serving, turn the broiler to high. Sprinkle the crèmes with the rest of the sugar and caramelize under the broiler.

Of course you can use a real crème brûlée torch, if you have one! That actually works better. Though for years I used a paint burner, you know, with one of those little propane gas tanks attached. Only last year did my mother give me one of those professional torches.

Works just a tad more precisely. I'm just saying.

Croquembouche with
Cardamom Orange Filling & Salty Caramel

FOR about 20 choux pastry balls
PREP 1 hour and 45 min.
BAKE 25 min.

FOR THE CHOUX
PASTRY BALLS
7 tbsp (100 g) butter
2 tbsp (25 g) sugar
pinch of salt
1¼ cups (150 g) all-purpose
    flour
4 or 5 eggs
1 recipe Orange Pastry
    Cream (page 36)

FOR THE CARAMEL
2½ cups (500 g) sugar
1 tsp sea salt

Preheat the oven to 350°F (180°C). Line a baking sheet with parchment paper.

Make the choux pastry balls: Bring the butter, sugar, salt, and 1 cup (250 ml) water to a boil in a heavy saucepan. Add the flour all at once and stir with a wooden spoon until the dough comes away from the sides of the pan. Take the pan off the heat. Let cool while stirring occasionally.

With a wooden spoon, stir in all the eggs until you have a smooth batter that's thick but not fluid; depending on their size, you may need 4 or 5 eggs. The batter has the right consistency when it "tears" when you lift the spoon. You'll know what I mean once you try it.

Scoop the dough into a pastry bag and pipe little heaps on the prepared baking sheet. Use a wet finger to round the tips. Bake the balls for 25 minutes, until golden brown. Turn off the oven and let cool in the oven to prevent sagging.

Meanwhile, make the pastry cream according to the recipe and transfer to a pastry bag. Refrigerate until ready to use.

Put the *croquembouche* together right before you serve it. With a sharp little knife, make a small cut in the bottom of each pastry ball. Pipe in the cream until they are all filled.

Make the caramel: Melt the sugar with 7 tbsp (100 ml) water and the salt in a saucepan. Let the caramel simmer for 15 minutes, until it's tea colored. Don't stir, but do brush down the sides of the pan with a wet pastry brush to prevent the forming of sugar crystals. Place the bottom of the pan in a container of cold water to halt the cooking process.

Place a sheet of parchment paper on the counter. Dip the tops of the pastry balls one by one into the hot caramel and let them dry on the parchment paper, caramel side down. After about 20 minutes (try first) you can pull them off the paper and the pastry balls will have that recognizable flat, crusty layer.

Dip the bottoms in the caramel and stick them to a champagne bottle, until the entire bottle is covered. Tie a bow around it and place it on the table.

Mocha Crème Caramel

SERVES 4
PREP 20 min.
BAKE 30 min.
INACTIVE at least 2 hours

gluten-free

½ cup plus 2 tbsp (125 g)
    sugar
2 whole eggs
1 egg yolk
1⅓ cups (325 ml) whole milk
1 vanilla bean, sliced open
    and seeds scraped out
1 shot strong brewed
    espresso

Preheat the oven to 300°F (150°C). Place four ramekins in an oven dish or roasting pan.

In a saucepan, heat 6 tbsp (75 g) of the sugar with ⅓ cup (75 ml) water until the sugar has dissolved. Slowly bring to a boil and cook the caramel until it's amber colored. This takes about 10 minutes. Try not to stir, just gently shake the pan once in a while. Brush down the sides of the pan with a wet pastry brush to wash off any sugar crystals. After about 8 minutes, once the caramel is golden brown, take the pan off the heat and divide it among the ramekins. Watch out, as the caramel is very hot.

With a hand mixer, beat the whole eggs with the egg yolk and the rest of the sugar until the sugar has dissolved.

In a small saucepan, bring the milk and vanilla bean pod and seeds to a near boil, then stir in the espresso. Pour the hot milk over the egg mixture while stirring. Pour the mixture through a strainer and divide it among the ramekins. Pour boiling water into the oven dish to come halfway up the sides of the ramekins and place the pan in the oven. Bake for 30 minutes, until a thin knife inserted into one of the puddings comes out clean.

Remove the ramekins from the water bath (use oven mitts!) and let them cool, first on the counter, then in the fridge for at least 2 hours. Before serving, carefully run a knife around the edges of the pudding to loosen them from the ramekins. Place a plate over the ramekin and turn them upside down together, so the pudding ends up on the plate. Remove the ramekin; the fluid caramel will run over the pudding.

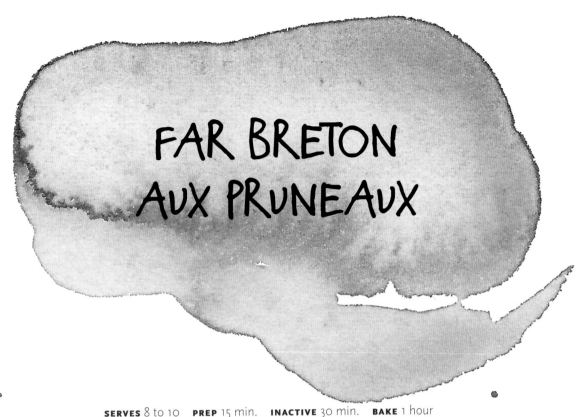

FAR BRETON AUX PRUNEAUX

SERVES 8 to 10   **PREP** 15 min.   **INACTIVE** 30 min.   **BAKE** 1 hour

7 tbsp (100 ml) good-quality rum
4 cups (17 oz / 500 g) prunes
butter, for greasing
2 cups (250 g) all-purpose flour
1 cup (200 g) sugar
pinch of salt
8 eggs
1 vanilla bean, sliced open and seeds scraped out
4¼ cups (1 L) whole milk

In a saucepan, heat the rum to a near boil, then turn
off the heat and add the prunes. Let steep for 30 minutes.

Preheat the oven to 400°F (200°C). Grease a 9-inch (24-cm) round baking pan and line
the bottom with a sheet of parchment paper cut to fit. Grease the parchment paper, too.

Combine the flour with the sugar and salt. Beat in the eggs, two at a time, and the vanilla
bean seeds until you have a nice thick, smooth batter. While whisking, pour in the milk.
Pour in the rum that hasn't been soaked up by the prunes and stir well.

Place the rum-soaked prunes on the bottom of the baking pan and pour the batter on top.

Depending on the height and the size of the baking pan, bake the cake for about 1 hour, or
until set. If you use a wider pan, the cake will be lower and you won't need to bake it as long.

Lemon Coconut Soufflés

SERVES 10
PREP 15 min.
BAKE 10 min.

½ cup plus 2 tbsp (125 g)
    fine sugar
¼ cup (½ stick / 60 g)
    butter, at room
    temperature, plus extra
    for greasing the ramekins
zest and juice of 2 lemons
2 eggs, separated
generous ½ cup (75 g) all-
    purpose flour
2½ cups (350 ml) milk
½ cup plus 2 tbsp (150 ml)
    coconut milk
2 tbsp grated unsweetened
    coconut

ADDITIONALLY
a small jug of heavy cream

Preheat the oven to 350°F (180°C). Set out a roasting pan on the counter and grease 10 ramekins with butter or baking spray. Check in advance whether they all fit in the roasting pan.

Whisk the sugar, butter, and lemon zest in a bowl until airy. Add the egg yolks and whisk until everything is well combined. Add, in dashes, the flour, milk, and coconut milk and whisk until you have a smooth batter. Whisk in the lemon juice last.

In a meticulously clean bowl using a spotless whisk, whisk the egg whites until stiff. Fold a spoonful of the egg whites into the lemon mixture in the other bowl and then fold in the rest until you have a smooth and airy batter.

Pour the batter into the prepared ramekins and sprinkle with the grated coconut. Pour boiling water into the roasting pan to come halfway up the sides of the ramekins and place the pan in the oven.

Bake the soufflés for 30 minutes. Serve immediately, with some cream to pour on top . . .

do not forget the dog

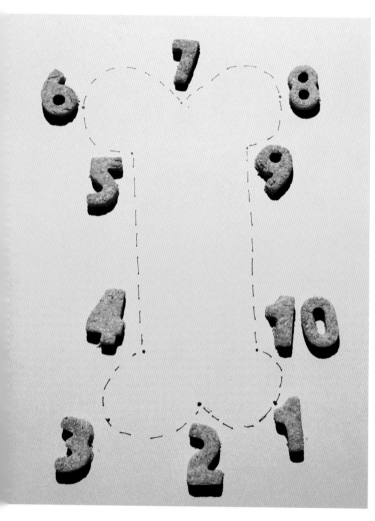

Marie's Munchies

FOR 30 cookies, depending on the size
PREP 15 min.
INACTIVE 30 min.
BAKE 25 min.

7 tbsp (50 g) wheat germ
1¼ cups (150 g) whole-wheat flour, plus extra for dusting
1 egg, beaten
about 7 tbsp (100 g) coconut oil, melted and cooled

Combine the wheat germ with the whole-wheat flour and make an indentation in the middle. Pour in the egg and two-thirds of the coconut oil. Knead swiftly into a cohesive dough. Add more coconut oil, if necessary, and possibly a few drops of cold water.

Let the dough rest for 30 minutes in the fridge.

Preheat the oven to 325°F (170°C). Line a baking sheet with parchment paper.

Roll out the dough on a lightly flour-dusted counter and use a cookie cutter or knife to cut shapes. Place on the prepared baking sheet. Bake in batches for about 25 minutes until golden brown and dry. Keep in an airtight box or container.

Flaxseed Cookies

Flaxseed is supposed to be very good for dogs' fur, I've been told. My Marie—mind you, a picky eater—loves these. That alone makes me happy.

FOR 60 small cookies
PREP 20 min.
BAKE 45 min.

1 cup plus 2 tbsp (100 g) rolled oats (not instant) from the natural foods store (see page 18)
⅔ cup (100 g) golden flaxseed
⅔ cup (100 g) cornmeal
7 tbsp (100 ml) low-sodium organic chicken broth (made from 1 cube)
1 egg
flour, for dusting

Preheat the oven to 325°F (160°C). Grease two baking sheets with spray or oil.

Combine all the ingredients into a firm dough. Roll out the dough on a flour-dusted counter and use a cookie cutter to cut out cookies. Place on the prepared baking sheets. Scrape the remaining dough scraps together and repeat. Continue until you've used all the dough.

Bake the cookies in batches for 45 minutes, until hard and dry. They barely rise, so you can fill those baking sheets.

Let cool completely and store in an airtight container. They will keep for weeks.

Marie

Salmon Cookies

Marie's joined to my hip once I open a can of salmon.

They are the best treats in the world, these cookies—it's so easy to bribe dogs, I wish everyone was like that.

My mother's cat loves these as well, provided they're chopped into small pieces.

FOR about 40 cookies
PREP 12 min.
BAKE 40 min.

1 (4½-oz / 130-g) can salmon
1 egg
generous ½ cup (50 g)
    rolled oats (not instant)
    from the natural foods
    store (see page 18), plus
    extra as needed

Preheat the oven to 350°F (180°C).

Drain the canned salmon and mix it with the egg and rolled oats into a thick porridge that's not very sticky. If it's sticky, add some more rolled oats. Set aside for a while so the oats can suck up all the liquid.

Line a small baking pan (about 7½ by 5 inches / 19 by 13 cm) with parchment paper and fill with the mixture.

Press with a fork until you have a smooth, even surface and score the cookies with a knife.

Bake for 40 minutes, until just light brown.

Let cool and slice the cookies through with a sharp knife. Keep in the fridge in a resealable plastic bag.

RECIPE INDEX

Paris, France

GENERAL INDEX

Connemara, Ireland

iNDEX FOR PEOPLE WiTH FOOD ALLERGiES

THANK YOU

Oof

Sophie, Guusje, Renske, and Horas for your unrelenting assistance, support, and advice.

*My mother, Mariëtte, who explained to me that ovens are hot and that
I had to be careful if I wanted to bake anything. I was four years old at the time.*

*Martin, Vera, Inge, Wouter, Rob, Hennie, Bartina, Michiel,
and Stephan of Fontaine Publishers for their trust and endless enthusiasm.*

And everyone at ABRAMS and Stewart, Tabori & Chang, too, for the same reasons.

Sandra, from the cool clothing brand Humanoid, who makes sure I look great.

Annemieke, for styling some of the photos and for her cheerful inspiration.

*All my family and friends for their patience, because each time there was some wonderful social
event I showed up late or bailed with the excuse that I needed to work on this book.*

&

Marie, you adorable little cookie monster.

Connemara, Ireland

Paris, France

VOLUME MEASUREMENTS

1 tablespoon = 15 ml
1 teaspoon = 5 ml
4 tbsp = ¼ cup = 60 ml
⅓ cup = 80 ml
½ cup = 120 ml
1 cup = 240 ml
2 cups = 1 pint = 475 ml
4 cups = 2 pints = 950 ml

OVEN

I bake in a convection oven. Your oven may take longer or shorter than I have indicated in the baking time. The baking times in this book are a *suggestion*. Trust your own experience with your own oven and always use an oven thermometer! Read more about this on page 15.

PRODUCTS

I use organic eggs, large ones, just so you know. Actually, I always use organic ingredients: butter, meal, flour, and dairy are more pure and honest if they're organic. On top of that, the organic baking or gluten-free sections usually have more choice in flour and meal— go have a look.

for

Sophie, Guusje, Renske & Horas

four tough cookies

Published in 2015 by Stewart, Tabori & Chang
An imprint of ABRAMS

Text, styling, layout & illustrations: Yvette Van Boven
Photography: Oof Verschuren
Editorial team: Martine Steenstra, Inge Huijs, Rob van Riet &
Hennie Franssen-Seebregts
Translation: Marleen Reimer & Victor Verbeek

For Abrams:
Editor: Holly Dolce
Designer: Liam Flanagan
Production Manager: Denise LaCongo

Library of Congress Control Number: 2014959144
ISBN: 978-1-61769-167-6
Text copyright © 2015 Yvette Van Boven
Photographs copyright © 2015 Oof Verschuren
Originally published in 2014 by Fontaine Publishers BV, Hilversum
www.fontaineuitgevers.nl

The text of this book was composed in Modern No. 20, Plantin, and Scala Sans.

Printed and bound in China
10 9 8 7 6 5 4 3 2 1

ABRAMS

THE ART OF BOOKS SINCE 1949

115 West 18th Street
New York, NY 10011
www.abramsbooks.com

HOME BAKED

MORE THAN 150 RECIPES
FOR SWEET AND SAVORY GOODIES